WORKERS
&
PROTEST

The European Labor Movement, the Working Classes and the Origins of Social Democracy 1890–1914

Harvey Mitchell

PROFESSOR OF HISTORY
UNIVERSITY OF BRITISH COLUMBIA

Peter N. Stearns

PROFESSOR OF HISTORY
RUTGERS UNIVERSITY

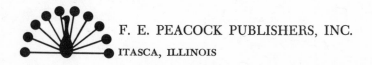 F. E. PEACOCK PUBLISHERS, INC.
ITASCA, ILLINOIS

Contents

GENERAL INTRODUCTION

Mr. Mitchell and Mr. Stearns have written an unusual book. I applaud their method, even if I do not share all their conclusions. By laying their essays side by side they have let the cat out of the bag and revealed how differently the history of the labor movement between 1890 and 1914 may be written. And they have had the courage to make these differences explicit in the comments with which they have closed the book. These comments might have been mere polite exchanges of compliments, the salutes of scholars from afar as their ships momentarily crossed courses. Instead, they force the authors out of their chosen positions and make them face the opponent's fire. The reader stands by and learns from the resulting confrontation.

II

Mr. Mitchell's essay brings out the striking differences in the development of the working-class movement in three European countries: England, France, and Germany. Merely to list a few of these differences is to explain why generalizations about European labor history in this period (and any other) must be made with extreme caution. In Germany Marxism was taken seriously and Marx was actually read; in France and England Marxism was never able to supplant indigenous ideological traditions. In England the trade-union movement preceded the Labour party; in Germany the Social Democratic party created the union movement; in France the most important trade-union organization—

the CGT—came into being as part of a reaction against the conservatism of the Socialists. In England and Germany the trade-union leaders were always pushing Socialist leaders toward the right and protesting against revolutionary rhetoric; in France the CGT was always criticizing the Socialist party from the left and trying to goad it into revolutionary action. The working-class movement in Germany and England commanded a mass following; in France in the period studied by the authors it never succeeded in mobilizing more than small, if noisy minorities. The English working-class leaders had confidence in their ability to influence the state and make it bend to their demands; the Germans feared and admired the state and avoided direct confrontation with it; the French found the state expendable and looked forward to the day when they would do away with it and get on to more human types of social organization. In Germany socialism was a way of life; in England it was a method of political action; in France it provided one of the best ways of getting a political career underway. An impressive set of contrasts. And if Mr. Mitchell had included Italy, his picture would have been even more complex.

Mr. Stearns's effort is to convince us how overly simplified labor history has been in the past. No longer, he says, is it necessary to write the interminable and dull history of Socialist and syndicalist debates. That work is done. The time has now come to look beyond ideology. However we feel about this argument—and I myself have written the history of enough such interminable and dull debates to be initially sympathetic to it—we cannot deny some of his accompanying points. It is essential, he reminds us, to distinguish between workers, working-class movements, and working-class leaders. Workers did not always react to their conditions as their leaders said they should or as doctrine indicated that they would. Moreover, not even working-class leaders can be lumped together in a single group. There was sometimes a world of difference between Socialist deputies, who specialized in doctrine, and local militants who had to respond to local pressures and the nonideological concerns of their immediate clientele. National debates were mainly the frosting on a many-layered cake. It is also true, as Mr. Stearns points out, that not all workers were organized, a fact that is far too often forgotten. And many workers who were organized belonged to company and Catholic unions, quite different in aims and methods than the better known central trade-union organizations. Thus one of the major problems that working-class leaders had to face in this period was their relationship to the working masses. Indeed, the French Socialists on more than one occasion debated seriously whether or not it was proper for them to interfere in strikes. Far from being at the head of a band of revolutionary workers, Socialist and even union leaders were often in their train.

Mr. Stearns forces upon us a second distinction. Not all workers behaved alike. "Printers," he tells us in a striking phrase, "behaved much more like printers than like Germans or Englishmen." In the process of substantiating this assertion Mr. Stearns gives us a thumbnail sketch of the attitudes and behavior patterns of some of the occupational groups that were dominant in the early working-class movement. Artisans, he says, tended to be better educated than industrial workers and more interested in doctrine. They were also pragmatic and quick to compromise. Miners were isolated, devoted to their families, religious, and had gardens. Dockers were given to fits of anger and were irregular in their working habits. Textile workers were doctrinaire but not aggressive. Railwayworkers were relatively satisfied with their lot and did not always identify with other industrial workers. These points have been made before. Scholars working on the French working-class movement, for example, had long ago noted that revolutionary-syndicalist leaders tended to be printers, that construction workers were inclined to anarchism, and that metallurgical workers were more sophisticated in their acceptance of large-scale organization and their methods of struggle. But no one has ever pleaded this point with Mr. Stearns's fervor.

For me the most interesting part of Mr. Stearns's essay is his discussion of changes that took place in the nature of working-class demands and tactics during the decade between 1895 and 1905. Before 1895 wor'ing-class movements had been movements of defense. Workers rose up in indignation when their existing benefits were threatened. There is much evidence to suggest that workers did not question their downtrodden state, but rioted when misery increased and became literally intolerable. After 1895 working-class demands and methods became more sophisticated, and workers took the offensive. They struck in times of relative abundance. They began to protest the lack of improvement in their conditions of life. There was what Mr. Stearns calls a "revolution of expectations."

Looking for the possible causes of this change, Mr. Stearns points to an improvement in diet and an increase in spare time. After 1890 workers had more energy, and they also had more time to devote to the reading of revolutionary literature and the attendance of meetings. The Social Democratic movement in Germany with its hundreds of newspapers, its thousands of paid bureaucrats, and its constant activity would be unthinkable in the circumstances of the early industrial revolution in England. In Dickens's England workers had no energy, no time, no money. Now in Wilhelm's Germany they had increasing quantities of all three. Yet at the same time that they stood ready to benefit from liberal Europe's progress, they also had to cope with new burdens—notably, inflation and demands for a faster pace of work. It is this coincidence of improvement and keenly felt pressure that accounts for much of the agitation of these years. Though the material conditions of workers were improving, they were losing ground in terms of their share of the national wealth. Wages were rising, but profits were rising even faster and inflation was cancelling a good part of the workers' advance. Although hard to measure, the relations of workers with their employers were probably also becoming more impersonal and hence leaving an impression of increasing authoritarianism in the society at large. Inevitably these developments affect the attitudes of workers and the methods that they choose to adopt. The labor movement is one measure of this change in attitudes and tactics, and Mr. Stearns devotes a fascinating section to the analysis of the strike phenomenon. Many would contest his conclusion— that the adoption of the strike as a tactic represented an index of increasing moderation—but as in so many other cases, whether he convinces us or not, he makes us reconsider and to some extent revise our former conception. His is a most subversive mind.

III

So far I have discussed those areas in which the two authors' essays overlap, or at any rate those areas where their arguments do not conflict. Mr. Mitchell follows Mr. Stearns in believing that we must devote more attention to workers. Where the authors disagree both implicitly and explicitly is in their attitude toward national differences in the labor movement. Mr. Mitchell feels these differences are important enough to make essential a separate discussion for England, France, and Germany. "Any account of the labor movement in Britain, France, and Germany in the generation before the First World War," he writes, "would suffer from serious distortion if it rested on the proposition that industrial capitalism elicited a uniform response from the working class." Mr. Mitchell's essay is accordingly full of distinctions between the labor movements in these three countries. Mr. Stearns is convinced that these differences are relatively unimportant; or to put it more accurately, he feels that the similarities deserve more attention than the differences. Historians of the working-class movement, he maintains, have failed to see the broad outlines of the forest because they have concentrated so single-mindedly on the separate national trees.

What is at stake here is no mere historians' quarrel over emphasis or shades of interpretation. The authors disagree over what the content of working-class history should be. After some generalizations about working-class development in Europe, Mr. Mitchell goes on to discuss the movements that arose to represent workers. These movements were led in great part by men who stemmed from the middle class. Mr. Stearns does not think these movements should occupy the center of the stage in a working-class history. He is interested in what the workers themselves felt, thought, did. His premise is that working-class leaders seldom reflected the real ambitions of workers. Leaders, he submits, were influenced by political and cultural factors, while workers were more concerned about their own material welfare. And he does not hesitate to take the further step of arguing that workers seldom followed the men who claimed to be their leaders. For Mr. Stearns, Mr. Mitchell is a traditionalist because he feels that ideas and politics are important. Mr. Stearns is trying to grasp the evolution of the working class as a whole. Though he does not say it, his premise is that a man is what he does: I am my occupation. Seldom has a materialist interpretation of history been pressed so far. And seldom has any historian distinguished so sharply between elites and masses. For Mr. Stearns the two seldom met.

There is one central issue on which the authors agree. Workers and working-class leaders, they submit, were getting more reformist and less revolutionary on the eve of the First World War. Mr. Mitchell notes this change on the level of ideology. Mr. Stearns feels that ideology merely reflected the pressure of the workers themselves. He observes, rightly I think, that workers had ambiguous attitudes toward the state. The state oppressed them. Yet it also offered them certain benefits such as pensions, unemployment insurance, and the right to collective bargaining. The policies of trade unions mirrored this ambiguity. They generally opposed radical political action and their major concern was to control industrial conflict rather than to inflame it. On the basis of this evidence, Mr. Stearns does not hesitate to affirm that ideological concerns were diminishing in importance for most working-class leaders on the eve of the First World War. Mr. Mitchell comes to a similar conclusion; yet with his close attention to the politics of the working-class movement, he cannot fail to note that sizable (or at least noisy) radical minorities remained stubbornly opposed to reformist policies and practices on the eve of the First World War.

The thesis of an increasingly reformist labor movement put forward by Mr. Stearns and Mr. Mitchell is persuasive. It connects neatly with working-class development since the Second World War and explains why workers have ceased to constitute a revolutionary threat to neocapitalist society. As an observation of what happened to workers in Western Europe over a period of a hundred years, it is certainly correct and deserves to be brought to the attention of students. But as an historical inter-

pretation of the working-class movement between 1890 and 1914, the Stearns–Mitchell thesis has a serious flaw: it consigns Western workers to reformism on the eve of the collapse of the reformist position; it does not prepare us to understand what happened to the working-class movement after 1914. The First World War led to the radicalization of the working-class movement. Communist movements, after all, were the product of the disintegration of prewar working-class organizations. They arose in the immediate aftermath of the war. The period between the wars, moreover, was characterized by savage combat between reformists and revolutionaries and by attempts to devise a neosocialism or third way. However you interpret the developments of these years it is hard to think of them as years of diminishing ideological concern. Indeed, Mr. Mitchell is quite right to raise the question as to whether the expectations and legitimate aspirations of workers were realized by the neoreformist program which can be said to have triumphed in the three countries with which he dealt. Note that I write "neoreformist," because the programs of prewar reformists in England, France, and Germany have only been realized *in part*. And the part that has not been realized—a change in the quality of life—was for most prewar Socialists the most important element in their program, the goal to which they had dedicated their lives.

IV

The failure of the authors' interpretations to explain the labor history of the period following the one with which they deal is, in my opinion, the result of their narrow definition of the labor movement. Working-class leaders and workers had to respond to pressures that came from outside the labor movement itself. Printers may have acted alike in many respects, but printers were not printers twenty-four hours a day. Moreover, a man could cease to be a printer and become something else—a soldier, for example. The fact is that the working-class movement was only one aspect, if the most important, of a general tendency toward the organization of the masses. Large groups of people were on the move. They were being uprooted, moved into cities, thrust

into new occupations that their fathers and grandfathers had never dreamed of, threatened and tempted in ways they had never been threatened and tempted before, and organized by men who aspired to be their leaders and ideological guides. Movements of youth, women, ethnic minorities, writers, *and* workers were all, in their own way, responses to this upheaval— an upheaval that was transforming in unsuspected ways an entire society.

Different nationalities reacted to these phenomena in different ways, for the simple reason that their situations were different. Mr. Mitchell is wise to be on the outlook for national peculiarities, and Mr. Stearns would no doubt have had even greater difficulty in drawing his general picture if he had attempted to include countries like Italy, Spain, and Sweden. He is right, however, in arguing that certain general developments affected all countries and created general problems that were European and not specifically national in scope. Indeed, in my view, both writers underestimate the force of international considerations. Reformism as a viable ideological position was destroyed after 1917 by the experience of the war and the impact of the Russian Revolution—despite the workers' concern for their material welfare. Everywhere workers were torn by feelings of national solidarity, their desire to improve their material position, and their aspirations toward a new and freer society.* What happened in one European country more often than not influenced the way these various priorities were weighed in other European countries. Social Democracy never recovered from the failures of the German party, the largest Socialist party in Europe and the model for all other Socialist movements before 1914.

Mr. Stearns's attack on ideology does not convince me that ideology was of no concern to workers. But it does suggest that the distinction between reformism and revolutionary orthodoxy

---

* Even Russian accounts of the working-class movement now acknowledge that bonds of class solidarity were sometimes undermined and superseded by other considerations like the war experience. See B. R. Lopukhov, *Fashizm i rabochee dvizhenie v Italii, 1919–1929* [Fascism and the working-class movement in Italy, 1919–1929] (Moscow, 1968), 53, who criticizes the Italian Socialists for their failure to rally working-class veterans after World War I.

is not sufficient for understanding the situation before 1914. I agree with Mr. Mitchell that Mr. Stearns has gone astray in identifying ideology with revolutionary action. Ideology refers both to attitudes and the attempt to systematize attitudes into a program. Attitudes limit programs, but it would be a mistake to argue that programs, once formulated, do not in turn affect attitudes. The crucial question faced by working-class leaders after 1900 was the need to devise a program that would correspond to the new socioeconomic situation and that would attract widespread working-class support. Anybody who dismisses Jaurès and Jouhaux as simple reformists has misunderstood completely their attempt during the years before 1914 to create a new, radical alternative to the overly rigid positions that dominated the Socialist and revolutionary syndicalist movements around 1905. If Jaurès and Jouhaux were ready to abandon certain aspects of the doctrines of their respective organizations, it was not because they had ceased to believe in a thoroughgoing transformation of French society: they had rather become convinced that new times required new methods—a position, by the way, with which Lenin, inexorably opposed to Jaurès and Jouhaux's *methods,* agreed. All too often Mr. Stearns confuses pragmatism, which to me suggests an openness to new solutions and a lack of rigidity, with moderation and a rejection of radical goals. Jaurès and Jouhaux (like Lenin and Mussolini) were pragmatists; they were not, however, moderates, if by moderation is meant a willingness to accept the *status quo.*

The hinge of Mr. Stearns's argument is his analysis of French revolutionary syndicalism, which he insists did not truly represent the aspirations of French workers, even before 1914. The question is a complex one and cannot be discussed here in the detail that a fair response to Mr. Stearns's thesis would require. It is easy to sling stones, but infinitely more difficult to construct buildings. Mr. Stearns has erected an edifice of interpretation that deserves the most careful study and attention. Nonetheless, I am persuaded that in his zeal to indicate the gap between workers and doctrinaires, a praiseworthy undertaking, he has misunderstood the importance of French syndicalism. True, the CGT never represented more than a fraction of French industrial workers. True, the undemocratic nature of the organization made it possible for radical leaders to silence their reformist opponents who then went on to pursue more moderate policies on the local level. But to all this must be added that the revolutionary-syndicalist leaders who dominated the CGT before 1914 captured the imagination of the French workers and crystallized their opposition to bourgeois society in a way that no subsequent working-class organization in France has ever been able to do. And the creation of the Communist party and the success of the Communists in gaining control of the CGT after 1936 suggest that the legacy of revolutionary syndicalism was far from dead in 1914.

V

The great value of this book is that it forces us to rethink these questions, to bring them out into the open, and to reconsider the way working-class history should be written. As Mr. Stearns reminds us, it is no longer sufficient to produce a set of figures and then to assume that workers reacted to material conditions in some eternally determined way. People will want to know how workers actually reacted, and not how ideology or some economic theory said that they were supposed to react. Nor will people be able to wield the term *worker* with the same facility. They will have to specify what kind of worker they are talking about, in what country, at what point in time. And Mr. Stearns has laid to rest once and for all, I should think, the sloppy practice of labeling European countries in this period as nations of heavy industry, small workshops, or backward farms. There were plenty of small shops in Germany and plenty of large factories in France. The level of economic development in Europe was, to a great extent, a regional question. Henceforth historians will have to be more careful; sweeping generalizations linking nationalities, the average size of economic enterprises, and attitudes will no longer be sufficient to explain working-class movements and their evolution; connections between these factors will have to be established, and not merely taken for granted.

All these distinctions will not prevent generalizations. They should, however, change the nature of the generalizations which we make and improve their quality. And for that we may be grateful to Mr. Mitchell and Mr. Stearns. They have aired their differences in public, and we all—students and scholars alike—stand to benefit from the debate. Let us have more of such polemics in the future, if they can be as well informed, as frank, and as intelligent as this one.

November, 1970   ROBERT WOHL
                                                 University of California
                                                   at Los Angeles

Labor and the Origins

in Britain, France,

of Social Democracy

and Germany, 1890–1914

by Harvey Mitchell

CHAPTER 1.

INTRODUCTION

Any account of the labor movement in Britain, France, and Germany in the generation before the First World War would suffer from serious distortion if it rested on the proposition that industrial capitalism elicited a uniform response from the working classes. Such a view would also totally ignore the immense variety of economic development, social structures, political traditions, and cultural peculiarities, which, together with other factors, helped create a multiplicity of experiences difficult or impossible to reduce to a convenient formula capable of capturing the truth about the working classes in the three industrial societies that will be surveyed in the following pages. (1)

Nevertheless, it is difficult to avoid the use of certain terms that are now well entrenched in the vocabulary of historians and social scientists. One such is *industrial society;* another is *capitalism.* For the purposes of the present study we can characterize the first such category as the mechanized production of commodities in factories and enterprises in an overwhelmingly urban environment; and the second may be regarded as a description of one form of industrial society—that is, a society in which there is "private property in means of production and regulation of the productive process by private contract (or management or initiative)." (2) It will be recognized at once that both of these categories are "on a high level of generality," (3) and that one of them, capitalism, has acquired an ideological connotation or has been endowed with a specific meaning, usually pejorative. It is obviously necessary to qualify them before they can be used to some advantage.

Let us begin with the term *industrial society.* All three societies under scrutiny in the present study possessed certain common features by 1914, so much so that the term *industrial* can be applied to them. However, the origins, pace, intensity, and impact of industrialization were not the same everywhere. The force, development, and consequences of industrialization were greatest in Britain first; they then became discernible in Belgium and France; but by the outbreak of the First World War, they had in many respects proceeded furthest in Germany and overseas in the United States. (Explanations for industrial takeoff (4) and the industrial primacy of one state as against another at different points of time need not detain us here.) It is sometimes also assumed that Britain's industrial development created the pattern for subsequent industrialization elsewhere. While, to be sure, British industrial society found many conscious imitators on the continent who felt that it was necessary to duplicate the sources of British industrial power in their own countries in order to match or exceed it, several factors proved the impossibility of absolute emulation. The resources of the different states—natural and technological—were not always the same, at least in the beginning; and their deployment and allocation were in turn dependent on the nature of the state's human resources—the size, age, urban-rural distribution, education, and skills of its population, if we isolate only the quantitative aspects of the human factor. What is more, countries that undertake industrialization will if at all possible "concentrate at a relatively early point of their industrialization on promotion of those branches of industrial activities in which recent technological progress had been particularly rapid. . . ." (5) The essential point is that our inquiry into the nature of the labor movements would not profit too greatly from an assumption that whatever differences industrial societies might exhibit in their early development, as they mature, they all more or less tend to assume identical features so powerful and pervasive as to negate the impact of other equally forceful environmental factors, including discrete national traditions.

Besides, the legacies of the preindustrial era were not the same in every state nor uniform within states. We have only to look at the sources of the labor force—one of the factors in the industrial process. The enclosures of eighteenth-century Britain revolutionized the countryside and created a pliable labor force for the new industries, while the Revolution in France delayed throughout the nineteenth century the depopulation of rural areas and may even have made labor too costly a factor of production. (6) The same Revolution in the Rhineland helped consummate the creation of a free peasantry, but it made no impact in Prussia where the state, together with the powerful landlords, commanded a docile peasant population and allowed it to be channeled into industry when needed.

The role of the state was often decisive. In Britain, resistance to the new industrial and commercial elites from the landed aristocracy was not great enough to require measures to repress the latter to the advantage of the former. The repeal of the Corn Laws, while favoring the new industrial sectors of the economy, did not spell the doom of the agriculturists who turned to a more rational exploitation of the land. In many respects the landed upper classes in Britain took on bourgeois and capitalistic characteristics. In Germany, on the other hand, the state did infinitely more to promote industrialization. It is doubtful whether the industrialization of Germany could have progressed without state intervention, so strong was the opposition of the landed aristocracy to a process which they feared might deprive it of its powers. In promoting German industry, however, the state did not deprive the aristocracy of its social and political privileges so that the industrial elites, to a much greater degree than in Britain, tended to assume the life-style of the aristocracy. The French position was somewhat between those of Britain and Germany. Certainly the Second Empire encouraged the new banking institutions that did so much to industrialize the country, but the state did not serve to mobilize the resources for industrialization nearly to the same extent as in Germany. Nor was there an overpowering landed interest which could intimidate French industrialists and hence force the state to take the initiative.

This rapid review does not exhaust the varieties of industrial experience. One more example should suffice to make the point. Even if all the major industrial states suffered from the slowdown which interrupted expansion for some two decades beginning in the 1870s, their individual recovery, however much they owed to technological advances, was nevertheless closely related to developments that preceded this major spurt of industrialization. In Britain, the first of the industrial giants, innovation was never absent, but as David Landes points out, "the marginal product of improvements diminished as the cost of equipment went up and the physical advantage over existing techniques fell;" moreover, Britain failed to take full advantage of the "cluster of innovations earning the name of the Second Industrial Revolution." (7) By contrast, Germany made the most of these opportunities, and indeed, because more of her industry remained to be mechanized, she gave the "impression of an uninterrupted rise" in her industrial growth. (8) France's industrial expansion was the least spectacular of all, but it is inaccurate to say that she never had an industrial revolution. "After the relatively rapid expansion of the Second Empire, the Third Republic was a period of autumnal advance, accelerated finally by the upturn of 1900–13, which was based partly on the new technology, partly on the opening of valuable iron deposits in Lorraine." (9)

Having sounded these cautionary notes, the same reservations must be observed in a discussion of the meaning of the term *capitalism*. Most students concur in the designation of these three societies as capitalist, but they are rightly wary of equating the term and the realities of the forms of investment within a particular capitalist economy. It matters a great deal if the investment is in heavy or light industry, if a family firm generates the capital, and whether excessive competition is considered unfair. The last feature has been peculiarly characteristic of French capitalism, though the presence of oligopolistic competition in many industries was by no means an isolated phenomenon. This is not to say that these were the only entrepreneurial forms in France, for she also possessed a few cartels in iron and steel. But it was in Germany that the cartel was most highly developed, because of a combination of factors peculiar to German institutions —psychology, high tariffs, and bank control, to name but a few. The cartel form of industrial investment was no stranger to the British scene either, but where it existed, as in metallurgy, milling, chemicals, and glassmaking, it was not as effective as its German counterpart; nor did it dominate the investment landscape, for common law forbade restrictive trade practices, tariff barriers were lacking, and the private firm was still the most prevalent form of capital formation.

It would certainly be wrong to deny that conditions of labor in industrial societies under capitalism exhibited many common characteristics. Indeed, the more investigators have been able to penetrate the nature of labor problems in the early stages of industrialization, the more convinced they are that they were essentially the same in all western European countries. Moreover, by extending their researches into the beginnings of industrialization in newly developing countries, they have also found that labor conditions in such societies are not very different from those of early industrializing western Europe. (10) As we move from the early to the later stages of industrialism, we find additional similarities between the various working-class protest movements. In their desire to achieve an appropriate status in industrial society, the working classes pursued similar tactics. Everywhere they struggled for legal recognition from the state for the right to organize and to strike. They sought from the state protective legislation—that is, laws protecting them in the factory from excessive exploitation: laws regulating hours and conditions of work; accident, disability, sickness and unemployment insurance; and holiday and pension pay. At the same time, they demanded an increasing share of the goods they helped produce. At one time or another, they engaged in violent demonstrations against both employers and governments. Some occupational groups, regardless of nationality, proved more susceptible to radicalism than others. For example, men who worked in hazardous trades or who did not have steady work or who worked in isolation from the larger community—e.g., dockers, seamen, lumbermen, and miners—often made more radical demands than other types of workers. On the other hand, radicalism was often associated with the more skilled members of the working population—men working in the printing trades, building craftsmen, metalworkers, and railroad workers. It also seems to be true that at certain times—though the exact relationship of working-class activity to economic causes is not yet clear—skilled and semiskilled workers took the lead in the protest against the threat of technological change. Yet there is also evidence for the militancy of other skilled workers who did not face such threats or who were in occupations of uninterrupted prosperity. (11)

We are still far from being able to assert with finality that the similarities of labor protest nullify the differences between labor movements. What is striking in any comparative study are the many different forms of labor protest. In the first place, the numbers of organized workers varied from a rather impressive proportion of the total working population in Germany to a much less significant ratio in France. The forms of organization differed a great deal too. In Germany, at the national level, labor unions were highly centralized, while in France, organization was based on a loose federation permitting a high degree of initiative to the *syndicats*, a state of affairs that would not have been tolerated by the powerful General Commission in Germany. French unions furthermore made a virtue of low membership dues, while German unions stressed the strength to be derived from well-stocked reserve funds. Both British and German unions showed unmistakable signs of bureaucratization, whereas French unions were on their guard against such tendencies.

As for ideological* commitment, the French Confédération générale du travail (C.G.T.) developed early its own amalgam of Proudhonist and Marxist doctrines, and sharply contested the various French Socialist groups' claims to dominate French unionism structurally, ideologically, or in terms of practical politics. In Germany, there was for many years an unwilling subordination of unions to the Social Democratic party, but by 1906 the unions finally succeeded in ending this dependence and were

---

* The term *ideology* is best and most briefly described by Maurice Cranston in a review article, "Ideology and Mr. Lichtheim," *Encounter,* XXX (October 1968), 70–74. According to Cranston, the concept of ideology has five characteristics. First, an ideology embraces a coherent theory capable of explaining the human experience; second, it sets out a general and often abstract program of political and social change; third, the program conceived by the ideology will be achieved only by struggle; fourth, the ideology demands "commitment" from its followers; and, finally, while it is meant to appeal to a mass following, it reserves a special place for the intellectuals who are thought of as the persons who will lead the masses in the conquest of the program. Mr. Stearns and I use the term for the most part in the above sense. The terms *doctrine* and *program* are sometimes used as its equivalent, but mainly in the subsidiary sense suggested by Cranston.

able to force the S.P.D. to give them an equal voice in the labor movement, and, by this stroke, considerably weakened the influence of its theoreticians, however much they differed among themselves on labor's need to adjust theory to practice. In Britain, very few unions acknowledged socialism as their goal, although many of the leaders of certain unions were themselves members of various Socialist groups and, with the assistance of a few leaders of the latter, worked to create the conditions favoring the establishment of the Labour party. Nevertheless it should be noted that the Labour party would have been helpless without support from the unions, and that the muted socialism which it espoused was as much due to the cautious leadership of the Independent Labour party as to the more conservative views of the union leaders. In short, the leaders of the British labor movement were only vaguely committed to a form of socialism and approached most problems in a pragmatic, nondoctrinaire way. Of all the labor movements, the British was the least affected by Marxist ideology. Indeed, its leaders scarcely felt the need to refer to a comprehensive social and economic analysis as a guide to action. In the realm of ideas, they relied more on the writings of the later Mill whose turning away from economic liberalism was prompted by his conviction that political democracy would either be incomplete or impossible without some form of social and economic democracy. Besides, Marxism's impact was hardly felt in a movement conceived in the Nonconformist ethic and in the Puritan gospel of work.

One must not lose sight of the total environment of national political life which affected the development of labor protest. The legacy of revolutionary violence was, for example, strongest and deepest in France. The Great Revolution and those that followed in the nineteenth century, including the traumatic consequences of the Commune, influenced the forms of protest in several ways. The revolutionary tradition was a living reality in the conscious activities of labor militants; the experience of the Commune, especially, was a point of departure for many of its survivors who not only influenced a generation of workingmen but also assumed positions of authority and power both in the unions and in some of the Socialist sects. Both union and Socialist leaders referred to France's revolutionary past in almost reverent terms, as somehow endowing France's laboring population with a virtue denied to others and so placing them in the advance guard of European labor and socialism. They could also point with pride to the revolutionary conquest of universal suffrage by midcentury. The class consciousness of the French labor movement was also derived from French revolutionary struggles which predated Marxism; indeed, Marx's theory of the class struggle was nurtured by his study of the eighteenth-century Revolution and his analysis of 1848. Finally, the revolutionary tradition stimulated in French labor, and to a lesser degree, in French socialism, a deep distrust of the state and authority.

Britain's revolutionary tradition had another kind of significance. "The symbols appealing to the nineteenth-century British worker," it has been suggested, "were a replica of the Socialistic sermons expounded by the leaders of the radical sects in the Puritan revolution. The Levellers and Diggers of that era were duplicated in the nineteenth century by the Labor Churches, Guilds, Chapels. Here labor leaders in their dual capacity of lay preachers and political ideologists expounded Socialist doctrine." (12) The early Owenite experiments and the heroic Chartist days had also left a stock of memories, and, of course, strains within Chartism had their genesis in the movement for parliamentary reform and the founding of working-class reform societies just before, during, and after the French Revolution.

More characteristic of British labor, especially after 1848, was its capacity to make gains through the ideology of self-help and enforcing demands by applying pressure on the properly constituted authorities. This belief in the fairness of authority was broken only twice. The first such example was the "new unionism" of the late 1880s and early 1890s. It represented a challenge to the older more settled labor ethic because of its direct and fearless confrontation with the state. But it soon lost its vitality, not, however, without altering the complexion of the labor movement which became more receptive to the needs and demands of previously unorganized sections of the working class and to the simultaneous movement toward independent labor politics. The second challenge occurred in the few years before the

1914–18 War when the syndicalist-inspired wave of mass strikes disturbed the industrial peace and frightened the more conservative union elites and the cautious parliamentarism of the Labour party's leadership. Both the Trades Union Congress (T.U.C.) and the Parliamentary Labour party were commanded by men who preferred to tackle labor's problems in the more discreet atmosphere of the convention hall and Parliament. Class war was anathema to them and, what was more, a foreign excrescence. The Fabians were similarly disturbed by this uncharacteristic evidence of violence; they, more than most, favored the indirect approach. There is a remarkable affinity of views to be found among the Fabians, conservative trade unionists, and the leaders of the Parliamentary Labour party. Labor's protest, it was maintained, would best be answered by cooperation with the ruling class whose acceptance of working-class demands was only a matter of time. In fact, there was, on the whole, a good deal of middle-class empathy for the labor movement nurtured as it was on many of the same Utopian symbols bequeathed by the seventeenth-century revolution. Moreover, a group such as the Fabians, with their entrée to the drawing rooms of their social peers, did a great deal to popularize and make acceptable the more moderate aspirations of the working classes.

German political life did not revolve around an axis of revolutionary traditions. Indeed, the failure of 1848 to ruffle the sensibilities of Germany's ruling elites left the Liberals feeling uneasy but did little to impede their ultimate absorption by the semi-authoritarian statism perfected by Bismarck and the aristocracy, or to extinguish their hopes of achieving a constitutional form of government by legal methods. Living outside this national consensus were the trade unionists and the Socialists for whom 1848 meant something more. From its embers they fanned to life some of the Socialist ideas, and by 1875 the Eisenachers and the Lassalleans were able to unite in the Socialist Labour party; but the Gotha program which enshrined their fusion was far from being revolutionary in Marx's sense. Despite the evident reformism of the new party, the Socialists were cast into the wilderness by Bismarck's anti-Socialist Laws in 1878 and were forced for the next twelve years to lead a semilegal existence. During this period of repression, the revolutionary pronouncements of the party and its improved electoral performance—by 1890 the Socialists were able to poll almost 1.5 million votes—determined the future posture of the reorganized Social Democratic party after the anti-Socialist legislation was abandoned. The Erfurt program, handiwork of Karl Kautsky, was a curious mixture. On the one hand, its revolutionary ardor, analysis, and prognosis were typically Marxist, while on the other hand, it recognized the need, by the pursuit of reformist methods, to protect and extend the immediate interests of the working classes.

Of all the labor movements, the German was the one most racked by the bitter polemics of its two extreme wings. The revolutionaries, of whom Rosa Luxemburg was to become the key figure, consistently urged the S.P.D. to stress its revolutionary role in the face of the growing weight and power of the Free Trade Unions which retreated increasingly from the maximum to the minimum goals of the Erfurt program. Both the growth of party and trade-union membership and the steady increase in the S.P.D.'s electoral strength—only once interrupted at the time of the 1907 elections—fortified the reformist rather than the revolutionary elements in the German labor movement; the more so as Eduard Bernstein's revisionism, repudiated earlier by the S.P.D., was vindicated by the practical successes of a reformist policy, and as the southern wing of the party refused to pursue the politics of pure opposition. Yet as the movement gained strength, the contradictions of its position within the political framework of imperial Germany become painfully apparent. However hopeful the leaders were of eventually assuming power by constitutional means, they could not, under pressure from the revolutionaries in their midst, deny that the absence of genuine democratic representative institutions both at the federal and provincial levels—including a discriminatory suffrage system—was an obstacle which was not likely to be overcome even if their electoral power gave them a majority in the Reichstag. It is therefore necessary to underscore the stubborn realities of the German political scene which never ceased to irritate and would finally prick the integument that scarcely concealed the divisions within

the German labor movement. Consensus in the party was pre-
served until 1914 by the Byzantine permutations which were
grafted to the main body of Marxism by such theorists as
Kautsky, the conciliatory statements of the revered party leader,
Bebel, and the key positions held by trade unionists like Karl
Legien. The tolerance shown the Cassandra-like warnings of the
Luxemburgists barely softened their harsh criticism of the party
and the unions.

My chief aim in the following chapters, as the preceding observations suggest, is to discuss the politics of the British, French,
and German movements—that is, to examine how their leaders
perceived their relationship with the working classes as significant sections of them became a more potent force in society
through more effective organization and as a result of having a
political party speak and act on their behalf. What did this unprecedented growth in power but not so obvious process of social
integration—at least certain ranks of the laboring population
began in some respects to accept the morals, manners, and outlook of the middle classes—do to the ideological content of the
movements in question? Was the gap between professed aims
and actual programs widened or narrowed? Did militancy increase or decrease? Such questions will entail major concentration on the elites of the movement, the union leaders, political
bosses, and intellectuals who tried, not without severe struggle
among themselves, to shape its development and its relationship
with society as a whole. These and other questions can, I believe,
be most profitably dealt with by looking at the movements in
each of the national settings under analysis. To believe that
industrial society generates inflexible laws of development is undoubtedly productive of new and useful insights, but if taken
too far such an approach is likely to be too clinical and abstract,
neglectful of persistent traditions emerging from a particular
national experience.

CHAPTER 2.

GREAT BRITAIN:
THE DENIAL OF IDEOLOGY

The best-known features of British working-class life in mid-Victorian times are well documented. What struck people in the late Victorian period and in the Edwardian era was the wide-spread poverty brought to light by social surveys undertaken by wealthy philanthropists—Charles Booth who investigated urban workers in London in the late 1880s and early 1890s and Seebohm Rowntree who did the same in York a few years later. Despite some reservations by recent scholars, who question the standards used to judge poverty levels and who also point out that neither London nor York was typical of working-class life, (1) the persistence of destitution during a period of general material improvement was nevertheless real and blighted the lives of millions. Whether the figure is estimated at 10 or some 30 percent of the population, those who fell into the category of the destitute or the very poor were a sorry testament to the alleged benefits of industrial civilization. But how did the achievements of British industry express themselves, at least in the shares held by different classes of the population? However low Chiozza Money's estimate of the immediate prewar total national income may be, the great bulk of the nation's wealth was in the control of a minute proportion of the total population. According to his calculations, 0.4 percent of the most affluent possessed over one-third of the national income. (2) Taken as a whole, the middle classes absorbed a large portion of the national income. What of the working classes? From 1870 until about 1900 their material benefits continued to rise. Accurate statistics before 1880 are hard to obtain, but it is probable that wage rates were higher in that year than ten years earlier. In the next twenty-year period ending in 1900, real wages rose mainly because the increase in money wage rates was accompanied by a 15 percent decline in retail prices. The situation remained almost stationary during the next decade; the rising retail prices which marked this period and the last years before the war more than consumed any rise in wages. While Clapham is able to discern a slight improvement in real wages by 1913, his reservations (3) are supported by the more recent investigations of Deane and Cole who claim that ". . . there seems to have been a tendency for real wages to decline in the decade or so before the First World War." (4)

It is, of course, impossible to draw up a balance sheet of the quality of working-class life based purely on quantitative criteria. To be sure, the bulk of Britain's laboring classes lived in better material circumstances in 1900 and immediately before the war than at the midpoint of the previous century. Hours of work had been reduced in many industries, as a result of both union pressure and legislation, but the intensity, fatigue, and frustrations of work, however hard they are to measure, cannot be neglected in any assessment of conditions; and, in the notorious sweated trades, hours of work had hardly been altered. The state was becoming more and more involved in the manifold aspects of labor, and was assuming a more interventionist role by extending its supervision not only over hours and conditions of work, but also by taking responsibility for the victims of industrial accidents, unemployment and sickness, not to mention the progressive enlargement of the franchise and the extension of educational opportunities to which all parties now paid heed. Local authorities also contributed to the improvement of the general population's welfare. Yet while in gross terms all these measures made a real difference to the lives of many, national averages cannot convey how different sections of the working classes really lived in pre-1914 Britain. There remained for too many of them the recurrent threat of unemployment, inadequate housing, poor health, and only the rudiments of education. Significant disparities continued to exist between that large sector of working-class families that lived at or near the poverty level, stretching their weekly eighteen to twenty-one shillings to maintain a bare subsistence, and the fortunate 15 percent with incomes of £2 or more. The more-favored groups felt the ravages of industrialism less, of course, and, with the advantages of skill, education, and new forms of employment in clerical and lower managerial grades, their perceptions of the industrial system could hardly have been the same as those below them in status —a situation analogous to an earlier period with its divisions between an aristocracy of labor and the larger mass of the marginally skilled and unskilled. Social and economic improvement were, in fact, less marked than is commonly supposed. As late as 1917, when a medical survey of the male population was undertaken, only a little over one-third of the young men were found to be in satisfactory health, while more than two-thirds were classified as suffering from marked or partial disabilities. Consequently in the struggles of the working classes to improve conditions, perspectives, prognosis, and prescriptions differed, but it would be hazardous to draw a direct line between relative affluence and reform, disadvantage and radicalism, for the coincidence between such pairs is never exact nor so logically accommodating. As in other industrial societies, the controversies between reformers and radicals were most bitterly debated within the working-class movement itself, not without the powerful and often persuasive arguments and examples of personalities from the dominant social groups.

II

Just before the onset in the midseventies of a depression that was to endure for over two decades punctuated only briefly by periods of recovery, the British trade-union movement had achieved considerable success both by extending its membership and by gaining a legal status that was to be strengthened by additional legislative enactments before the decade was over. That the consolidation of trade-union strength was so rapid was due to a number of causes almost wholly specific to Britain. The most obvious was the economic climate which stimulated trade-union growth. With the exception of a few isolated periods of slackening activity, the 1850s and 1860s constituted a single time bloc of great industrial advance favoring the efforts of skilled workers to organize themselves into fairly effective bargaining units. Economic expansion alone does not account for the unique strength of the skilled British working classes. There was nothing comparable on the continent, even in France and Belgium which were also experiencing industrial transformation. Just as decisive in Britain was the virtual abandonment by working-class elites of the earlier forms of working-class protest. Neither nationwide and indiscriminate groupings of workers on the Owenite models of the 1830s nor the political agitation of Chartism served as the basis of trade unionism in the calmer, relatively more quiescent atmosphere of the fifties and sixties, although the legacies of each were not so thoroughly interred as to prevent the class consciousness of the one and the organizing ideas of the other from being revived in a later period of working-class agitation. For the moment, however, Owenism found expression in the formation of cooperatives, and Chartism in a kind of nostalgic mental refuge for a few pioneers who kept alive the memories of its heroic days. Little of their spirit and few of their goals animated the more practical-minded men who emerged as the leaders of trade unionism in the mid-Victorian period.

Of the million or so trade unionists who were affiliated with the Trades Union Congress in 1874, the most recent recruits were semiskilled and even unskilled workers but these soon withdrew in large numbers under the pressures of the depression. Most members belonged to craft societies in printing, building, and metalworking, or to unions in industries in which the necessary skills were more closely tied to the changing demands of the machine age, as in the railways, coal, iron, cotton, and wool. In the first, a prescribed form of apprenticeship regulated entrance to the trade, while in the second, skills were acquired by work on the job. Whether through apprenticeship or experience, trade unionists were men whose skills set them apart from the larger, more heterogeneous group of unskilled and unorganized laborers. By restricting the number of apprentices and enforcing other regulations, the craft unions aimed to determine wage rates; by exacting heavy fees, they could also promise material benefits, including unemployment payments, which were also often used to conceal strike pay. Originally local groups, many of the craft unions soon became amalgamated and gained national status, the chief advantage of which was to centralize finance and, to a much lesser extent, to coordinate strike action, although the local constituents of these "new model unions" were left free to determine wages and conditions. An even greater degree of centralization developed, most notably in the typographical, engineering, shipbuilding, and building unions. Instead of conducting their bargaining sessions with individual employers, these unions sought collective agreements with employer representatives covering entire districts or towns.

The regulatory devices enforced by craft unions were found inapplicable by the second major type of union which organized coalminers, workers in the iron trades, operatives in textiles, and railway workers. Price fluctuations tied to export markets, the existence of large reserves of labor, resolute employer resistance, technological innovation, methods of promotion within the trades, stricter discipline—these were some of the obstacles to unionism in coal and iron and in the railways. In the coal mines, such impediments did not operate simultaneously nor were they real barriers in the good years in the 1850s and 1860s when the unions made considerable headway. But with the coming of the depression, they were forced on the defensive and membership fell disastrously. Most of their leaders believed that survival demanded a new wage policy, and accordingly they adopted the sliding-scale device whereby wages were tied to the selling price of coal. At the same time, they attempted, largely without success, to set a floor below which wages would not fall. Powerful employer resistance forced the unions in the iron trades to adopt similar tactics. The unions themselves, moreover, were desirous of ending the wage conflicts that had marked industrial relations in the 1860s and had ended in defeat. Not even the sliding scale, achieved by negotiating machinery and by arbitration when necessary, was acceptable to the railway owners who refused to recognize the unions. But by the 1880s some companies were at least prepared to listen to deputations of workers airing their grievances. By contrast, the cotton spinners were very well organized. Their grip over the industry rested on their enforcement of discriminatory practices similar to those utilized in the craft unions against the promotion of less skilled workers and wage bargaining based on standard lists for piece work which were set by the chief spinning centers of Oldham and Bolton. The cotton weavers were not nearly as successful in obtaining uniform lists nor in organizing.

Union government in this period was shaped by the nature of demands and weapons. Since the amalgamated craft unions relied overwhelmingly on adherence to their regulations rather than on the strike, it mattered less that their affairs were in the hands of powerful general secretaries with little or no check from executives representative of the membership, so long as the centralization of their affairs ensured the payment of benefits. However, as collective bargaining at the district or town level became more common, this pattern of government came under fire from members who wanted a greater share in policy decisions. In the national coal and cotton unions where collective bargaining on a wider geographical basis had been the rule for much longer and the strike was frequently used, the union executives were representative from the beginning, and delegates from the various associations met regularly in the national bodies to elaborate policy.

The Trades Union Congress, which dates from 1868, avoided the attempts of the earliest national federations to press on the ideological front. Instead it reserved its energies for gaining legislation for greater union freedom from existing legal restraints, which became the chief goal of its Parliamentary Committee. However, a good deal of the preliminary work that led to the 1871 Trade Union Act was due to the efforts of the conservative London-based "Junta" whose arguments before the Royal Commission on Trade Unions had prepared opinion for the change in law that now removed some of the most discriminatory features under which trade unions had operated. Further legislation—the Conspiracy and Protection of Property Act and the Employers and Workmen Act—was enacted in 1875, and the Act amending the Trade Union Act of 1871 became law in 1876. The position of the unions was strengthened as never before, and can be considered the outcome of skillful lobbying by the Parliamentary Committee and the increasing attention which successive governments saw fit to pay to the influence of labor. Additional labor legislation in the same decade and during the 1880s extended the protective arm of the state to various occupations.

Such was the overriding objective of the unions—to enhance their economic power. It was achieved by the union leaders' espousal of economic ideas which did not violate the principles of *laissez-faire*, and by growing sympathy among both Liberals and Conservatives for labor leaders whose middle-class sentiments matched their own. On the political front, the unions were similarly self-effacing, for while they were active in the Reform League's agitation for franchise reform in the 1860s, and subsequently put up a token list of candidates in the 1868 elections, their Labour Representation League, established in 1869, was within a few years swallowed up by the Liberals. Its successor in the 1880s and 1890s, the T.U.C. Labour Electoral Committee, remained firmly in the hands of the old guard despite efforts to transform it into an independent party. By then, the unions had a small contingent of working-class men in the House of Commons, none of whom, however, dreamed of challenging their subordinate position within the Liberal party. Indeed, no greater admirer and supporter of the Liberals could be found than Henry Broadhurst, who, as secretary of the Parliamentary Committee, revealed both within the Congress and in the Commons how determined he was to maintain that political connection and to prevent the unions from being dazzled by dangerous Socialist ideas.

III

The absence of political militancy in the ranks of labor during the mid-Victorian period helps explain their uneasiness over and resistance to socialism in the years that followed. Despite the efforts of Socialists to change this, the trade unions were able for the most part to determine the shape of independent labor politics and mold them to serve their more limited aims. The prior achievements of the trade unions were sufficient to ensure this outcome. The future Labour party was never allowed to forget how fragile its foundations were without trade-union support. At the same time, an articulated Socialist program capable of imposing its will on the unions was not likely to emerge for two reasons: British socialism suffered from both organizational and doctrinal fragmentation; and few labor leaders in positions of power were ready to commit themselves directly and publicly to Socialist principles. The persistent vitality of the Liberals was in some measure responsible for these inhibitions. The successive challenges to liberalism were indeed formidable, but few of them came from the established forms of trade unionism or the Labour party which in part reflected its goals in the House of Commons. So long as the paths to economic and political power seemed to encounter no overwhelming obstacles, so long as the Liberal party itself appeared to stand for social and political reform, (5) so long, finally, as the labor movement believed that its progress was dependent on the achievements of these reforms, its leaders, both in the unions and in the party, were unprepared and unable to become the proponents of radical action.

Whatever the exact temporal origins of the "new unionism" were and however justified are the qualifications which have been raised about its novelty in the labor movement, it is generally recognized that at some point in the mideighties, dissatisfaction with existing labor institutions led to the founding of a number of new unions which, in spirit and organization, were marked off from those that had commanded acceptance in older labor circles. The major impulse for this new development was provided, with few exceptions, by men and women whose analysis of the traditional forms of trade unionism was informed by their contact with and experience in the small Socialist sects of which the Social Democratic Federation, the Socialist League, and the Fabian Society were the most important. (6) Although these groups were divided from each other in doctrine and tactics, each provided a pool of ideas which the leaders of the "new unionism" adapted to the problems connected with the task of organizing large numbers of unskilled workmen. Will Thorne, Tom Mann, and John Burns shared H. M. Hyndman's contempt for the entrenched power of the trade unions, but they believed that their structure and objectives could be changed by setting up labor unions in rivalry with them. Hyndman's aloofness, together with his illusion of building a political party without first seeking a mass base for it, the "new unionists" rejected as profoundly shortsighted. Socialism, they held, would penetrate the consciousness of the British working class only when the exploitative nature of capitalism was reduced to symbols with immediate meaning for workers who had neither the skills, education, nor previous organization to improve their conditions. (7)

The time for labor's renewal was propitious. The unemployment rates of skilled workers had risen steadily from 1884 to 1887, but more serious was the incidence of unskilled unemployment; it was considerably higher, and it was to these groups of workers that the S.D.F. and the Socialist League addressed their appeals, without however, going far enough to satisfy the most militant of their members. With improving economic conditions beginning in 1887, the militants saw their opportunity to articulate the grievances of large sections of workers who were outside the ranks of organized labor. Noteworthy too were the attacks launched on the leaders of the Trades Union Congress and its Parliamentary Committee at precisely this time by members whose denunciation of capitalism revealed some acquaintance with Socialist ideology or was at least similar in tone to the demands made by the "new unionists." In almost every instance of renewed labor agitation among the unskilled, Socialists of various persuasions took the lead in organizing strikes. The eight-hour day, a minimum wage, and the right to work formed a triad of demands of enormous appeal to the strikers. That demands issued by organized miners and cotton operatives were largely identical would appear to call into question the innovations of the "new unionism." But the established unions in these industries clung to their exclusiveness and saw no reason to question their traditional alliance with the Liberals. Moreover, in those parts of the country in which the coal and textile industries had been poorly organized, the "new unions" also made headway. To these workers whom the older unions had neglected or had been unable to organize, and to the unskilled whom

they had deliberately excluded, the invidious distinction between skilled and unskilled labor was felt to be intolerable, and
they eagerly accepted Burns's analysis that the new technology
was erasing labor status based on skill as an explanation for their
plight and as a rationale for action. (8) This was decidedly
Marxist in orientation as was the 1892 Gasworkers' statement of
aims in which the principle of the class struggle and the belief
in the self-emancipation of the workers were stated in hard and
biting words. (9) There was a good deal more of this kind of
talk than is generally admitted. The task of trade unionism, as
Tom Mann and Ben Tillett saw it, was to become "the all-
powerful instrument for abolishing poverty. . . ." (10) Accordingly "trade unions shall be the centres of enlightenment, and
not merely the meeting-place for paying contributions and receiving donations." (11)

The "new unionists" sought to create an organizational structure that would ensure "the solidarity of the workers—employed
and unemployed, skilled and unskilled." (12) What they desired
were general unions comprising the workers of several industries.
The Gasworkers, the Dockers, and the National Amalgamated
Union of Labour were general unions of this type. But this was
not the only structural form assumed by the "new unions." There
were also single-industry unions, such as the Leeds Builders'
Labourers and Mahon's Postmen's Union. The original structures
envisaged were soon altered if only because both leaders and
workers found that practice demanded it. Structural innovation
was in any case less significant than the fact that the "new
unionism," by powerfully challenging the foundations of the old,
tried to destroy their spirit of compliance. If the leaders of the
"new unionism" were more conscious than their predecessors of
the need to adapt unionism to the changing structure of the
economy and the newly emerging technological society, then it
must be said that they were far from successful. (13) What they
achieved was the organization of workers, skilled, semiskilled,
or unskilled, who had been outside the unions and who now
became members of both the "new" and the older unions. For
a time, they succeeded in shaking the complacency of the older
union leaders, who, as it turned out, proved to be the chief

beneficiaries of the "new unionism." For ironically, after the first enthusiasm which inflated the ranks of the "new unions" during the brief upturn of the business cycle, their membership fell with the return of economic difficulties; and while they began to rise again by 1900, reaching a figure of 204,000, they were still some 150,000 short of the workers who had been organized in 1890. (14) By contrast, the older unions saw a considerable expansion in membership. From 750,000 in 1888 just before the full impact of the "new unionism" was felt, the older unions more than doubled their membership to some 1.8 million by the turn of the century.

IV

Diverse as the roots of British socialism were, it was hardly "a slumgullion of fads and dissensions that could accommodate any view, so long as it was unconventional," as an unkind critic, trying to describe it as it appeared in 1906, recently dismissed it. (15) That there were in socialism's ranks men and women whose eccentricities amused and often outraged respectable Victorians is surely no criterion for assessing the worth of the ideas they espoused nor the activities in which they were involved. Hyndman cannot be considered quite *déclassé*, for he continued his activities in the world of business even as he attacked its ethics. The Webbs never lost respectability; their links with society were never broken. Of great importance was the relative openness of politics in Britain, for difficult though it was, there were no insuperable barriers to the adoption of new ideas provided they met the tests of political practicability. This was an old tradition and the way in which both Liberals and Conservatives, ever attentive to their political fortunes, received new forms of thought and adapted them to serve their purposes.

In Britain, a rigorous Marxist body of thought was lacking. Engels's residence in London, as Marx's involvement in the First International, made little direct impact. Hyndman's S.D.F., later the Social Democratic party, was the only Socialist group to style itself as Marxist, but while its members believed in the imminent collapse of ₁apitalism and relied on some of the sim-

pler Marxist formulations to support their predictions, most of
them neither made an effort to grasp the full thrust of Marxism
nor used it as a foundation for analyzing the further development of industrial capitalism. In other words, in Britain "Marxism
was as yet unrepresented in the theoretical field." (16) Although
Das Kapital had not been entirely neglected by a few intrepid
souls, especially by a small group of Jewish Social Democrats in
the early 1900s, (17) its intricacies remained a mystery until
after 1918. To point out that George Bernard Shaw and Hyndman
had both read it is not to prove a great deal; Hyndman's understanding of it was never profound, and Shaw soon rejected some
of its chief principles. On the other hand, William Morris's grasp
of Marxism was probably unmatched in Britain, even if he publicly shrugged off its difficulties.

However slender was the S.D.F.'s grip on doctrine, it would
be a mistake to dismiss the Federation as an alien anomaly with
no roots in Britain—a species of political myth making indulged
in by the Fabians. Despite the series of eruptions that led to
defections and personal rivalries, the S.D.F. was a vital force in
British socialism. (18) Apart from making some real progress in
Lancashire, the S.D.F.'s progress in the provinces was limited.
Its greatest strength lay in London where it established several
branches in the principal working-class districts and gained a
following chiefly from workers who had once been the mainstay
of London radicalism. Its successes occurred in such areas as
West Ham, which was heavily industrialized—perhaps more so
than a great many provincial towns, though London's industries
as a whole were smaller in scale than those in the North and the
Midlands. Its antireligious tone did not alienate London working
men, the great majority of whom were neither church nor chapel-
goers. In any case, with the passing of time, its secularism gave
way to a kind of vague religiosity associated with the ethical
movement before the war. Much of its direction was in the
hands of middle-class and self-educated working-class leaders.
In the local politics of London's districts, these men, either alone
or in cooperation with trade unionists and radicals, sought to
change conditions in the workhouses, campaigned for better
housing, the extension of education, and many of the reforms

generally associated with the credo of municipal socialism. In fact, Hyndman's pamphlet, *A Commune for London* published in 1887, appeared before Webb's own contribution to the cause of gas and water socialism. The solid work of the S.D.F. in the area of municipal politics is perhaps its most enduring legacy, and but for its inability to work in a larger labor group after 1900, it might have made even a larger impact. For all that, the Social Democrats retained their primacy in the London Socialist movement down to 1914.

If Marxism as a dynamic doctrine played a minor role in the S.D.F., it was an entirely negligible element in the thought of the Fabians. Beatrice Webb's reasons for accepting the Marxist analysis of the breakdown of capitalism just before the outbreak of the war is proof enough that until then, she and Sidney as well as the majority of Fabians deliberately excluded Marx's contributions from their vision. As Mrs. Webb put it, "the Fabian Society studiously avoided any quotations from Karl Marx, preferring indeed Robert Owen; they translated economics and collectivism into the language of prosaic vestrymen and town councillors." (19) Shaw, to be sure, had for a while been a convert, but his dismissal of the labor theory of value in favor of marginal utility ended his brief flirtation. In only one respect did Fabianism approach Marxist analysis. In both can be found the prediction that the changes induced by industrialism would in due course destroy the foundations of capitalism and set up in their place those of a Socialist order. But the Fabian belief in the Socialist future, best expressed in the original *Fabian Essays,* was rooted in the late philosophy and speculations of John Stuart Mill, who thought of socialism as the probable outcome and desired objective of modern industrialism. Like Mill, the Fabians maintained that society was surely moving in this direction, but unlike Marx, they were certain that Britain's political institutions would permit the advent of socialism by a gradual and nonviolent process. Since for them existing political institutions were capable of being transformed rather than destroyed, the chief task lay in convincing the political potentates of their duty to accept the formulations required for introducing necessary and inevitable changes. They thought of themselves as intellectual shock-troops, social engineers, or the founders of a social science based on empirical investigations of social and economic problems to be solved by groups of experts dedicated to planning the future.

If the Fabians are important, it is because of their contributions to the creed of collectivism—the direction by the public authorities of most aspects of industrial society. Yet if they urged the state to assume the direction of major sectors of the economy —the planning of production, distribution and exchange—they were hardly perfunctory democrats. It is true that they were impatient with any proposals for democratizing the industrial process, with workers sharing in the management of factories and plants. Such a scheme was neither efficient nor practicable. Their central government was to be anchored to the wishes of a democratic electorate whose desires and needs could also be served by full participation in trade unionism and cooperatives. While it was essential for the efficient operation of certain industries and services and necessary to ensure social justice, the Fabians did not conceive of it as the sole or single most important repository of public ownership and control. They preferred, at least in their earliest proposals, to vest the bulk of authority in the hands of municipalities and hoped to advance their ideas by converting the new county councils to them. It was only during the 1900s, when some of the Fabians realized that the councils and municipalities lacked the resources to cope with all the problems of planning the financing and administration of the largest industries and services, that they considered establishing new regional units to direct them. The Webbs, at least, were not as convinced as their fellow Fabians, Emil Davies and Chiozza Money, that nationalization was the best form of collectivism.

It would be tempting to believe that these intellectual labors were immediately influential. A reading of Beatrice Webb's diaries and autobiography, for example, seems to leave no doubt that a number of key politicians in both the older parties and in the Labour party, trade unionists, and Socialists of various schools, were the principal means whereby the Webbs and their closest colleagues gained acceptance of their main ideas and plans. It is certainly difficult to measure their impact. Probably the popularizations of Fabian views—largely the work of Shaw and Wells—forced their way into the consciousness of a wider public. The same cannot be said of the more technical essays and books which were in any case not designed to reach the same audience. The Fabians refused to lend themselves to new political ventures, holding themselves aloof from the Independent Labour Party (I.L.P.). They became involved in the Labour party only reluctantly and with many reservations. They believed that more lasting results would be achieved by working through or permeating the traditional political institutions. Hence, they cooperated with the Progressive party in London, became members of Royal Commissions, sought to gain the confidence of leading unionists, and did their best to lay their plans before the guardians of the Liberal party. Many of their schemes, such as municipal socialism, were not original with them. The Webb's Minority Report on the Poor Law Commission was virtually ignored by the Liberal party, and its inauguration of policies aimed at the solution of urban problems and unemployment controverted some of the basic Fabian principles. Mrs. Webb had no sense of compassion for human failure; Winston Churchill showed not only greater tolerance but a deeper understanding of the wastage of the industrial system. (20) In many fields of welfare legislation, as A. M. McBriar has demonstrated, (21) the Liberals formulated their own concepts which in point of time preceded those of the Fabians. And the leaders of the Parliamentary Labour party, if touched at all by Fabian ideas, were above all receptive to those counseling caution and collaboration with the Liberals.

By the 1890s, Socialists were making some headway towards planting the roots of widely based independent political action, but neither the S.D.F. nor the Fabians were responsible for it. The former, as we saw, was chiefly a London phenomenon and conserved most of its energies to organizing the working classes in the city's far-flung districts. As for the Fabians, they too were largely London-centered. After a few brief but abortive attempts in 1892 and 1893 to organize an independent political party, they scrupulously avoided any new political commitments. If this was the attitude of the London Fabians, it was not emulated

by the Society's branches elsewhere, where in both composition
—it was working class—and outlook, they differed from the
parent body. Similarly, provincial members of the S.D.F., as well
as others who had been in its ranks or still retained ties with it,
were not as inhibited as the stalwarts in the Federation about
the prospects of a separate party representing the combined
interests of the labor movement. Indeed, tiny splinter groups
comprising former Social Democrats and Socialist Leaguers tried
to create by various means the nucleus of an independent party,
but the difficulties were too great. Unsuccessful as these efforts
were, the essential point is that Socialists joined forces for this
purpose, whatever it was in socialism they chose to stress and
however different were the paths along which they had traveled
to it.

While none would deny that a good deal of the propaganda
favoring the creation of an independent party was the work of
Londoners—Champion, Eleanor Marx and Edward Aveling, Keir
Hardie, J. H. Mahon, Thorne, Mann, Tillett, and even Burns—
the problems involved were solved in Yorkshire, and it was there
that the I.L.P. was finally set on its course in 1893. All the conditions for success seemed right in the textile regions of the
West Riding: "A close-knit community. . . . An industry facing
readjustment and competition. Declining wages and appalling
social evils. Tremendous problems in the way of effective trade-
union organization. A strong tradition of campaigning for legal
protection in industry and limitation of hours. And . . . the tradition of the *political* independence of labour." (22) And lest
there remain the impression that the Methodists assisted in the
birth of the I.L.P., John Trevor's Labour Churches, so important
to the diffusion of Socialist sentiments, were nondenominational
and acted as a "unifying influence," closing the gap between
"moral enthusiasm and the hard cutting intellect. . . ." (23) Sin
was identified with merciless and wicked capitalists, and salva-
tion with the just aspirations of the workers. Robert Blatchford,
writing under the name of Numquam in the weekly *Clarion*,
published in Manchester, attracted readers for similar reasons.
His *Merrie England*, summarizing his beliefs in a new Socialist

society free from the restraints and injustices of industrial capitalism, had enormous appeal.

The I.L.P.'s goals were openly Socialist. "The collective ownership and control of the means of production, distribution and exchange," were stated clearly in its program, while the struggle for the achievement of immediate social and economic changes was articulated in a number of demands including the eight-hour day, a minimum wage, the right to work to be guaranteed by projects undertaken by local governments, state pensions for those over fifty, free secondary education, and confiscatory taxation of unearned incomes. At first, more stress was put on its ultimate objectives and less on piecemeal reforms; later, at the urging of leaders like MacDonald and Glasier who were impressed by the progress of municipal reforms embodying what they regarded as the essentials of municipal socialism, the emphasis was reversed. At first, too, the party organized branches rapidly in Yorkshire, Lancashire, and Cheshire, Scotland, and the Midlands, where it was strongest, but later found resistance elsewhere, particularly in London where it encountered the rivalry of the S.D.F., the Fabian Society, and the Progressives. The T.U.C. also offered opposition, though gradually the leaders of the "new unionism" made their views prevail in a number of unions (24) which consequently became receptive to the idea of joint action, until finally the Congress in 1899 endorsed Keir Hardie's long-nurtured hopes of creating an organization reflecting the strengths and wishes of the entire labor movement. Many in Congress were prompted more by the recent court decision threatening the right to strike and picket than by real sympathy for socialism or for an independent labor party. What moved them equally was the coercive power of a number of employers' organizations dedicated to the curtailment of aggressive trade unionism.

It was almost predetermined that the Labour Representation Committee should address itself primarily in the first years of the century to the problems faced by the unions. The unions' presence in the L.R.C. was overwhelmingly determined by utilitarian purposes—the removal of the unexpected legal restraints that had been imposed on them, as well as their expectation that united labor action would help them in their struggle against the counterattack of the employers. The primacy given union demands arose from the same L.R.C. rationalization that had led to its formation—that labor as an independent political force would be stillborn without the financial and numerical strength of the unions. By 1901 only forty-one unions representing some 350,000 members had become affiliates of the L.R.C. The majority of unions—over 1200 with a membership totaling 1.3 million—remained outside. (25) The L.R.C.'s determination to obtain full trade-union support was stimulated by this reticence.

The persistence of trade-union hesitation was due to the poor showing of the L.R.C.'s candidates in the 1900 elections, when only two of its fifteen candidates, Hardie and Richard Bell, general secretary of the Railway Servants, were elected to the House. Not even the Taff Vale railway decision in the following year did much at first to change the thinking of a good many trade unionists. Bell, against whose union the courts had granted an injunction, warned the 1900 T.U.C. that an adverse decision by the House of Lords, where the case was being heard for the third time, would emasculate the unions. When the House of Lords handed down its decision, however, he took a more sanguine position, similar to that of others including Sidney Webb who felt that Taff Vale would have the beneficent consequence of extending to unions "full corporate status, legally enforceable agreements and compulsory arbitration." (26) There were others in the unions who shared such views. They were particularly impatient with what they felt were the rash actions of a number of unions infected by the propaganda of militant Socialists; they preferred to eliminate any ideological overtones from the unions and to transform them into respectable bodies seriously and pragmatically attentive only to the orderly and legitimate demands of their members. It was the apprehensions of the rank and file at the 1901 Congress that induced the passage of a resolution urging all unions to use their pressure to reverse the implications of the decision. However, the leaders were not bound in any way to pursue a concrete course of action. In the meantime, the Parliamentary Committee sought to regain some protection for the unions by pressing, in and outside the Commons, for new legislation, but the attempt in 1902 to ensure the legality of peaceful picketing failed, and later that year the T.U.C. still left the question of union-fund protection unsettled. The more conservative unions were obviously not as troubled by Taff Vale as were the leaders of the L.R.C. Towards the end of 1902 and especially during the following year, the unions succumbed to pressures for a complete reversal of the offending court decisions. Some of the credit for the policy change must be given to the L.R.C whose trade-union affiliation had increased during this period (27) as a result of the fears that the Taff Vale decision had inspired. The L.R.C. was thus partly responsible for the unions' demands for complete legal immunity. Nevertheless its zeal on this question is not to be construed as proof of its ascendancy over the unions. The unions were impelled to reverse their earlier reluctance to contest the Taff Vale decision for other reasons as well. The magnitude of the damages imposed on the Railway Servants and the composition of the Royal Commission on Trade Disputes and Trade Combinations which the Balfour government had packed with men hostile to unionism were doubtless decisive. Webb's inclusion in it was small comfort because of his well-known support for the idea of making unions legal entities. Besides, the unions' new outlook hardly meant an endorsement of the L.R.C.'s total program. In any case, by this time the L.R.C. was subordinating its earlier, more far-reaching goals to the task of furbishing an image that would attract all sections of the labor community—above all the trade unions. What is more, the Parliamentary Committee and the individual unions continued their own campaigns for new labor legislation; quite understandably, too, since they hardly felt absolute confidence in the political strength of the L.R.C.; and then, they could also exploit their established lines of communication with the Liberals from whom they expected and received promises to enact the necessary protective legislation once the elections of 1906 returned a Liberal government.

That the L.R.C. accepted the political maneuvers of the Parliamentary Committee with some equanimity and with little criticism was due to two developments. The first was the establishment by the L.R.C in 1903 of an electoral fund based on a voluntary levy—made compulsory in 1904—of a penny a member from each of the affiliated societies. This ensured that a portion of the electoral expenses of L.R.C.'s candidates would be covered; in addition, an annual grant of £200 was to be made available for successful candidates endorsed by the L.R.C. The fact that the unions in the L.R.C. gave their approval marked a step forward in its goal of becoming a party with solid backing. The second reason for the L.R.C.'s acquiescence arose from its own political bargaining with the Liberals with whom MacDonald secretly negotiated a *quid pro quo* agreement on a division of constituencies between the Liberal and Labour candidates in the 1906 elections. At the same time, representatives of the L.R.C. executive met with members of the Parliamentary Committee and the General Federation of Trade Unions—which had been set up by the T.U.C. in 1899 to consolidate strike funds—and agreed to support one another's candidates. It was clear that on the eve of the elections the unions were prepared to make the fullest use of their resources to overthrow the government, to the extent of recognizing its parity with the L.R.C.—a body that was ostensibly the voice of labor elements other than their own. It was equally obvious, however, that in the minds of those who established policy in the L.R.C., those elements were less important than the trade unions. Parity was achieved, to be sure, but at the price of virtual subordination to the unions and of ensuring the electoral ambitions of the Liberals.

The elections appeared to justify the calculations of the policy-makers in the unions, the Liberal party, and the L.R.C. For the unions, the victory was perhaps most meaningful. On whatever basis one computes the number of successful Labor candidates, nearly three-quarters of them were members of trade unions. (28) If thirty of the new Members of Parliament (M.P.s) were members of the L.R.C., twenty-three of them were also trade unionists. Seven of the successful candidates had been sponsored by the I.L.P., and an additional eleven were members, but this did not mean a commitment to Socialist ideas except in the most general way. (29) The Liberals were returned with an enormous number of additional seats; their absolute majority over all other parties stood at eighty-four. Therefore, despite the enhanced standing of the L.R.C. in the new House, its presence was in large part due to the votes of the unions and the Liberals, and, equally significant, to the dilution of its long-term objectives. It adopted the name of Labour party and devoted itself chiefly to the tasks of removing the ill effects of the Taff Vale decision and of supporting legislation aimed at extending additional protection to labor, the Workmen's Compensation Act being the best example. In return it received little aid for such wider measures as would have guaranteed employment.

Unless the Labour party was prepared to revive some of the explicit Socialist aims which it had discreetly dropped, there was virtually nothing to distinguish the Labour M.P.s from the Liberals. The absence of division was of no concern to the leaders of the Parliamentary Labour party, particularly after Hardie resigned from its leadership, while those who increasingly managed the affairs of the party—men like MacDonald and Henderson— operated wholly in pragmatic terms and contributed little if anything to Socialist theory or to working out plans for economic reconstruction. It was enough for them to act as the tolerant watchdogs of the Liberal party from whom they expected little more than timely concessions which they believed were the most practicable way of improving the condition of the working classes. Society for MacDonald was moving inevitably towards some form of socialism. The Liberals, by accepting some of labor's demands, were assisting this development; and the time would come when men from all classes, whether Socialist or not, would vote for a Labour party dedicated to social amelioration. Similar reasoning motivated Henderson, a former Liberal for whom socialism as theory was irrelevant. His vision of a mature industrial society under socialism never went beyond expecting greater state intervention and control. Their smooth cooperation with the Liberals and the Parliamentary Committee of the T.U.C. irked men like Snowden, Jowett, and Lansbury. Although Snowden's socialism was not unlike Henderson's, he was a much more consistent and frank, but dogmatic, advocate of nationalization. Jowett's socialism was felt more deeply, and he had no patience with tortuous parliamentary procedure. George Lansbury who found the pre-

vailing views unpalatable, dreary, and unimaginative, threatened
to resign from the party. But neither he nor the others could
force themselves to do so because of their loyalty to the party
and their hope of changing its direction.

Within the Labour party efforts to exercise some control over
the activities of its M.P.s were not lacking. After 1907 they were
bound in theory to carry out the instructions of the Annual Conference, but in practice they were allowed considerable freedom
in their execution. Similarly, there emerged a wide divergence
between the Party Conference resolutions and the course actually
followed. Victor Grayson's campaign in the Colne Valley by-
election in 1907 focused the discontent. He ran without support
from the national executives of either the Labour party or the
I.L.P. His success was a rebuke to both, and his subsequent performance in the House where he flouted the rules and assumed
the role of an independent Socialist critic was a source of em-
barrassment to the custodians of party respectability. For many
he became the symbol of rank and file's discontent with the
official policy of compliance. When other independent candidates
presented themselves at by-elections during the next two years,
the party leaders were faced with the problem of halting the
growing disaffection. The defeat of these locally sponsored candidates partially restored their confidence, but did not stifle internal
criticism. Ben Tillett's lavish denunciation of the party's lassitude
and hypocrisy (30) was countered by a fresh endorsement in
1909 of the I.L.P.'s freedom of action; and in the same year a
resolution at the I.L.P. conference to secede from the Labour
party was heavily defeated.

If the attacks upon the leadership continued, especially after
the affiliation of the Miners' Federation with the Labour party
strengthened the counsels of moderation and compromise, the
party could derive no small comfort from a policy aimed at
creating a stable front based on the financial power of the unions.
The Osborne Judgment—by which the House of Lords decided
that the unions' participation in politics and financial support
of a political party were illegal—was of course, a threat to the
Labour party and the unions, but paradoxically it provided a new
battlecry for both. It also justified the continued reliance on the

Liberals for support in the two elections called in 1910, for without their assistance the Labour party would have found the campaigns financially beyond its means. The leadership also argued that only the return of a Liberal government could ensure the reversal of the Osborne decision and restrict the powers of the Lords. Thus the advantages of political symbiosis preserved the working alliance of Liberals, trade unions, and the Labour party. During the next four years, political bargaining, with Lloyd George virtually determining the terms, restored to the unions and the Labourites most if not all of their rights and powers, for while new legislation was introduced in 1911 to provide salaries for M.P.s thereby reducing the Labour party's financial burden, the Trade Union Act of 1913 restricted union freedom to engage in political activities by requiring them to earmark special funds for that purpose. Moreover, such political funds could not be constituted without seeking the approval of a majority of the union membership. Though this proved irksome, the union leadership was reasonably content, as was its counterpart in the Labour party.

For many others, however, the record of the established organs of the labor movement appeared dismal and unpromising. Voices of protest of varying degrees of militancy urged new policies aimed at restoring to the labor movement its original goal of working-class emancipation which, they believed, would not be achieved by the deadening hand of parliamentarism. Such views were already being expressed, as we have seen, within the party. They had been a much more consistent part of the S.D.F.'s program and remained so during its various transformations, the last being its emergence as the British Socialist party in 1911. The same distrust of parliamentary reform inspired the advocates of industrial unionism and syndicalism. Stimulated by a series of mass strikes which began in 1910 and continued until 1914, they called into question the entire ethos of the decision makers in the unions and in the Labour party. Condemning the practice of collective bargaining, the compromises inherent in the machinery devised for conciliation and arbitration, and the divisiveness of fragmented unionism, they expected to transform the nature of industrial society by militant strike action involving

entire segments of the labor force, the various industrial constituents being subsumed under "One Big Union." There were
differences among the various militant leaders. Some insisted
on complete reliance on revolutionary industrial action; others
pressed for a combination of industrial strike action and a militant
Socialist party; and still others wanted to form a revolutionary
party dedicated to direct industrial attack on the economy. All,
however, believed in the efficacy and practicability of democratic control and management of industry by the workers, and
none any longer reposed much hope in the nationalization of industry by the coercive organs of the state. Even if it could be
reformed to serve the interests of producers and consumers, it
would not cease to control their lives and would not abolish the
wage system. It was this aspect of the new labor militance that
was stressed most by the Guild Socialists who, in the pages of the
New Age, Lansbury's *Daily Herald,* and in a number of books
and pamphlets, envisaged the reconstruction of an industrial
society in which production would be determined by national
guilds based on the unions, the interests of consumers would be
guaranteed by Parliament, while the state would, in case of conflict, act as final arbiter.

The rank and file who participated in the great wave of strikes
in the mines, docks, railways, and transport industries were eager
to accept much of this analysis of the ills of industrialism under
capitalism, but they were doubtless moved more, at least in the
first instance, by traditional grievances. Prices had risen alarm-
ingly, at first slowly between 1902 and 1908, and then more
rapidly from 1909 and 1913; no wage increases of substance had
been gained to meet the rising living costs. The displacement of
skilled by unskilled workers and the attempts of management
to erase differences between them intensified labor unrest. In
some of the larger industries, the failure to devise an effective
system of industrial relations could not but help tip the balance in
favor of violence. In other industries, workers had long been
trying to establish unions and took advantage of the feverish
climate of strike action to lay down their tools and fight for
recognition. Most of the strikes were authorized through the
normal channels of the unions' leadership; a few were more

purely spontaneous and lacked union authorization. The more conservative union leaders would have preferred to achieve their goals without resorting to strikes and violence, but could neither ignore nor withhold their approval from the gains made by the strikers in several industries. They were, however, alarmed by the propaganda of men like Tom Mann who were in the vanguard of the new agitation and were worried lest their more patient efforts to bargain with management and to seek the good graces of the government be thwarted by the hotheads in the unions. In this they were supported by the leaders in the Labour party. While making the customary genuflections before the altar of successful strike action, they adamantly reiterated that Parliament would remain the ultimate arbiter of social and industrial improvement. Both were assisted by the government's efforts to establish the necessary machinery for the settlement of disputes. The great increase in union membership—it jumped from two and a half to four million during the years 1910 and 1914—and the formation in 1914 of the Triple Alliance of Miners, Railwaymen, and Transport Workers held both a threat and a promise for the labor establishment. The possibility of additional strikes and even a general strike could dislodge them from power; on the other hand, skillful guidance of the new mood in unionism could result in more sophisticated conciliation procedures and the "promise of stability at a new level, not of upheaval." (31)

Stability, not class struggle, was the *summum bonum* of the Labourites and the union hierarchy. Neither the one nor the other was committed to a militant Socialist creed; indeed, the most powerful men in both were either discomfited by allusions to socialism or hostile to it. Their opponents in the labor movement were divided among themselves not only before 1910, but after as well. The older groups on the Left held themselves aloof from the new militancy, the Fabians retreating more and more to their favorite tactic of seeking change through discreet means, while the British Socialist party denounced the anarchosyndicalism of the militant labor leaders. The I.L.P. survived despite the secession of dissatisfied elements. These groups, especially the Social Democrats in the London area with their roots deeply embedded in the working classes, retained sufficient vitality to prevent the consolidation of a strengthened and unified movement on the new Left. Of course, the militant labor leaders felt that they could storm the bastions of tradition in the labor movement without the support of the older Socialist splinter groups. At the time, the scent of even greater victories flowing from direct action served to minimize the differences between the various groups of the new Left. Had the challenges to the established order not been interrupted by the war, the divisions among the militants would certainly have come to the surface, with what results it is difficult to say. In the event, the resolution of these problems lay in the future.

CHAPTER 3.

FRANCE: THE USES OF IDEOLOGY IN AN UNDERDEVELOPED INDUSTRIAL SOCIETY

An industrial society with older, static elements, based on small units of production, yet developing alongside them large concentrations of factory labor, could not but produce a wide variety of responses from its working classes. At the risk of simplification, we may think of the French labor force as being divided into four categories. At one end of the spectrum was the homeworker, who usually produced for the clothing trade, suffered excessive exploitation, and worked in isolation. The artisanal workers in the book, building, small metal and woodworking trades worked side by side with their *patrons* (employers) and were often on friendly terms with them. Then there were the large concentrations of workers, usually women, in the textile factories. The highest labor density was to be found in heavy industry, such as steel manufacturing and mining, and in the newer automotive and chemical concerns.

The widely ranging qualifications, labor traditions, and the extent of urbanization of the labor force must also be taken into account in plotting the reflexes of the working classes. Highly skilled workers in the printing or metal trades, for example, were relatively well paid, conscious of their superiority and of belonging to a group or class materially and psychologically armed for struggle with employers. They were nevertheless reformist rather than revolutionary in their outlook. The textile workers, at the other extreme, had no skills, performed simple machine operations, earned little, were subjected to harsh factory discipline, and were obsessed with fear of unemployment. Resigned and passive for the most part, their consciousness of being a class apart fed belief in a future transformed by revolution. Whether or not the working classes were reformist or revolutionary in turn depended somewhat on their mobility. In such older industries as textiles and metal production, for example, it was customary for generations of families and whole areas to serve as an unchanging supply of labor. Such conditions helped generate a heightened sense of class consciousness. On the other hand, new sources of labor of recent peasant origin were recruited in the newer industrial regions and in newer industries, such as rayon and chemical manufacturing; in the latter a combination of intense employer resistance and labor suspicion prevented the easy penetration of unionism and socialism. Thus mobility or its absence was a factor in the shaping of labor protest. Nor can one ignore the responses of workers in small towns specializing in a single industry as opposed to those of workers in larger urban areas with a wider variety of industrial structures.

No discussion of the structures of labor would be complete without making brief reference to the longer- and shorter-term conditions of economic growth and the impact they made on working-class aspirations. It must be noted first that the period extending from the early 1870s to the mid-1890s was marked by economic sluggishness which expressed itself in a rather considerable decline in prices. For the period as a whole, the French labor movement, under enormous psychological as well as economic pressure, exhibited revolutionary features associated with the older Jacobin tradition. (1) From about 1876 to 1878 a recession affected particularly the silk, textiles, mining, and metallurgical industries, and had serious repercussions throughout the economy. This was followed by a brief period (1879–82) of economic vigor inspired by the Fréycinet railway-building plan, only to give way to an even more serious crisis affecting all sectors of the economy and leaving in its wake a deep hatred of foreign labor which had been imported during the railway-building boom. It is not surprising therefore to discover that General Boulanger, regarded as a savior by a wide spectrum of French society, should, because of his promise to rid France of foreign workers, attract working-class support in the later 1880s, the more so as many of the artisanal trades felt themselves threatened by the application of new techniques in industry. (2) The industrial system under capitalism appeared to its critics, especially Jules Guesde, the major personality in the Socialist movement in this period, to be reaching its end with the collectivist society of his dreams waiting to take the center of the stage. (3)

From about 1895 to 1914—the period which has been dubbed *la belle époque*—the French economy moved forward. Price levels advanced rapidly; profits rose; and wages increased. The exact nature of the impulses given French economic development in the last twenty years before the war is still a subject of debate. For our present purposes it is useful to stress a number of factors of special relevance to the evolution of the working-class profile. While, to be sure, working-class living standards improved, rising wages were more than offset by the increase in prices which reached rather spectacular heights between 1910 and 1914. (4) Inflationary periods and relatively full employment, however, are more conducive to more practical forms of labor protest, such as were beginning to be urged by some sections of French syndicalism after 1909. Perhaps more important in modifying labor's attitudes were the advantages derived from the introduction of social legislation, which, all the same, were rather niggling in comparison with the greater social benefits in Germany and

Britain. Yet together with greater educational opportunities as well as those connected with openings in tertiary employment, at least some of the better-off workers experienced improved conditions. The share in the economy's growth was certainly not felt equally by all sections of labor, but what could be discerned was the greater portion of some working-class budgets given to a more varied diet and better clothing, signs both of better wages and of an expectation of social amelioration. (5) More difficult to assess is how these workers whose portion of the national income had increased, however slightly, viewed their relative social and economic position. There are some indications to suggest that as the opportunities for greater social mobility increased, some of the more advantaged sections of labor may have become more willing to accept the existing social order and therefore less receptive to its Socialist critics. (6) In turn, the latter, as we shall see, were trying to devise a program more relevant to the altered social structure. But the process of the labor movement's accommodation, especially that of the militants, to changing conditions, was not tied in absolute fashion to shifts in the economy, and even if adjustment was in the air, the persistence of the more traditional economic structures ensured the survival of the older ideological traditions. Often, at the same time, the attitudes based on such traditions bore little relationship to the objective facts.

II

Before the 1890s when both the French trade-union world and Socialist sects began the process of consolidating their organizational forms and of elaborating coherent programs, they were hampered by excessive fragmentation. For almost a decade after the Commune, the French labor movement remained virtually leaderless and unorganized. If any one figure may be singled out as having decisively changed the direction of French labor and socialism in this period it is Jules Guesde. Armed with a doctrinaire version of Marxism, the subtleties of which he only dimly comprehended, Guesde and his closest companions, including Marx's son-in-law, Paul Lafargue, sought to capture the embryonic unions for a Socialist political party that would dictate such tactics as would facilitate and hasten the assumption of economic and political power the moment capitalism died of its own inanition. In this they were only partly successful, because of clashes of personality within the wider Socialist movement. (7) More telling as an explanation for Guesdist failure to monopolize the labor movement was the refusal of many unionists to subordinate themselves willingly to a political party which had collective ownership as its objective—a resistance which was extended by most branches of organized labor to the other Socialist parties no matter how sympathetically inclined they were to accord a large measure of autonomy to the unions.

Proudly but intolerantly announcing themselves as the sole French interpreters of the Marxist legacy, the Guesdists could not conceal the threadbare quality of their Marxism nurtured as it was, their historian tells us, (8) on only a few elementary Marxist texts which had been translated into French. Indeed, the intellectual sources from which Guesde and Lafargue drew their beatific vision of the future society probably owed more to the thinkers of the eighteenth century and the Utopian Socialists. (9) Guesdism had an all-or-nothing quality; social and economic reforms were for the Guesdists a lure set by the bourgeois masters of the state to trap the workers. On the foundations of this dismissal of social amelioration by gradual reform, the Guesdists created France's first modern political party and armed it with a national program, a central organization, and local and regional branches. From a membership of 2,000 in 1889, Guesdism's strength rose to nearly 20,000 members in 1902, after which the number of the party faithful declined slightly and remained stationary. Party membership in France is not as useful a guide as electoral results to an understanding of political strength. From some 25,000 voters in the 1889 national elections, Guesde's party, the Parti ouvrier français (P.O.F.), attracted 295,000 supporters in the 1898 elections or 40 percent of the total Socialist vote. Electoral victories in several municipalities had preceded the steady improvement of the Guesdist party at the national level.

From what sections of the working class and from what regions did the Guesdists derive their following? When their star shone brightest from about 1893 to 1899, the bulk of their support came from industrial workers in textiles and the small metal trades; from artisans in the building, shoemaking, and woodworking occupations; and from small shopkeepers whose clientele was made up of working men. A smaller number of peasants, viniculturists, and gardeners of petty but independent means also added their strength to the Guesdists. Geographically Guesdism's greatest strength lay in the departments of the Nord and the Pas-de-Calais, old and important textile regions, whose labor force was organized in the Fédération du Nord, one of the most powerful regional unions. Within the Midi, departments such as the Bouches-du Rhône, Aube, Gironde, Hérault and Gard elected more than half of the twelve successful Guesdist deputies in the 1898 elections. There the older Jacobin traditions were the chief reasons for Guesdist influence, but it had to compete with the Radical-Socialists for support. The third zone of Guesdist power stretched across four departments in east-central France: Allier, Loire, Rhône, Isère, where workers in industries such as textiles, metallurgy, and leather provided a following. (10)

Challenges to a Guesdist-oriented labor movement came from within the movement itself, although in 1902 the Socialist group led by Edouard Vaillant (11) joined forces with the Guesdists to form the Parti socialiste de France. The Vaillantists, organized in 1881 as the Comité révolutionnaire central (C.R.C.) and later, in 1898, as the Parti socialiste révolutionnaire (P.S.R.), combined reverence for a revolutionary patriotism inspired by Jacobinism, belief in direct democracy, hope in internationalism, and commitment to the class struggle at home. But no systematic body of theories underpinned the Vaillantist appeals, perhaps because Blanqui their patron saint had primarily been an activist rather than a social analyst. Their stronghold was in the working-class *arrondissements* and suburbs north of Paris where they commanded a dedicated following among metal workers and other artisans for whom the tradition of combat in earlier revolutionary struggles was a living reality. Apart from the Paris region, the P.S.R.'s strength was dispersed in three or four departments on the northern fringe of the Massif Central of which the Cher was the most important, in the urban centers of Lyon and Toulouse, in the lower Loire valley, and in certain areas of the west. (12)

Like the Vaillantists, the Broussists or Possibilistes, who had early in the 1880s broken with the Guesdists whose dogmatism they dismissed as pure intransigence and whose revolutionism they abhorred as dangerous, were chiefly a Paris-centered phenomenon particularly after 1890 when the Broussists lost most of their support outside the capital. (13) Organized as the Fédération des travailleurs socialistes de France (F.T.S.F.), the Broussists were hostile to Guesdist collectivism which they felt denied the yearnings of French workers for a decentralized and autonomous grouping of communes in the tradition of 1871. Moreover, they refused to support the violent overthrow of society. Instead they stressed the municipalization of public services managed by workers who, gaining administrative experience in this way, would prepare themselves for the tasks of running the entire industrial framework of the nation. Thus would socialism transform the capitalist armature of the state.

The explicit reformism of Broussism led to the departure from its ranks of Jean Allemane who set up the Parti ouvrier socialiste révolutionnaire (P.O.S.R.). What divided the Allemanists (14) from Broussism was its negation of the spontaneous revolutionary will of the working classes. For the Allemanists, the lessons of the Commune were to be found in labor's instinctive response to carry on the struggle against capitalist oppression. Even more vital to the Allemanist position was its distrust of the political process as enshrined in the parliamentary system. Much of this denigration had its origins in the Proudhonist legacy which they took up and shaped to justify their beliefs in the virtues of working-class action through the medium of the unions. In the full flowering of socialism, the unions would be responsible for the administration of the economy. It is because of the primacy given to the unions and to the weapon of the general strike as the only way to deliver the final blows against capitalism that the Allemanists can be said to have added an original component to French socialism. Like the Broussists, and, to a lesser degree, the Vaillantists, the Allemanists gained most of their support in Paris and from scattered pockets of followers in a few provincial outcroppings such as the Jura and the Doubs where the heirs of

Bakunin found a congenial home in the P.O.S.R. After the mid-1890s the Allemanists lost their identity as a separate party, but became an important constituent in the revolutionary syndicalist movement.

In spirit the Allemanists were closest to the anarchists. (15) Few in number, the anarchists were nevertheless able to strike a deep chord of sympathy in working-class circles because of such commanding personalities as Jean Grave and Sebastien Faure. Their detestation of all authority and of all restraint, above all of the state, led them to stress the absolute necessity of striking it at its weakest points and so to hasten its destruction. This, they felt, would be achieved by working-class solidarity, especially the united action of labor's elites. Given such an outlook, all institutions such as universal suffrage and parliament which recognized the legitimacy of the state, its laws, and its army, had perforce to be destroyed and their place taken by a free and voluntary association of social and industrial units built up from below with mutual aid as their guiding principle. The principles of anarchism rested on the writings of Proudhon and its action on the memories of Bakunin's struggle against the Marxists in the First International. Together with some of the Allemanists, the anarchists would bring their views of the industrial social order to revolutionary syndicalism.

For the Independent Socialists, (16) such a conception of the existing social structure was as foreign as it was to the Radical-Socialists with whom they shared a few basic postulates. Heirs of the earlier social republicanism associated with the struggles of 1848, they spoke of the triumph through parliamentary measures of social justice and the end of labor's exploitation. Led by men from the ranks of the lower and middle bourgeoisie—lawyers, intellectuals, professors, and journalists—their specific programs of social reform were drawn up in response to the needs of the regions from which they came. Nondoctrinaire, opposed equally to the revolutionism of the anarchists and the rigidities of Guesdist collectivism, they were attracted to the theories of integral socialism advocated by Benoît Malon, (17) who, in founding the *Revue socialiste* in 1885, made it a forum for the free discussion of the various strands of socialism. He aimed to reduce the centrifugal tendencies of French socialism and to forge a synthesis that would appeal to all Socialist sects. Such eclecticism naturally alienated men like Guesde but attracted others like Jean Jaurès, (18) whose own thinking was closest to Malon's. Indeed, in his mature years, Jaurès would erect a more complex structure of socialism by a subtle blending of Marxism, humanitarian idealism, and appeal to the symbolism of the French revolutionary tradition. In these early years, Jaurès had not yet achieved pre-eminence in the Independent Socialist camp. Alexandre Millerand and René Viviani headed the group in its first organized attempt to win seats in the 1893 parliamentary elections.

It is necessary to pause at this point to inquire into the extraordinary divisions within French socialism. French socialism was fed by numerous currents whose main tributaries had risen in a period of nascent industrialism. Their capacity to endure was due in very large part to the persistence, as we have indicated, of significant archaic sectors of the economy in which the artisanal worker's sympathies and aspirations were still tied to patterns of protest which can best be described as heroic and spontaneous, with revolutionary upheaval as its goal. In the 1880s and for a time in the next decade this was almost as true of the Guesdists and the Vaillantists as the Allemanists and anarchists. What was common to these four groups—the Broussists and Independents cannot be considered in the same way—was their belief in the imminent collapse of capitalism, and it is well to be reminded of conditions in the latter 1880s and early 1890s when the economy appeared moribund and when the French political scene was rocked by scandals and undermined by corruption. If such an analysis of conditions created a common pool of hopes, the competing Socialist groups were yet cut off from one another, as we saw, by their assessments of how best to achieve the total transformation of society.

The most obvious and perhaps also most telling reason for the diversity of means urged by the various groups was their domination by personalities whose very names were synonymous with the sects they led. Loyalty to a specific doctrine really meant loyalty to specific leaders. Their differences did not lead to a broadening of the theoretical base of socialism to which they were all pledged, and their respective followings consequently viewed socialism in terms of slogans narrowly identified with a few outstanding persons. The support given each of the groups, as we have seen, came from similar socioeconomic strata. This was clearly true of the Paris region where almost clanlike structures and historic traditions ensured the tenacious hold of the various leaders. In the provinces a similar pattern of personal loyalties was maintained, not excluding the textile regions of the Nord with their ineradicable devotion to Guesde. At no time were these personal rivalries as painfully evident as during election periods. Candidates from the various Socialist parties competed with each other, refusing to collaborate except in the run-off elections when the least-favored Socialist candidate withdrew.

For all the confusion in this testing period, a kind of polarization was, however, beginning to take place. On the one hand, the anarchist and Allemanist strains would assume a new role in the growing unionization of the labor force. On the other hand, despite their protestations to the contrary, the Guesdists and Vaillantists moved closer to reform and parliamentarism, which was almost predictable in light of their eagerness to win places for themselves within the political institutions of the state. What propelled the Guesdist and Vaillantist parties to take part in political contests was the growing realization that the working classes required some assurance that their conditions would be improved not in some distant future but in the present. Problems of housing, food prices, unemployment, hours of work were acute, so that when, for example, the Broussists began a campaign in Paris to set up municipal-housing schemes, the Guesdists, at first opposed to partial remedies, soon altered their views when the workers began to show their approval of the Broussist plans. For the former hostility to reforms were now substituted words praising their efficacy not only as the means to improve conditions but as a self-educative device for workers. Similarly, attention was now devoted to the agitation for the eight-hour day as the solution to unemployment, better wages, and the improvement of the health of workers. From these demands, it was but a short step to urging Socialist members on municipal councils to cease using them as pure sounding boards for revolution in favor of working

towards the achievement of practical programs of reform. Municipal socialism in the local councils of the Nord became almost as
important a part of Guesdist goals as for the Broussists in Paris,
where, in addition, Vaillant himself was a member of the municipal council. Thus almost imperceptibly the Guesdists and Vaillantists were setting up a countercurrent of immediate reform to
their professed revolutionary objectives which over the next decade would undergo further attenuation.

III

Reformism bred its own triumphs in the Socialist successes in the
1892 municipal elections. The Guesdists now predicted that the
road to socialism lay through universal suffrage. The Guesdist
mayor of Roubaix spoke of plans to provide meals for schoolchil-
dren, set up free public bathhouses, maternity hospitals, and
homes for the aged. (19) More decisive was the impressive showing of Socialist candidates in the 1893 parliamentary elections;
some fifty Socialists, the Independents making up the largest contingent, took their seats in the Chamber of Deputies. For Guesde
the results amounted "to the beginning of the Revolution which
will make free men of you." (20) Not a small part of his party's
gains was due to the patriotic appeals of its election platform in
which a Socialist France was envisaged as freeing the world of
tyranny—words reminiscent of Jacobin rhetoric a century before.

The P.O.F.'s confidence in the electoral process may have
aroused serious misgivings among a few of its more relentless
doctrinaires, especially as they witnessed the growing prominence
of the Independents, who were able to throw their net much
wider than the Guesdists. But such doubts were not expressed
when both Guesde and Vaillant subscribed without reservation to
Millerand's summary of Socialist strategy and goals in the famous
Saint-Mandé speech delivered in 1896 following even greater
Socialist victories in municipal elections. Millerand spoke of a
future collective society achieved by means of the ballot. France's
destiny, as that of all modern states, lay, he said, in the collective
ownership of the means of production and distribution in as much

as the economic and technological trends of industrial society were leading to capital concentration which would in progressive stages come under the ownership and direction of the people.

This prognosis of future industrial society humanized by the Socialist ethic found no more receptive listener nor more fervent advocate than Jaurès. No one in socialism's ranks had a greater capacity to weave together the disparate strands of French Socialist traditions, the dialectic and the economic arguments of Marx, the liberal, republican, democratic, and Jacobin legacies of the revolution, and the philosophy of idealism. For him Millerand's statement of principles was only a skeleton; Jaurès fleshed it out in numerous editorials and speeches in the process of which the former dichotomies between reformism and collectivism were transformed in a typical Jaurèssian synthesis. In the 1890s he was building the foundations for his future efforts to solve the complex and tangled problems facing the Socialist party and the unions. In his highly personal way he dealt with what he conceived as France's unique contributions to the eventual victory of socialism. Universal suffrage and republican institutions he did not regard as mere weapons to be brandished in the conquest of a Socialist society. True, they had been perverted by selfish interests serving a bourgeoisie singularly lacking in conscience and concern for humanity. Nevertheless they were of intrinsic value and ought not to be dismissed out of hand by Socialists; they were worth preserving, for though they were historically linked to the triumph of the conquering bourgeoisie, they would continue to show their vitality in a Socialist society. His criticism of bourgeois society was similarly nuanced. His theory of socialism, with its appreciation of past traditions, did not amount to a total condemnation of the bourgeoisie, some elements of whom he saw as constituting valuable allies in a common assault on the hateful survivals of a preindustrial society—clericalism, militarism, race hatred.

This refusal to bow before a narrow sectarianism or to deny sentiments of humanity and ideals of progress to groups within the bourgeoisie made it easier for Jaurès to argue the necessity of defending Dreyfus. The forces supporting the antirevisionists represented all that was retrograde and evil in French society and their eradication was as much the concern of Socialists as non-Socialists who lived by the ideals of liberalism and democracy. To this end Jaurès devoted his enormous energies of mind and oratorical skills. No less convinced of Dreyfus's innocence, Guesde and Vaillant yet held themselves apart from the Socialist campaign led by Jaurès. In their eyes collaboration between Jaurès and non-Socialist politicians and intellectuals was proof of his superficial commitment to Socialist realities. More dangerous was the possible domestication of the working classes which such maneuvers might achieve. The greatest threat, however, was Jaurès's undeniable attractiveness to many in the working classes; if unchecked, Jaurèssism could possibly penetrate Guesdist territory. It was this fear that led the Guesdists towards the end of 1898 to welcome a proposal to discuss the union of all Socialist forces. Guesde doubtless believed that the P.O.F. would emerge strengthened. Jaurès, who actually took the initiative, was motivated by a sincere desire to end the factionalism.

Unity was to be delayed. In 1899 the supple maneuvers leading to Millerand's acceptance of a cabinet post in the Waldeck-Rousseau ministry were the chief causes for the continuing divisions. For Guesde and Vaillant, Millerand's participation in a bourgeois government amounted to a betrayal of socialism. To sanction it, to regard it as a victory for the workers, would only end in the subtle emasculation of socialism. Jaurès thought otherwise. Millerand's presence in the government would be of inestimable value to the Socialist and working-class movements and was no more to be considered an alarming innovation than similar moves in the past decade. The two points of view narrowly missed collision at the Japy Congress of all Socialist groups in 1899 when two motions, one condemning Socialist participation in a bourgeois government except in extraordinary circumstances, the other declaring that such participation was incompatible with the class struggle, gained assent. The issues had been clearly and deliberately glossed over for the moment. They were raised again in the following year when the Guesdists departed from the meetings. (21) In 1901 Vaillant's group also quit the discussions.

What had begun as an effort to resolve differences had ended in rupture. The antiministerialists—Guesdists, Vaillantists, and an offshoot of the Allemanist faction—joined forces to form the Parti socialiste de France, while Jean Jaurès, now uncontested leader of the ministerialist faction, established the Parti socialiste français. At the very center of the Bloc des gauches, he labored in the press and in the hemicycle to liquidate the debris of the Dreyfus affair, the prelude, he believed, to even greater gains for the cause of socialism. His contacts with the larger intellectual world of Paris gave him the necessary prestige and resources to carry on the fight and to justify it in his optimistic belief that unity would one day come. Working towards the same end was the important group of Socialist polemicists, headed by Hubert Lagardelle, the editor of *Le Mouvement socialiste*, founded in 1899 to examine the foundations and direction of socialism. (22) No less important in its influence on Jaurès was *La Vie Socialiste* where men like Francis de Pressensé were urging Socialist union. With their support and the increasing attention they were giving to economic problems and the emergence of a national trade-union movement, Jaurès felt more than ever that the future of socialism required a firmer and more extended basis of popular support. The establishment of *L'Humanité* in 1904 gave Jaurès a fresh opportunity to sound opinion on the issue.

It was his ardent wish for and belief in Socialist unity that led to Jaurès's submission to the demands made at the 1904 Amsterdam Congress of the Second International to end Socialist divisions and to condemn ministerialism. He accepted the Amsterdam resolutions because of his loyalty to the concept of international socialism and his belief in the International's prerogative to guide the strategy of the national parties. (23) In 1905 Socialist union was at last achieved. Guesde was triumphant, but the true victor was Jaurès. It was his conception of socialism upon which the united party would base its tactics and strategy. No one but Guesde's most devoted followers could claim that his loyalties to and nostalgia for revolutionary socialism were viable in the changed circumstances of the twentieth century. In terms of Guesde's avowed revolutionism there had been precious little in his party's action to match it. Moreover, Vaillant was also changing his outlook. The remnants of his Blanquism could not survive the impact of an altered industrial society.

IV

One year later, the Confédération générale du travail (C.G.T.) at its Congress in Amiens overwhelmingly voted in favor of a resolution embodying the creed of revolutionary syndicalism, which, for many of the delegates present, meant not only independence of all political parties, but also a defiant declaration that the unions alone represented the true interests of the working classes. Those who maintained the latter view were not content to confine the C.G.T.'s activities to the narrow pursuit of economic gains for the workers. They possessed a well-articulated if exclusivist ideology designed to transform society. They believed that they, not the parliamentary leaders of the newly unified Socialist party called the S.F.I.O., were the true heirs of socialism, and they were equally impatient with those union leaders who warned workers against the needless sacrifice of their economic rights for a revolutionary program.

It was not until 1902 that the unions, (24) by fusing the C.G.T. and the Fédération des Bourses,* succeeded in establishing a center of authority rivaling those of the Socialist parties. Dating from 1895, the former suffered from financial poverty, absence of effective leadership, and defective structure. The latter, on the other hand, was the true locus of union life; by 1901 it had seventy-four affiliated Bourses numbering over 1,000 dues-paying local unions. (25) Without the Bourses, the extension of union activity at the national level would have remained doubtful, and the C.G.T. might well have foundered.

It was in the Bourses—the first was founded in Paris in 1886— that the ideology of revolutionary syndicalism was shaped. Its contours were determined by the melding of a few key ideas and traditions some of which were common to protest groups in other

---

* The Bourses du Travail were organized on a local basis and brought together workers in all trades. Originally established to find jobs for workers, they rapidly assumed educative functions and became a forum for the discussion of working-class problems.

parts of Europe. But these common elements were joined with others particular to France. France's revolutionary past was an essential ingredient; violence as the necessary midwife of social change was accepted but not cultivated as some theorists outside the movement urged; neither Sorel, Berth nor Lagardelle was responsible for revolutionary syndicalism's belief in violence; it owed much more to practice than to theory. (26) The idea of a revolutionary *avant-garde,* a small active elite as the catalyst of mass action, came from the examples of Blanqui and Bakunin. Marx provided the theory of the class struggle as the justification of working-class aspirations and history's chosen instrument of social change. The weapon of the general strike was by no means new either, since it had figured in the manifestos of several radical workers' groups for over two generations. Yet of all the springs from which revolutionary syndicalism fed, the teachings of Proudhon were the main creative force. From him the revolutionary syndicalists took their faith in the laboring man's capacity to create a society in which his dignity and superior virtue would be recognized, a society which would have as its basic unit the workshop managed and directed by workmen freely associating with other such units, free also from the deadening impact of the state with all its powers of coercion. Many of these views were, it was pointed out earlier, held by the Allemanists and the anarchists, who, assuming positions of power in the unions in the 1890s, ensured the survival of and gave new life to Proudhon's ideals and the Bakuninist style.

The young Fernand Pelloutier, secretary of the Fédération des Bourses from 1895 until 1900, became, both as leader and person, identified with the methods and goals of revolutionary syndicalism. Before he died from overwork at the age of thirty-three in 1901, Pelloutier left his imprint on the development of union life in France. He was, it must be stressed, not only a theorist; his organizational abilities were responsible for the wide diffusion of the Bourses. (27) But he believed that the Bourse as the focus of labor protest was futile unless it also served as the laboratory of the worker's self-liberation—the precondition of his moral and social regeneration. Pelloutier's ideology of unionism was suffused with a moral vision rooted in the conviction that the corruption of bourgeois society fattening on the exploitation of others and the deceptiveness of false ideals must be replaced by a society responsive to the wishes of the workers enlightened by the purifying force of education. His belief in the superior virtues of the workers made it imperative to keep before them their responsibility as the historic and moral instruments of freedom. Prudence and compromise were not for him. That way lay the death of the working man's spirit and purpose. He refused to be tricked into accepting concessions from employers and the state; they were handouts meant to lure the worker away from his revolutionary role. "We are eternal rebels," he wrote, "men truly without God, without master, without country, the irreconcilable enemies of every form of despotism, whether moral or material, individual or collective— that is to say, of laws and dictatorships (including that of the proletariat)—and the passionate lovers of the cultivation of the self." (28) What he feared most was that the workers would not have the resources for the struggle; that they would not develop the virtues necessary for their own liberation. As for the claims of the Socialist parties to further the goals of the workers, they could not be taken seriously; Pelloutier dismissed them categorically as the vote-gathering techniques of a group of politicians for whom adjustment to the demands of the bourgeois state was more important than fulfilling the goals of the revolution. Their talk of revolution was mere rhetoric by which, even if they did not deceive themselves, they hoped to deceive the working classes.

Pelloutier's successors had to deal with the problem of extending the range and effectiveness of union organization while never losing sight of the ultimate goals of revolutionary syndicalism. In short, the C.G.T. was engaged in the day-by-day struggle to improve the material conditions of the working classes, and at the same time in projecting its revolutionary goals of creating a society freed from economic exploitation and political oppression. Leaders of revolutionary syndicalism—men such as Griffuelhes, Pouget, Delesalle, Yvetot, Monatte, Merrheim, and Jouhaux—claimed that there was no contradiction between these two aspects of their work. The methods of union struggle, they insisted, were in every way relevant to the realization of both immediate and long-range objectives. The truth is, however, that more often than not the former were sacrificed to the latter. Rather than reacting defensively, the revolutionary syndicalists until the last years before the war raised what critics saw as shortcomings in their ideology to a synthesis embodying virtue and promise.

This can be seen in their attitudes to a number of questions affecting the working classes. In the first place, no action could be deemed authentic—that is to say, revolutionary—unless it issued from the collective will of the workers. Nothing of permanent value could be accomplished by laws of social amelioration, since they were not a product of the active struggle of workers for their rights; similarly, compromises with employers meant accepting the very framework of a system they were dedicated to combat. This meant, secondly, that the working classes must forever adopt a posture of defiance—ready to choose their own weapons and alert to the opportunities for advancing the cause of the classless and stateless society. Defiance implied a war of attrition against authority—the state and its chief defensive organs, the army and police, the instruments put at the disposal of capitalist employers to crush the workers. Aimed at undermining the very fabric of society, the war could best be carried on by means of direct action which included agitation for the eight-hour day, the boycotting of nonunion goods, slowdowns on production lines, sabotage, bad workmanship, and wastage. Most important was the strike, which could be directed against individual employers or against an entire industry. In its most revolutionary role, the general strike was seen as bringing the entire productive force of the state to a halt. The latter weapon was thought of in near-Messianic terms, as the culmination of a series of struggles in the course of which the coercive powers of the state would be weakened and hence fail in its task of defending capitalism against the superior *élan* of workers in the final revolutionary struggle. Faith in the power of the general strike to deliver the *coup de grâce* to a rotting structure was the linchpin of revolutionary syndicalism. No matter how few the victories in the daily combat, no matter how few the numbers engaged, the workers would surely triumph in the end by the steady accumulation of experience in the relentless struggle.

The structure of the C.G.T. reflected these ideas since its chief posts were held by the revolutionaries, and also because the small workshop was still an important unit in the industrial structure, while many workers in heavy industry remained unorganized. Accordingly the Confédération put a premium on the autonomy of each of its constituent units with the result that at conventions each had a single vote regardless of size. This was rationalized on the grounds that far from the desirability of recognizing the superiority of numbers, it was necessary to avoid a structure which would become inert under the dead weight of false democracy. By the same token, overcentralization would inhibit, not release, the spontaneous will of the workers. A rigid and heavy fee structure was condemned on similar grounds—nothing would ensure sclerosis more than a full war chest which its protectors would be committed to safeguard rather than risk in combat.

With such a body of beliefs and operating within such a structure, the growth of the organized working class was not spectacular. Of an estimated 7,440,000 workers in industry and commerce in 1906, some 11 percent were members of unions, but only 4 percent were affiliated with the C.G.T. (29) Nevertheless the impact of the C.G.T. on the life of the nation was greater than its numerical and financial weaknesses indicated. Successive governments adopted harsh methods to break strikes and in general tried to discredit the revolutionaries. In other respects, the power of the C.G.T. to disrupt the economic life of the state was exaggerated both by its own leaders and governments. The numerical weakness of the unions was a serious handicap in the daily struggle. It was not unusual for union strength to increase at the time of a major strike, only to fall drastically when it was over. Moreover, thousands of workers in the new industries remained outside the unions, while the rural masses were suspicious of them. Within the C.G.T. dissatisfaction with this state of affairs was voiced by two groups. The Guesdists argued that autonomous union action could have only limited success. Without the establishment of a close liaison between the C.G.T. and the S.F.I.O., the former's claim to improve the condition of the workers was doomed to frustration and failure. The reformists wanted the C.G.T. to shift its attention from revolution to the conquest of concrete gains for the workers. If the strike was a legitimate weapon, so was collective bargaining, and the contemptuous dismissal by the revolutionaries of social legislation was shortsighted and ultimately destructive. One of their spokesmen, Auguste Keufer of the Fédération du Livre, pointed to the solid gains made by his union and asked that the C.G.T. be reshaped both in its organizational and fee structure. But at the Amiens Congress, Keufer voted against a motion by Renard of the Textile Federation to cooperate with the Socialist party, and the revolutionary concepts triumphed. (30)

For Griffuelhes, secretary-general of the C.G.T. until 1909, the Guesdist position meant the permanent subordination of the unions to the S.F.I.O. and in consequence the end of the only authentic voice of socialism. The reformists with their insistence on piecemeal change were also a menace, because they would duplicate in France the experience of the German trade unions which, despite their financial resources, had accomplished less than the C.G.T. "Money," Griffuelhes wrote, "is not enough by itself to ensure success. The spirit of combat which has been developed among us and which is lacking almost totally in other countries is necessary." (31) On one point, however, both revolutionaries and reformists did not differ. They were united, despite their differences, by the determination to defend their dignity as craftworkers and to gain the right to direct and manage the productive process. As yet the C.G.T. was hardly representative of the new, still embryonic working class, characteristic of a more advanced stage of industrialism. (32)

In the last ten or so years before World War I both the C.G.T. and the S.F.I.O. underwent changes which were to create the foundations of a consensus within the labor movement. It is not easy to discuss these developments without giving the impression that the movement as a whole was heading in that direction. Many of the previous patterns of behavior both within the unions and the S.F.I.O. retained their vitality and were in large part responsible for the failure to create permanent lines of communication between them. What we must now do is to examine the forces and personalities within both branches of the labor movement desirous of ending its isolation in the nation without omitting from our analysis the counterforces to, and the opponents of, these developments.

Within the S.F.I.O. unity did not erase differences, for it was accomplished at the price of permitting almost complete freedom of expression for the party's various voices. At least five such tendencies lived side by side in the S.F.I.O., but the Guesdists alone possessed something like a consistent outlook on most matters. With the ultimate revolution as their avowed aim, they did not, however, project a youthful image and even made a virtue of their inflexibility. They maintained their rigid opposition to the C.G.T.'s political pretensions. In 1911 two Guesdist deputies, Compère-Morel and Ghesquières, even aired the dispute in the Chamber, and in 1912 their views received overwhelming support from the party congress at Lyon. (33) The general strike was condemned by Guesdists as a naïve and self-destructive weapon injurious to the causes of labor and socialism. Socialism, they never tired of saying, could be advanced only by the steady accumulation of electoral strength—the straight path towards the final capture of the state. The Allemanists were not without support in the S.F.I.O. It was largely due to them that the party's constitution limited the independent action of Socialist deputies and required them to submit to a discussion of their public activities at the annual congresses. If this requirement was designed to exercise the party's control over the deputies, it largely failed since the exigencies of parliamentary maneuvering created their own environment. Increasingly, as the number of deputies grew, they, rather than the party, began to impose their wishes on its members. By 1913, they were permitted to have up to one-third of the seats on the Permanent Administrative Commission from which they had previously been excluded. On the Left the Hervéists constituted another subgroup. Gustave Hervé's supporters urged a permanent psychology of insurrectionism and deplored the legalism and caution of the party leaders. On the Right were such Independents as Albert Thomas, Edgar Milhaud and Pierre Renaudel, fearful of rash action, committed to parliamentary tactics, and convinced of the superiority of gradual social reform. The picture is, of course, more complex than that conveyed here.

It was not uncommon for members of the various subgroups to cross lines or to take up unexpected positions.

Membership in the party was never high before 1914. From some 50,000 members in 1906, the party rolls registered only an additional 40,000 new members by 1914. On the other hand, its electoral support moved up from 877,999 in 1906 to 1,398,000 in 1914, and the number of its deputies rose from 51 to 103 during the same period. By the latter year, 17 percent of the French voters were throwing their support behind the party. (34) The significant trend was the party's gains in rural areas with a Radical tradition. Although it also strengthened its hold in such industrial regions as the Nord, the Paris basin, and the Pas-de-Calais, it made little impact in other industrialized parts of the country, such as Lorraine. It was becoming more and more evident that the S.F.I.O. could no longer be considered a purely working-class party when in fact it drew so much of its strength from other social groups. Intellectuals, peasants, civil servants, teachers, and small businessmen were becoming as important to the party as the workers. Nor should it be forgotten that the most prominent men in the party came from a middle-class milieu, which, by itself, was a factor in the movement away from the militancy of earlier times. (35) Still more significant was the growing attention given by party leaders to what they now saw as their responsibility: socializing the republic not by means of the dictatorship of the proletariat, so dear to Guesdist hearts, but by winning over a majority of Frenchmen of all classes.

Such was the task to which Jaurès gave all his energies. There is some danger in identifying that last decade of the S.F.I.O.'s progress before the war with Jaurès, but it is nevertheless true that the new directions of French socialism cannot be fully grasped without attributing to him a key role, virtually unique in the history of Socialist parties before 1914. If he, above all others, seems to incarnate the search for consensus, it is because he was ready to allow all the elements within the party full scope to express themselves. His own views were not without their contradictions; he never tired of saying that revolutionary violence would perhaps be necessary if the inevitable march toward socialism were halted by the short-sighted action of the bourgeoisie. He spoke too of the historic role of the working classes in socialism's quest for the liberation of mankind. More than the other leaders of the party, perhaps with the exception of Vaillant, he understood the yearnings of the revolutionary syndicalists for independence, and he never failed to come to their support in the series of strikes which were launched so frequently between 1906 and 1913. He went so far as to open the columns of *L'Humanité* to the leaders of the C.G.T., to the great disapproval of the more orthodox members of the party. On the best means of opposing international conflict, he unhesitatingly supported the weapon of the general strike, and by doing so he gained even greater sympathy from the syndicalists. His understanding of their motives and their style did a great deal to create the environment for a *rapprochement* between party and unions. The Guesdist attacks against the C.G.T. irritated him. Working-class unity, he said, could be achieved only as a consequence of mutual understanding. At the same time, he had his doubts. Like Pelloutier, he wondered whether the workers would be able to take the lead. There was in him the gnawing knowledge that the journey would be slow and risky, that the ardor and determination of the workers might wane under pressure and setback.

If Jaurès was prepared to advocate revolutionary means in the face of intense and concerted opposition to Socialist demands, he nevertheless felt that the struggle need not necessarily take a violent turn. Acting as it were from the center, he sought to bring to it all the groups in society that could strengthen it. If he acknowledged the primacy of the proletariat, he did not neglect the peasants for whom he held out the possibility of bringing about an end to their exploitation. He spoke too of a society in which the cooperatives would play their rightful part and hoped that the *petite bourgeoisie* would join them. He was even encouraged by the appearance of large-scale capitalist enterprises, since he predicted that by accelerating the tempo of industrial activity, they would change the socioeconomic structure to the ultimate advantage of socialism. Every advance in social legislation for which the party fought would add to the list of social improvements. Such was his position, for example, on workers' pensions.

Within the C.G.T. from about 1910 to 1914, the former intransigence was weakening somewhat, and some forms of cooperation, albeit informal, between the Socialists and the unions on specific issues, were not dismissed out of hand by Jouhaux, the new secretary-general. This was due in large part to Jaurès's openness. The pages of *L'Humanité,* in which Jaurès tackled nearly every problem faced by the C.G.T., and those of *La Bataille syndicaliste* where Jouhaux carried on his side of the debate, reveal how the two men began to appreciate the other's point of view. Griffuelhes's earlier uncompromising opposition to any dialogue was not Jouhaux's way of dealing with Jaurès's view that the working classes would advance their cause by a simultaneous attack on capitalism by syndicalists, Socialists, and cooperatives. While refusing to acknowledge Jaurès's equation of Socialist and union action, he held out the possibility of collaboration. The C.G.T.'s desire for autonomy, he wrote, did not mean "that the C.G.T. ought to think of the political organization of the working class as an enemy and to treat it as such . . . . It may even be that in certain circumstances the two actions, political and economic, will come together in sympathy without however ever merging [*se confondre*]." (36)

There were other reasons for the changes in the posture of the C.G.T.'s militants. Although the general strikes called between 1906 and 1909 had failed, strike action on other fronts had been more successful. After 1909 strikes proved harder to win. Perhaps the best example is the 1910 railway strike when the strikers, hesitant to act and badly led, were forced to return to work without winning their demands. The other unions, save for those in the building trades, had not demonstrated their solidarity with the strikers, but the chief reason for the rout was the government's conscription of the strikers, its use of the army to disperse them, and its undisguised support of the railway owners. Similar defeats followed the strike of naval conscripts in the ports of Le Havre, Saint-Nazaire, Dunkirk, Bordeaux, and Marseille. While the leaders of the C.G.T. believed that the militance of the workers had to be maintained, the intervention of the state on behalf of the employers was tending to discourage and demoralize the workers. Clemenceau, followed by Briand, Caillaux, and Barthou, had not hesitated to call out troops to suppress the strikers. Of equal impact on the thinking of union leaders were the unmistakable signs of aggressiveness on the part of the largest employers. A few years before the Amiens Congress, employers in several industries had formed defense organizations to paralyze strike action, and after 1909 unionists like Alphonse Merrheim, Pierre Monatte, and Francis Delaisi were turning their attention to the growth of giant industrial combinations in France with the power to bring the unions to their knees. It was necessary, they said, to possess accurate assessments of employer strength before undertaking strikes; strikes should be launched only after the financial and managerial strength of industries had been analyzed so that the unions would know not only the rules of the game, but be able to play them better than the employers. (37)

Jouhaux also underscored the numerical weakness and structural anomalies of the C.G.T. and warned that the labor movement would continue to suffer defeats if changes were not introduced. A wider union membership was needed particularly of workers in the newer industries which were resisting organization. The declining importance of craft industries had already been recognized by the 1906 Congress in its refusal to accept in future any new craft-union affiliates and by urging existing craft unions to merge. But fusion was slow and incomplete by 1914. Only in 1912 did the C.G.T. proceed further by enacting new statutes requiring unions not only to join their respective federations and their Bourses or departmental unions, but also enjoining the Bourses of each department to constitute a departmentwide organization of unions. It was hoped that this rationalization of structure would be completed by 1913. At the same time, the C.G.T. declared that the Confederal Committee of the C.G.T. would not accept more than one delegate from each of the departments. Jouhaux summed up the new approach: "We are at a new moment in the economic life of France. For some years we have been witnessing a considerable industrial development . . . We must therefore adapt our movement's methods to the development and evolution of industry; if not, we will act in a vacuum. . . . We must not proceed blindly, it is necessary to know the possibilities of action presented in each region and to work hard to plan a useful effort." (38)

For all the signs of change in the attitudes of the acutest minds in the C.G.T., the old syndicalist suspicion of political socialism persisted. Apart from collaboration in 1913 between the C.G.T. and the S.F.I.O. to oppose the proposed three-year military-service law, and agreement on the use of the general strike to meet the threat of war, there were no other projects upon which the two bodies were prepared to take joint action. Even on these crucial problems, Jouhaux was not single minded. An unalloyed policy of antimilitarism and the traditional stress on a general strike, he was afraid, would alienate large numbers of the working classes at a time when the C.G.T. was trying to gain new recruits. This same concern would probably have led him to seek closer ties with the Socialists. After the 1914 elections, he could not ignore their increased strength, a substantial part of which rested on the votes of the working classes. Yet Jouhaux, like his closest colleagues, was hesitant. The old revolutionary traditions could not be so easily displaced by the new realism.

That there was less hesitance among the Socialists was due almost entirely to Jaurès's patience and understanding. But he had to cope not only with the claims of the C.G.T. to speak for the working classes, but with the doctrinal divisions within his own party which made the task of seeking a lasting agreement with the unions enormously difficult. The more percipient of the Socialists were aware of the changing socioeconomic structure of France and were trying to adjust themselves and their ideology without, however, betraying its humanitarian and moral foundations. They were also being impelled to do so by the prospects of assuming power in the future and were beginning to grasp upon what popular social and economic groups that power would rest. But whatever strides France was making towards the modern industrial age and however intelligent were some of the labor movement's adaptations to it, the older revolutionary reflexes identified with the earlier forms of industrialism continued to exert their force and attractions. The French labor movement had not yet achieved its goal of creating a Socialist society in an industrialized economy.

CHAPTER 4.

GERMANY: ORDER AND AUTHORITY
IN THE GUISE OF IDEOLOGY

The particular forms of the German labor movement cannot be understood apart from the unique processes of Germany's industrialization; hence we must pay some attention to them. It was not only that the government took the initiative in modernizing the economy; it did so almost wholly on its own terms. It was not only that a few large banks and cartels, trusts, and syndicates came to dominate significant sectors of the economy, but that they were encouraged to do so by the government, with the consequence that there was little room left for smaller capitalists. The government's impact upon the economy was reinforced by the fact that it was itself a very important entrepreneur. It also became the most significant force in the country's social structure by introducing measures of social legislation which were designed as yet another means of cementing the nation together. Indeed, the German government, with its benevolent attitude towards the great bankers and industrialists, its paternalism towards the working classes, and the forms but not the substance of parliamentary government, was guided by the goal of serving the nation's destiny in a hostile world.

Some scholars trace the veneration of the nation-state in Germany to the founding in Prussia of an "authoritarian tradition of the military-bureaucratic authoritarian state." (1) Others point to the failure of the commercial and industrial classes in 1848 to create a viable policy based on bourgeois liberalism with the result that, as Marx and Engels put it, they abdicated their will and ideals to the landed aristocracy and royal bureaucracy. (2) Still others see the triumph of Prussianism as coming only in the aftermath of the Austrian War and the victory over France in 1871. However disputed the exact timing, there can be no doubt that, as Veblen wrote in 1915, "the dynastic spirit of the Prussian State has permeated the rest of the federated people, until the whole is now very appreciably nearer the spiritual bent of the militant Prussian State of a hundred years ago than it has been at any time since the movement for German union began in the nineteenth century." (3)

In "the absence of a revolutionary breakthrough by the peasants in combination with urban strata," (4) the changes needed to modernize the German economy were engineered from above. Not only did the government intimidate, isolate, and defeat the liberals whose will to resist was in any case never strong, it was also able, when necessary, to force the landed aristocracy whose social and political preeminence it wanted to maintain to accept the industrialization of the economy. In both cases the goal of fortifying the state overcame all opposition. The deliberate preservation of the old power elite of landlords and bureaucrats, who were as essential to the state as it was necessary for them, weakened an independent bourgeois ethic and ensured the assimilation of the upper ranks of the industrialists within the aristocracy. One writer calls this process the "feudalization of the upper bourgeoisie . . . [which] buttressed the conservative landed class in a period when it no longer had an economic hegemony." (5) The same view is advanced by another analyst of the German scene in a much more extended treatment of the failure of liberalism and democracy in Germany. (6)

In every crucial situation in which the German labor movement found itself, the government loomed almost overwhelmingly large. The anti-Socialist laws, the restrictions on the unions, the introduction of welfare legislation, the existence of emasculated parliamentary institutions, the closing of the alliance between Junkers and industrialists—these were some of the issues which begged for a direct confrontation between the Social Democrats and the state. And they were often posed in terms which were seductive for large sections of German Social Democracy, to the extent of infecting even such veteran leaders as Bebel and Kautsky, however much they protested their fidelity to the inevitable revolution. This is not to suggest that the German labor movement succumbed to the blandishment of the government by some iron law of necessity, nor that there were no Social Democrats who fought both the state apparatus and those in S.P.D. who accepted it. The path to 1914 was a tortuous one, and those who were involved in the struggles within the German labor movement could, at various points along the road, discern the dangers to it.

II

From the 1891 Erfurt Congress there emerged a vigorous and powerful Social Democratic party, proud of its battlescars and confident in its mission. It had not only survived the years of adversity under the anti-Socialist laws but had seemingly been able to deal effectively with its own internal sources of dissension. Although the manner in which the S.P.D. approached the crises which lay ahead owes much to the specific environment of the 1890s and later, the patterns of its responses can be traced to the earlier period of its existence. The Socialists were far from being a united group, despite the fraternal launching of the Socialist Labor party at the Gotha Congress in 1875 soon after the Grunderjähre had ground to a halt. The Lassalleans, whose origins date from 1863, and the Eisenachers whose leaders, August Bebel and Wilhelm Liebknecht, founded the Social Democratic Labor party in 1869, had been prompted to unite their forces to face mounting legal action against them and by the conviction that labor protest against the high cost of living and wretched housing conditions—violent strike action and bloodshed were common in the 1871–73 period—demanded a common Socialist front. That decision brought almost immediate results. Membership grew, electoral popularity was strengthened, the treasury of the party was filled, and, on the eve of the anti-Socialist laws, the party could boast of publishing forty newspapers of which thirteen were dailies. (7)

So strong had been the desire for unity that neither the previous differences between the Lassalleans and the Eisenachers nor the strictures of Marx and Engels against the Gotha program (8) carried sufficient weight. The Lassalleans had not divested themselves of their belief in state initiative on economic and social questions. Indeed, the Lassalleans brought with them to the united party their faith in the existing state as the medium of change and the midwife of socialism. Before Gotha, the Eisenachers disputed these contentions vigorously; they realized the dangers of effecting social change by a repressive state and stressed the need for change from below; they expected nothing nor would they accept anything from an oligarchic government. After Gotha they continued to deny the Lassallean assumptions, but the exigencies of the repressive period of the anti-Socialist laws forced them to take up positions which brought them closer to the Lassalleans.

Lassalleanism retained its vitality not only because of the popularity of the theories of state socialism, but also because of the challenge to the party offered by Bismarck's social insurance laws. Socialist deputies such as Hasenclever, Frohme, and Kayser were deeply impressed by the Bismarckian legislation and expressed their satisfaction in terms that bore the imprint of Lassalle's doctrines, as the following quotation from Frohme illustrates: "It is the State—that means, the ever-enlarging union of individuals which encompasses all particularized strength in an ethical whole—which has the function of bringing about the evolution of humanity to freedom and well-being." (9) So pervasive was this train of thought that even the most influential anti-Lassalleans in the party, in expressing their disquiet, felt powerless to counteract it for some considerable time. Bebel, (10) Kautsky, (11) and Eduard Bernstein, the editor of the Zurich-based *Sozialdemokrat,* regularly reported their anxieties to Engels. But it was not until the 1883 Congress at Copenhagen (the party was forced by the anti-Socialist laws to hold its conferences abroad) that the condemnation of Bismarck's social reforms became party policy.

If, by the end of the 1880s, the Social Democrats were learning how to confute the theories of state socialism by leaning increasingly on Kautsky's writings in *Die Neue Zeit,* they faced another dilemma—how best to reconcile their activities as revolutionaries and as members of a political party operating within the framework of the German Empire. During the enforcement of the anti-Socialist laws, the deputies, who alone possessed a significant measure of immunity, focused the hopes of the party and the future of socialism upon their activities in the Reichstag and in the state assemblies. They were determined to avoid offering the government any pretext for the complete elimination of Social Democracy. At the same time, there could not but be a close connection between the parliamentary Fraktion and its illegal organizations and press outside the country. By itself this created tensions and misunderstandings between the internal and external members of the party. For the most part, the former counseled strict adherence to parliamentary measures of opposition, while the latter became increasingly critical of what appeared to them as excessive accommodation to the existing regime. (12) Bebel and Liebknecht made heroic efforts to establish a balance between the moderate and radical forces, but by the close of the anti-Socialist phase they had taken giant strides towards the repudiation of their antiparliamentary critics.

Events appeared to justify their tactics. Their scrupulous avoidance of conflict with the authorities and their pressure in the Reichstag to safeguard and extend benefits for the working classes enhanced the prestige of the party. At the same time, the party's influence on the trade unions (the *Fachvereine*), which flourished in the 1880s during the milder phase of the anti-Socialist laws, remained unchallenged. Thus when the party's strength increased both in the 1883 and 1887 elections, its leaders could attribute it to a correct evaluation of the objective political facts. When, after the abrogation of the anti-Socialist laws in 1890, the party doubled its popular vote, the stalwarts could say that they had led the party successfully through the period of the *Wanderjahren*. Despite their self-congratulatory mood, they were somewhat uncertain about the tasks that lay ahead, although each of the leaders had his own interpretation of what these were. Bebel, at times, believed that parliamentary action would in time be overtaken by the revolution at the right historic moment, while, at other times, he agreed with Kautsky and Bernstein that socialism could be achieved through the establishment of authentic parliamentary institutions. Yet the overriding impression is that the period of repression had prepared them less for conflict than for adjustment to the society they detested. They had shied away from becoming involved in the wave of strikes that swept the country in 1889, and a year later they cautioned workers against abandoning their work to take part in mass demonstrations scheduled for May 1. A faith in order and organization, compromise and compliance, had become the natural reflex of German Social Democracy.

III

In 1891 the leaders of the party could look back with pride to the survival of the party in the face of onslaughts both from the imperial government and from its own critics. What was to be their policy in the years that lay ahead? Largely the work of Kautsky, the Erfurt program combined on the one hand an analysis of the impending demise of capitalism and its replacement by a Socialist society, and on the other, a list of the immediate goals to be obtained for the workers, the achievement of which was seen as marking the way to realizing the final aim. But nowhere in the program were there any allusions to revolution or to the specific forms of polity of the future Socialist society. Engels understood that it was obviously impossible to refer to the revolutionary overthrow of the imperial German state, but he urged the drafters of the program to say something about the nature of the revolutionary state. If the word *republic* could not be used with impunity, why not specify that political power would be concentrated in the representatives of the people, he asked, as a prelude to the communist society? (13) Engels's recommendations were held to be impracticable, and indeed they were, but it cannot be denied that few Social Democrats understood the distinctions Engels drew, nor did their encounters with him sharpen their own thinking on the problems with which they would inevitably have to grapple when, as they predicted, their party gained a majority in the Reichstag.

Thus at the very center of Social Democratic thinking and action there lay a dilemma: how to construct a bridge with strength and flexibility to move from the achievement of immediate objectives to socialism. Those like Bebel who believed that the problem would find its own historical solution according to Marxist laws of development, were concerned above all in maintaining party unity as the best bulwark against internal and external divisive forces and as the only instrument capable of directing society along the painful road to Socialist power. Others who were hardly agitated by the revolutionary implications of Marxist analysis urged the party to elaborate a policy of conciliation with other classes in society without which the conquest of power was impossible. Still others were intent on raising the revolutionary temperature as the only means of bringing the practice and theory of socialism together. It has been suggested that these two wings of German Social Democracy were attempting to end the self-absorption and isolation of the party by forcing it to deal with the objective conditions of society as each saw them, while the orthodox leadership only reluctantly and rather late sought to end the party's alienation from society. (14) The party's leaders, however, almost from the beginning, could not but become involved in the practical problems raised by the society in which they functioned; indeed, as we have seen, they had tried to do so at the time of the enforcement of the anti-Socialist laws.

If the leadership was committed to seeking solutions for the immediate problems affecting the industrial working classes, and was thereby becoming immersed in day-by-day politics, it was yet intent on preserving the purity of Marxist doctrine and all that it entailed. Again this meant adopting tactics that could be made to square with ideology, or at the very least those that would not be in conflict with it. In a negative fashion the hostility of the regime helped to fortify them in their struggles in the real world of imperial Germany. The end of the years of repression had not coincided with a fresh period of receptivity to Socialist principles and activities. Far from it. Socialism was beyond the pale of respectable society and hallowed institutions. The prospect that the imperial government might at any time initiate new legislation aimed at breaking the back of Social Democracy was a powerful stimulus to it to harbor and strengthen its resources—to build a structure that could survive such attacks. The leaders of the party thought of themselves as guardians of a besieged fortress. It would be incorrect, however, to conclude that the Social Democrats drew their sustenance wholly from the fact of a hostile environment. In a very positive way, they believed in the superior virtue of the society they were creating, and they took very seriously the Marxist prophecy not only that capitalism contained within itself the seeds of its own destruction but that they were already constructing the foundations of the future Socialist society. They aimed therefore to create *en miniature* the city of their dreams and held fast to their faith that, as they gained new recruits, the boundaries of their fortress would push out further and further until the Socialist society they were building supplanted the society they were combatting. They believed, in short, that the tactics they were pursuing within the capitalist framework of society were at one and the same time winning benefits for the working classes and ensuring their ultimate inheritance.

The difficulty lay in the choice of tactics. Would it not, it was asked, be necessary to seek allies in the non-proletarian world so as to increase the party's electoral strength? Had not the party already during the period of anti-Socialist laws attracted support from other social groups? Would rigid adherence to doctrine not mean sacrificing the prospect of enlarging the party's appeal to broader and broader sections of society? To what extent would tactics demand cooperation with the government? Such considerations were in the minds of the reformists in the party and were expressed almost immediately after the lifting of the anti-Socialist laws. In truth, the problems raised were not essentially novel, for the previous policy of parliamentarism had been elaborated with just such questions in mind, and we saw that before 1890 Bebel and his colleagues had led the party to the acceptance of tactics which they declared were not at variance with their long-term goals. After 1890 the more clearly defined final aims enshrined in the Erfurt program constituted a commitment to eschew the overt embrace of measures that appeared to negate the former. The party's leaders were sincerely determined to avoid policies that might infect the aims of Social Democracy with the virus of capitalist corruption. As protectors of Marxism, they acted not only as its watchdogs but as the men responsible for handing it on in its pristine form to their successors. Naturally this attitude made it more difficult for them to realize the extent to which they were isolating themselves from the society they were seeking to change.

The challenge to their authority came first from the reformists, the practical men in the party who during the 1890s were to use one argument with which the leadership itself could not take issue. The times were not propitious, they said, for revolutionary action; hence the party must adjust its policies and seek to introduce such reforms as were possible only by cooperation with other groups and even with the government. Among the reformers in the party who adopted this line, Georg von Vollmar, a member of the Bavarian Landtag, took the lead during the debate on the Erfurt program. (15) He urged the party to respond positively to progressive measures introduced by the government and to realize that all change is the result of slow evolution. Despite the party's condemnation of Vollmar's position as an assault on its very foundations, it was harder for the leadership to dispose of his pleas in favor of the large mass of peasants particularly in southern Germany to whom appeals based on protective tariffs were being made by conservative landed interests. The peasants, Vollmar insisted—and he found support for this view from Saxon and Hessian deputies—had to be assured that the party was concerned with safeguarding their interests. The theory that capitalist concentration was creating a large agrarian proletariat, while appropriate to Prussia, was not relevant to Germany as a whole; hence the party had a duty to initiate measures preserving and extending the rights of peasant proprietors. Momentarily the leadership was caught off guard, but in 1895 Vollmar's proposals were overwhelmingly defeated. Closely connected with Vollmar's agitation for a more flexible agrarian policy was his support of government budgets which included appropriations benefiting the workers and peasants in the different *Lander*; again he was not alone, for Social Democrats had done the same in Baden and Württemberg; but again the party congresses condemned budget-voting as contrary to the principles of Social Democracy. Nothing the party leaders could say, however, dissuaded the southern party members from forming their own electoral alliances, voting for state budgets, and increasing their participation in local affairs.

Just as alarming to the leadership were arguments advanced by members favoring Germany's colonial policy and industrial cartelization. Max Schippel, Wolfgang Heine, and Heinrich Peus welcomed the large-scale concentration of industry not only as the fulfilment of the laws of economic development, but believed that cartels, monopolies, and pools were the best means of avoiding violent trade fluctuations and economic crises which in the past had wreaked havoc in the lives of consumers and weakened trade-union activity. By the same token, Germany's colonial markets, which could be exploited best by industrial concentration, could raise the living standards of the working classes and thus mitigate social division. Such views gained wide currency in the columns of the *Sozialistische Monatshefte*, which became the journal of the reformist tendency in the party. Kautsky labored hard in *Die Neue Zeit* to counteract them, as did Bebel and Liebknecht in *Vorwärts*, but they preferred to maintain the party's unity rather than face up to the need of disciplining recalcitrant members. The authority of the central organs of the party was clearly not sufficient to stifle dissident opinion.

Even had the men at the top been more jealous of their authority and more determined to halt the drift to reformism, they were inhibited by their own fundamental agreement with many of those who were contesting the principles laid down in the Erfurt program. Besides they sought consensus, not conflict, within the party, and they were aware of the many different sources of party strength which they could ill afford to lose. They could not ignore the disparity between the party's total membership and its popular vote. The working class was obviously not the sole source of the party's foundations; a considerable number of petty bourgeoisie—shopkeepers, white-collar workers in government and industry—swelled the votes for Social Democracy. According to one of Robert Michels's studies, less than 20 percent of the voters in some thirty electoral districts in the 1903 elections could be properly classified as party members. (16) This trend had made itself felt throughout the 1890s. Whereas in 1890 the greatest source of the S.P.D.'s electoral strength lay within the working classes, the phenomenal rise in the popular vote in the elections that came later could not have been due to the votes of the faithful alone.

Most of the S.P.D.'s strength lay in those industrial parts of the country where the majority of the population was Protestant. Typical was Saxony, the chief Social Democratic region in the country, with its large urban agglomerates, Leipzig and Dresden. In the 1903 elections, the Social Democrats took almost 60 percent of the votes in this area. Berlin was another stronghold, as were Stettin, Hamburg, and Kiel. On the whole, workers in crafts and small industry were the main supporters of the party, although the workers in the textile centers of Saxony voted for the Social Democrats also. The party's strength diminished in the Catholic regions where a well-organized Catholic Center party maintained its hold over the population. The more heavily Catholic the city, the fewer inroads the party was able to make. To be sure, the party increased its strength in the cities of the Ruhr, but mainly among the non-Catholic workers. In Essen which was 60 percent Catholic, the party increased its votes from 1.3 percent in 1887 to 28.3 percent in 1903, while in Dortmund with some 42 percent of its population Catholic, the S.P.D. vote went up from 5.7 percent in 1887 to 42.8 percent in 1903. (17) In purely Catholic working-class regions such as Aachen and the Saar, with its large mining and metallurgical regions, the party made little progress. Nor was it more successful among the large number of Polish workers in the mines and in other hard kinds of occupation in the Ruhr and in upper Silesia. Catholic Munich was an outstanding exception to the general Catholic resistance to the S.P.D. In rural regions, the party fared worst of all, whether in Bavaria or among the landless laborers in Prussia, although in the Württemberg countryside where there were factory workers in small towns there was some degree of Socialist penetration.

Much of the party's electoral popularity was in addition not the result of its own efforts, but of those of the *Freie Gewerkschaften*, the Free Trade Unions. Originally the creature of the party, the Free Unions had suffered their fate during the anti-Socialist laws, but in the 1880s had been able to regain gradually their influence and strength through the so-called *Fachvereine*, local groups of skilled craftworkers. By the end of 1890, estimates reveal a total membership of over 320,000, the growth being in large measure due to the spurt of business activity in the 1888–90 period. (18) With the end of the anti-Socialist period, the Free Unions moved swiftly to set up a more permanent structure and to use it as a basis for the further organization of workers. (19) The *Generalkommission* or central committee of the unions was designed as a kind of supervisory body with coordinating functions throughout the industrial areas of the country. Since the General Commission had as its aim a highly centralized structure, it supported the existing *Zentralverbande*, the central unions, which were strongest in the metalworking, woodworking, mining, and construction industries, and proceeded to break the power of the so-called localist unions which tried to resist centralization on the grounds that it would lead to the attenuation and ultimate destruction of union autonomy and the spirit of class conflict. By 1896, when that struggle was settled in favor of the General Commission, membership in the Free Unions stood at nearly 330,000; but by 1900 membership reached 680,000. (20) More to the point was the smaller membership of the S.P.D., even though this was concealed by its increasing electoral strength. By 1906, however, when the first membership statistics of the party became available, the Free Unions had nearly five times the members of the party.

This numerical superiority of the Free Unions was not, however, the result of any large-scale penetration of the largest industries. While unionization was able to make headway in the smaller and medium-sized industries, the industries with the largest concentrations of workers were able to resist it. Sections of the steel industry provide a notable example of employer opposition. As the 1890s drew to a close, employers banded together to pool their resources against the unions. Under these conditions, union demands could be fought, and collective bargaining, while more common after 1900, remained a novelty. Where it existed, it affected the lives of skilled laborers much more than those of the unskilled, who, for the most part, were unorganized. The employers' defense organizations took fright rather easily. By comparison with union strike action in other countries, the German trade unions were reticent. There were scarcely any work stoppages in the four-year period between 1892–95, which can be explained by unfavorable economic conditions, but even after the increase in business tempo began, strike action, though rising precipitately in 1896, fell again in the following two years. Only in 1900 did the figures approach those of 1896. (21) France with a far smaller organized labor force had nearly ten times the number of men out on strike in the 1892–95 period, and over the next five-year period again outnumbered the German strikers, but by a diminishing ratio. (22)

Organization was the chief aim of the Free Trade Unions. Under the guidance of Karl Legien and Adolf von Elm, the Free Unions devoted themselves to asserting the General Commission's authority for which purpose a huge bureaucratic machine with paid officials was developed; to accumulating funds for unemployment and other forms of insurance for its members; to establishing their own cooperatives, restaurants, stores, press, labor school, and so on; to seeking cooperation with government agencies involved in factory inspection, state-insurance schemes, and other matters affecting workers. Increasingly as the Free Unions extended their manifold activities, they sought to free themselves from too close an association with the S.P.D., and, in fact, because of the latter's fear of dissension, union leaders were able to pursue what was termed a neutral political line indispensable in their view for the task of attracting non-Socialist workers and the wish to cooperate with non-Socialist unions. Realism, they insisted, dictated a hard, practical line. While in the early 1890s Legien and his colleagues protested that they had no intention of setting up the unions as rivals to the party, the contrary was in fact happening. The dramatic progress of the unions constituted a threat to the *raison d'être* of the party, but the leaders of the latter, instead of reacting sharply, chose to ignore the basic antagonisms, as for instance, when the unions ridiculed romantic revolutionaries or expunged from their vocabulary the honored references to class struggle and the revolutionary conquest of power.

The forces of reformism within the German labor movement were given an enormous boost by Bernstein whose critique of Marxism crystallized the practical efforts of the reformists under the name of revisionism. (23) Drawing from his first-hand experience of the labor movement in England where he spent more than a decade, he extolled the merits of Fabianism, progressive reform, and municipal socialism. The preoccupations of academics such as Sombart also appealed to him, because he felt that their predictions about increasing productivity and advancing technology as the best guarantors of social prosperity and peace were proving the necessity for Social Democrats to close ranks with all progressive forces in German society in the struggle for social justice. From his studies of economic trends, he concluded that the improvement in working-class standards, at least within the labor "aristocracy," was destroying the doctrine of the increasing pauperization of the proletariat. If this were not enough, Bernstein went on to deny the Marxist theory of labor and surplus value, the inevitable recurrence of economic crises leading to the explosive disintegration of the capitalist system, and the primacy of material forces in history. In their place, he proposed the marginal theory of value, measures to attenuate the duration of business cycles as the first step towards their elimination, and, as a substitute for what he believed to be the determinism of Marx's dialectic, he called for greater stress on ideas and moral forces in history. There was no longer any need in consequence to pursue a policy of class struggle to the death. Much more could be accomplished, he suggested, by a fruitful alliance between the progressive bourgeoisie and the working classes.

At first the party executive saw no reason to censure Bernstein. Kautsky, as the party's most eminent theorist, had made *Die Neue Zeit* available to Bernstein and welcomed the opportunity to put before Social Democrats the views of a distinguished comrade. Bebel and Liebknecht disliked controversy but were not averse to arguments among the theorists as long as the debate remained at the verbal level and did not damage the party's cohesion. The first shot in the campaign against Bernstein's revisionism was fired by Parvus, editor of the party newspaper in Dresden. (24) The more penetrating mind of Rosa Luxemburg (25) soon contributed to the polemics. While Kautsky, who was finally stung into action by Bernstein's apparent denial of

Marxist principles, was content to restate them, Rosa Luxemburg was determined to establish the primacy of theory and to show that the party's tactics must of necessity proceed from the former. It was not simply a matter of rehearsing for the orthodox the belief in the imminent collapse of capitalism; nor of reasserting the view that economic crises would continue and become deeper; nor that trade-union pressure could at best only defend wage levels but without being able to raise them in proportion to the growth of the gross national product; nor, finally, that the alleged liberalism of the bourgeoisie was a mere camouflage whereby socialism could be suppressed and ultimately defeated. She did not deny the efficacy of certain reforms provided they conformed to the historical and necessary laws of Marxism. Much more significant was her affirmation of Socialist upheaval as the aim of all social reforms, by which she meant a continuing struggle, one which entailed the necessary false tries, the premature seizures of power, upon the foundation of which the permanent capture of power would in the end succeed. Deviation from this goal would smother socialism's present tactic and future promise. Bernstein's prescriptions would lead down the slippery slope to bourgeois conformism; he might just as well align himself with the aloof and arid academic Socialists whose aim was at least clear for all to see. In her biting but amusing way, she wrote: "Fourier's idea of transforming the water of the seven seas into lemonade was very fantastic, but Bernstein's notion of changing the ocean of capitalist bitterness into a sweet Socialist sea by pouring individual bottles full of socialist-reformist lemonade is merely stupider without being one jot less fantastic." (26)

Revisionism was condemned by the party first at its Congress in 1899, and again in 1901 at Lubeck and in 1903 at Dresden, while the 1904 Amsterdam Congress of the Second International put its seal of approval on the decisions of the German comrades. It would be an error, however, to attribute the party's repudiation of revisionism to Rosa Luxemburg, Parvus, and Franz Mehring. While they thought of Marxism as a dynamic dialectic, the party elders saw it as a body of received beliefs, frozen for all time, immutable in its purity. At the same time, their sympathies, inclinations, and previous policies aligned them with the reformists. Yet now they appeared to be saying that the reformists were mistaken and that in the future all tactics would be governed by absolute adherence to theory. Why did the executive throw its weight behind the critics of revisionism? As before, the executive saw no contradiction between their reading of Marxism and current practice. For them, Marxism was little more—though they were quick to deny the imputation—than a prescription for the future. It was essential, they felt, to possess the armory of Marxist theory and the support of the party's most brilliant theorists, not because they were similarly concerned with maintaining an active dialectic between the theory and practice of Marxism, but simply to derive prestige for policies they had been pursuing—policies aimed at preserving their self-image as repositories of Socialist virtue in an unfriendly world. The arguments of Rosa Luxemburg and other radicals could sustain this self-esteem and help them resist the contamination of the external world. They could therefore continue to build socialism within their besieged fortress. The radicals believed that they had changed the thinking of the party leaders, but the revisionists instinctively knew that the executive's capitulation was more verbal than real. Theoretical weapons were powerless to halt their determined efforts to pursue practical policies demonstrating immediate success.

IV

For a brief period after the Dresden Congress (1903), the reformists remained on the defensive, but their forces were hardly exhausted. They continued to draw lessons from the electoral victory in the 1903 Reichstag elections which seemed to endorse their policies, and they pressed for a decentralization of the party's structure to give greater autonomy to the southern state organizations where they were strongest and where they had already achieved a fairly wide degree of freedom from central control. For the moment, however, the strength of the executive-radical alliance pitted against them was too great to be overcome. In the ensuing crisis, they would find it possible to dislodge their opponents from the alliance and substitute themselves. Indeed, in the long run, their success in the party was so great that it would be more appropriate to call this a fusion or absolute identity of executive and reformist views.

The crisis within the party had been gaining momentum even during the revisionist controversy, although at the time few could predict how it would affect the future of the labor movement. Strike action, so muted during the 1890s, assumed enormous importance after the recession in the first years of the twentieth century. This was due to the rising cost of living and to the determination of the employers to deliver a series of stunning blows to the labor movement by using the lockout in a coordinated manner and so destroying the will of the workers. The number of men who struck in 1903 was twice that of the previous year; the tempo was maintained in 1904; and in 1905 more than half a million workers went on strike—four times the 1904 figures. (27) As the militancy of the organized workers grew, the party found itself debating the merits of the general strike, both because of the support given it by its own members and its popularity at the theoretical and practical levels in France, Belgium, Holland, Italy, and Sweden. The most distinguished of the Localists, Raphael Friedeberg, asked for a full debate, and the Amsterdam Congress of the International asked member parties to consider the circumstances that might justify its use.

In Germany the Jena Congress of the party in 1905 was not the first open forum to debate the issue. Before it met, certain decisions taken elsewhere were destined to determine the nature of the debate and its outcome. Much against the wishes of the Free Union executive 200,000 Ruhr coalworkers struck the pits in January only to be exhorted by union leaders to return to work. (28) They did so sullenly and in the midst of continuing news of the Russian Revolution's gains against the Czarist regime. (29) In the eyes of the union leadership, there was now the danger of a fusing of economic and political demands expressed in mass-strike action, and it was fear of what they believed to be this suicidal course that impelled them to condemn the general strike at the 1904 Cologne Congress of the Free Unions. There they thundered against the general strike as general nonsense and reiterated their unshakable faith in the merits of organization and the amassing of funds as the best defense of the working classes. Their majority resolutions could not be broken by the opposition of the mining and metallurgical representatives. The fighting spirit of the militants could not be stifled that easily, for throughout the summer complaints both within the Free Unions and the S.P.D. against the Cologne decisions were heard; even Bernstein briefly joined in the criticism.

When the party met at Jena, however, the executive, with Bebel in the lead, revealed more clearly than previously how it proposed to deal with fundamental issues threatening to upset its hard-won equilibrium. How would Bebel respond to the grave crisis in German political and economic life, which, in the opinion of radicals like Luxemburg, Rudolf Hilferding, Mehring, and even Kautsky to their Right, presented the opportunity for an intensification of the struggle along open revolutionary lines? Bebel could not afford, nor would he indulge in subterfuge, to obscure the fact that the extension of the suffrage was not only in jeopardy but that in certain areas of Germany municipal and state authorities had restricted the suffrage in the face of the party's electoral successes. Unless decisive action were taken, the very means by which Social Democracy hoped in future to take power would be destroyed. The threat to equal suffrage had to be met. Yet Bebel was fearful of sounding a revolutionary note because of his repugnance for violence and his refusal to acknowledge Luxemburg's contention that Socialist tactics in Russia were relevant to the German situation. To do so would unalterably change the party's direction. What was more, he could not take up a position that would alienate the trade unions whose support was crucial to the party. Trusting that the delegates would as always believe in his sincerity and good intentions, Bebel spoke for three hours during the course of which he produced a synthesis of apparent concessions to each of the chief points of view expressed at Jena. On the surface, each could now claim satisfaction, for although the congress voted in support of Bebel's resolution favoring the general strike as a legitimate working-class tactic to be used defensively against any attempt by the state to limit the principle of universal suffrage

or the right of association, there was nothing in it to disturb
the trade unions or the reformists. The former were pleased that
the resolution contained nothing critical of their hesitant use of
the general strike for economic purposes; while the latter could
rest assured that the party would not condone the initiation of
revolutionary action.

The radicals, Rosa Luxemburg in the vanguard, were determined to exploit the Jena resolution fully, to use it as a basis
for a full onslaught upon the reformists and trade unionists at
the next congress, in short, to transform the general strike from
a defensive to an offensive weapon. Conditions in Germany
seemed to be favoring the efforts of the radicals. In Saxony
where the Social Democrats had not dared resist the suffrage
restrictions introduced in 1896, the workers organized huge street
demonstrations in the major cities; they were drawing moral
sustenance from the example set by the Russian revolutionaries
who were gaining substantial concessions from a frightened regime. (30) Almost without warning, men who had previously
urged caution were now shouting that their revolutionary cre-
dentials were every whit as genuine as those of their Russian
comrades. In Hamburg, workers by the tens of thousands left
their jobs on January 17, 1906 to protest the city council's plans
to prevent the Socialists from gaining control over the state
government. (31)

Rosa Luxemburg had meanwhile been appointed to the edi-
torial board of *Vorwärts* for which she wrote articles on the
Russian situation. Then towards the end of the year she left for
Warsaw to take part in the revolution in the Russian empire.
In August she was in Finland, living near the Russian revolutionaries, and preparing a pamphlet on the Russian Revolution
and the mass strike commissioned by the Hamburg provincial
organization of the party. She was anxious to complete it in
time for the meeting of the party congress in Mannheim in
September. She looked forward to a stormy reception, but even
she was not prepared for what was to come. The executives of
the party and the Free Unions had secretly agreed as early as
February to put the militants in their place. This much she suspected. Then during the sittings of the congress, it became ap-

parent that the party was prepared to extend to the unions full parity in all decisions affecting the working class. In other words, the traditional subordination of the unions to the party had been waived in favor of full equality between them. The Mannheim decision also meant that the party's hands would be tied on the key question of the general strike. Legien had flatly stated his opposition to it. Kautsky was horrified by Bebel's capitulation to the unions. Rosa Luxemburg was furious, and she used her superb logic and her powers of invective against the party's new course. She, as well as others, saw that henceforth the party would be unable to decide on any vital issues without first seeking approval from the unions—the party would in future be subordinate to them. Moreover, parliamentarism was the path, she declared, to which the party was committing itself to the exclusion of all other means of advancing the cause.

It was in her *Mass Strike, Party and Trade Unions* that she brilliantly developed her theory of revolution and her Socialist credo. Fresh from her experiences in Russia, she insisted that the chief battleground of the revolution had shifted eastwards from Germany. The Russian workers were fighting for workers everywhere. Since their victories and defeats were equally those of German workers, the latter had much to learn from them. Indeed, the year of revolution in Russia was worth thirty years of parliamentary and trade-union struggle in Germany. Above all, the lesson to be derived from the general strike was that it needed no advance preparations, efficient organization, or heavy war chests. Once set in motion—she was not interested in the initiation or mechanics of the strike—it must be supported by every means available to the party, for the mass strike or a series of such strikes is a form of revolutionary struggle. She had harsh words for the artificial separation of the revolutionary struggle into its economic and political components: "The economic struggle is the transmitter from one political centre to another; the political struggle is the periodic fertilization of the soil for the economic struggle. Cause and effect here continually change places. . . ." (32) The struggle of the working classes would die if it remained in the hands of the bureaucrats in the party and in the unions, committed to the *status quo,* afraid to take action, and respectful of authority. It is, she concluded, not in the inner circles of the directing bodies of party and unions that the revolution would be made, but "below amongst the organized proletarian masses . . . the guarantee of the real unity of the labour movement." (33)

Thus Luxemburg and the radicals, though remaining in the party, were at war with it and with the unions to which it had entrusted not only its destiny but the future of the working classes. Yet the disease which they believed had attacked the party and the unions proved to be irreversible. The elevation of Friedrich Ebert (34) to the post of party secretary in 1906 symbolized the triumph of all they detested. For them, he was a bureaucrat concerned with order, impatient of theorists, contemptuous of revolutionary prattlers, and most of all determined to maintain the close connection between party and unions and the ascendancy of the reformists in the former. Ebert used his position to refine the party's organization which he saw as his main task, thereby revealing how little weight was now given by the party leaders to the maximum goals of the Erfurt program. The minimum goals had assumed major importance; indeed the meaning of conflict, intrinsic to the Marxist vision of revolution, was more and more dismissed as extraneous to German Social Democracy. Similarly, the expectation that parliamentarism and moderate trade-union activity would bring Social Democracy to power in the near future obfuscated what was apparent to the radicals—namely, that the political structure of the empire was such as to prevent the realization of Social Democracy's aims as long as it pursued its old methods. The suffrage issue was a real one. The radicals had their preferred method of dealing with it—the revolutionary mass strike. The leaders of the party chose to believe that congenial circumstances would offer a nonviolent solution.

The bureaucracy created by the S.P.D. leadership was not by itself the cause of the party's loss of whatever revolutionary élan it had once possessed. Bureaucratization was a reflection of the change in the leadership's vision; they now regarded a powerful organization as the precondition of Socialist advancement. That this should have occurred is not surprising if it is kept in mind that the party had from its inception clung to the notion of unity and order as the best means of maintaining its identity. The self-proclaimed moral superiority of the party which came to embrace every facet of the lives of the faithful became a safe point of reference, a focus for loyalty and self-confidence. The satisfaction of members' needs within the Socialist dwelling became the chief function of the party. True, this role had in large part been thrust upon the party by a society hostile to it, but that role came to transfix the party, to paralyze it, to inhibit it from thinking of how to relate that role in the present to the demands of the future.

How truly formidable the bureaucratic apparatus of the party was can best be gauged by the following figures. By 1913 the party had 4,000 full-time officials, of whom 750 worked in Berlin. Central-party funds were not used exclusively for propaganda, election campaigns, and the press, for the party workers had to be paid, those in the top ranks drawing salaries that put them well into the higher reaches of the middle class. The officials of the party constituted only one element in the total bureaucratic structure. The party also administered a great number of subsidiary organizations. It ran 62 printing works, 90 daily papers, and employed over 10,000 workers in its publishing houses. Also under its direction and control were building societies, cooperatives, inns, a popular theatre, a training school for party workers, choral societies, etc. Alongside the party officialdom existed an even more impressive union organization with an annual income in 1914 of 70 million marks and assets of 80 million marks. The unions also had their own subsidiary organizations. In many cases, especially in the top echelons of party and unions, the administrators were the same men. (35)

It would be wrong, however, to conclude that bureaucracy in the party silenced the party's radical critics or ended democratic procedures at the congresses. Open discussion prevailed and the congress resolutions continued to be respected by the members and the executive. While no one dared to use the party apparatus as a juggernaut, the conventional wisdom of the party officials could be imposed in other ways. The preponderant strength in the congresses of compliant delegates either from the less-radical rural areas or from the ranks of party officialdom ensured this. More a sign of the changing times was the increasing weight given at the congresses to the wishes and opinions of the Social Democratic deputies. As they increased in number, they began to constitute a homogeneous body with more or less identical inclinations nurtured in the special environment of the Reichstag. With positions to defend, a status to maintain, and campaigns to run, they left an indelible mark on the party which came in large measure to identify its mission with the parliamentary group.

Two decisions in 1907 set the stage for the party's future policies. The first was the reduction in S.P.D. strength in the Reichstag following the elections of that year. The second was the nature of the antiwar resolution voted by delegates to the Stuttgart Congress of the Second International in the wake of the Morocco crisis. As a result of the 1907 elections fought by the party on an anticolonial platform, the reformists concluded that anti-imperialism was a luxury; (36) besides many of them, including Bernstein, had expressed themselves as favoring Germany's colonialism. The Stuttgart resolution, promising Socialist action to prevent the outbreak of war and to hasten the downfall of capitalism if war did break out, was nevertheless a compromise, since the majority of the delegates refused to endorse the general strike as the chief weapon to halt the threat of hostilities. These decisions served to give preponderant weight in the party to the reformists. At the party Congress in Essen later that year, Bebel went so far as to defend Noske who had promised Socialist support in the event of war on the grounds that it would be impossible to distinguish between defensive and aggressive wars.

Although in the remaining years before the war the reformists were able to determine the party's direction, the radicals took advantage of every shift in the political and economic situation to press their case. They denounced the reformists for their willingness to support the Bülow tax measures and voted against the 1909 resolution of the Leipzig Congress which countenanced the possibility of an alliance with liberal parties. In 1910 they made an even greater impact on the party by seizing on the unmistakable strength of the popular demonstrations which had been organized to end the inequitable suffrage system in Prussia to intensify their agitation on behalf of the general strike. It was the outbreak of strikes before and following the suffrage meetings that stimulated the radicals. The January strikes in the Mansfeld coal mines and the lockout in the building industry in April were the most spectacular since the strike activity of 1905. Luxemburg's articles on the general strike were answered by Kautsky who now felt that it would lead to disaster. The 1910 S.P.D. Congress, under strong pressure from the unions, attacked Luxemburg for her inflammatory statements. The next year, she again came under attack for daring to criticize the party's refusal to meet with Socialist parties of other countries to discuss the threat to peace arising out of the second Moroccan crisis. Radical success at the 1912 Congress, when the party voted to condemn the Socialist-Imperialists in its midst, was skin-deep. With the exception of the expulsion of Hildebrand, other members who supported his views on German imperialism were untouched. And at the last prewar Congress at Jena in 1913, the radicals were defeated on the issues of electoral alliances with bourgeois parties, the Social Democratic support of military taxes, and the general strike. The Ruhr coal strike of 1912 had meanwhile been crushed and the 1912 strike in the Hamburg shipyards failed to obtain support from the union leaders largely because of their antipathy for strike action which, they could now say, was more dangerous than usual due to the use by the government of military and police force and the enforcement of restraint sanctioned by the courts.

Certainly we have evidence that on many crucial questions the working classes revealed that they were prepared to go further than the men who led them. As early as 1889, and as late as 1913, workers went on strike against the wishes of the unions, and in the interval between these two dates they had shown that they were as interested in political agitation as in promoting their economic welfare. Each time, however, both party and unions, convinced that the pursuit of Socialist aims by provocative action would be injurious and fatal, imposed restraints. On purely economic issues, workers in various industries in 1913 and 1914, including the powerful Metalworkers' Union, were expressing profound dissatisfaction with union leadership and demanded structural reforms to give the rank and file a greater voice in decisions. To suggest that such demands were equivalent to a revolutionary current from below would not be justified. Rosa Luxemburg was firm in her belief that the working classes had a highly developed sense of revolutionary class consciousness, and her theory of the mass strike in which economic and political causes change places appeared to make sense in 1910 when the political demonstrations in Prussia for equal suffrage were followed by labor conflict on the economic front. Class consciousness for Rosa Luxemburg was the sole weapon which could crush the evils of nationalism and imperialism, and she invested all her emotional and mental forces to the task of stimulating it. How class conscious were the organized working classes in Germany? Many of their demands had been satisfied within the existing system; in many respects they constituted a labor aristocracy deriving greater benefits from the economic expansion than millions of other workers who were outside the organized movement. How effective was the antipatriotic doctrine in the ranks of unionized labor? To judge from the attitudes of the leadership within the party and the unions, it could not have made much of an impact, apart from the time devoted to its propagation by the radicals, but they were in a minority. One must conclude on a tentative and questioning note: the leadership failed to exploit to the fullest the occasions when the rank and file were ready to challenge authority with all their resources. Whatever revolutionary ardor existed was blunted by the leadership. This was not solely because of their correct evaluation of the forces ranged against them, but rather because they themselves unconsciously shared the values of the society they sought to change. The order and authority of the Wilhelminian Reich could not, they felt, be shattered by engaging in permanent conflict with it. (37) They believed rather that the order and authority they had created in their own organizations were the best means to supplant the other.

CHAPTER 5.

CONCLUSION

Much has been written about how the First World War brutally ended socialism's period of innocence. The veteran Socialist, Julius Braunthal, recently expressed this view again by observing that, "With the outbreak of the war in western and central Europe there began the integration of the Socialist movement with the capitalist state. . . ." (1) In 1914 Lenin was already disputing the spotless record of his fellow-Socialists. Although his admirers have cast him in the role of a major prophet, he was not the first to dissect the weaknesses of the Socialist movement. Others, such as Rosa Luxemburg, had taken up similar positions—and with greater justification. She had taken the lead among the German Social Democrats in pointing to the dangers inherent in the party's failure to challenge the state on every front. What she had feared since the turn of the century was the emasculation of socialism by its own leaders. Like her, others in Germany, France, and Britain had been criticizing the powerful men in the movement for their compromises and lost opportunities.

Luxemburg was a Marxist who shaped its doctrines in a highly individual manner to deal with the peculiarities of Wilhelmine Germany; and, because of her intimate involvement with the Polish and Russian parties, she was in a better position than most to place the German situation within the larger framework of European socialism. The leading French syndicalists, while plagued by doubts and suffering the anguish of reassessment in the last years before the war, rejected policies which they believed would lead to the strangulation of working-class *élan* in the coils of parliamentary socialism. Jaurès had greater confidence in the results of the parliamentary struggle, but increasingly towards the end of his life, he sought to understand and to cooperate with the syndicalists whose spirit of resistance he saw as a necessary and desirable counterweight to the deceptive lures of bourgeois society. In Britain the socialism of the Labour party could barely be discerned, yet both within its ranks and outside it, protest was loud against collaboration with the class enemy. Thus, even before the eruption of the war, the radicals—revolutionaries would be a more appropriate term in some cases, in other cases, the new Left would not be inappropriate—were deeply disturbed by the spirit of compliance which was pervading the labor movements in their countries.

In Germany, labor's retreat from dynamic challenge was only in part due to the trade unions. While originally the creature of the S.P.D., the German unions soon achieved an equal voice with it, not only because of their numerical and financial power, but also because the party itself had acquired characteristics remarkably similar, both in its bureaucracy and outlook. The S.P.D. had been psychologically scarred by the memories of the anti-Socialist laws. Both during their enforcement and after, the German Social Democrats subordinated revolution to parliamentarism in a vague hope that ultimately they would have political power thrust upon them constitutionally. In their frankest moments, however, they acknowledged that imperial Germany would never permit this to happen. Yet they were paralyzed to act. Over the years they had created a formidable apparatus and formulated a Marxist ideology to justify a policy of quiescence; they were accordingly more receptive to tactics promising protection of their gains than to arguments counseling a direct revolutionary confrontation with the state. They had, after all, acquired a stake in the power structure they had carefully constructed and felt no need to test its resilience in an encounter with a government which they feared would not hesitate to disperse its enemies with military force. The unions, similarly concerned to protect their gains, reinforced the pressures of moderation and conciliation within the party. Indeed, the leadership of the latter for all practical purposes increasingly shed any real commitment to ideology. But for the unceasing attacks from the revolutionaries in the party, its veterans who still commanded respect—men like Bebel and Kautsky whose attachment to the forms of revolutionary rhetoric was a matter of pride as well as of sentiment—would probably have been displaced earlier by the bureaucrats who had assumed real control in the S.P.D. and the unions. The force of the revolutionary critique of established policy was, moreover, weakened by the fact that its authors had not succeeded in establishing a rival-power base by forging an alliance of dissidents within the unions and the party, and sections of the working classes outside them.

In France, the syndicalists came to admire and envy the power of the German trade unions, but they felt that the measures necessary to establish a well-disciplined and solidly financed organization would vitiate their revolutionary goals. Uneasy over their slow progress, they sought to expand their organization, to end their isolation, and in the process found themselves reevaluating some of the premises upon which they had acted in the heroic, earlier times of absolute defiance of society. This was not easy. Nor was it less difficult for them to entertain the thought of working with the Socialists of whom they were so distrustful. Partly because of the succession of political crises which kept France in turmoil for so long after the founding of the Third Republic, partly because much of what the unified party stood for attracted support from former Radicals, partly because of the ascendancy of the Independent Socialists, and partly because of the accumulation of social and economic advances at the municipal level, the S.F.I.O. was, in many respects, as much a *petit bourgeois* and bourgeois party as one securely and uniquely founded on working-class support. These features alienated the syndicalists who thought of themselves as the only authentic Socialists, laboring to nurture working-class consciousness, and believing in self-emancipation as the prologue to total emancipation from bourgeois society. In Jaurès's vision of a wide Socialist front, including an independent unionism, the newer leaders of the C.G.T. saw the possibility of fruitful dialogue and, in some instances, they undertook active cooperation with the S.F.I.O. Unlike Germany where the unions were pragmatic to the core, those in France had set themselves in firm opposition to the political arm of the labor movement and served to remind it of its historic revolutionary role. This was one reason why Jaurès and Vaillant, while the leaders of a curious coalition of Socialists and near-Socialists, were genuinely attracted to the unreserved *ouvrièrisme* of the syndicalists; and why it would be an error to think of the S.F.I.O. as having completely surrendered itself to reformism before 1914. The anti-reformists among the French Socialists could not only occasionally expect support from men like Jaurès and Vaillant; they possessed a point of reference outside the party as well, and because their words were matched by power—albeit in its essentials static rather than dynamic power—they prevented the S.F.I.O. from grasping at reformism whole-heartedly.

Labor's experience in Britain was more complex. There the Labour party was almost overwhelmingly the instrument of the trade unions which had an unrivaled tradition of struggle, achievement, and power. For years politically neutral, they had gained concessions from the established political parties and therefore saw no reason to dissociate themselves from the dominant social ethic. The emergence of the Labour party, which owed its appearance to disparate groups of Socialists and sympathizers intent on creating a mass political organization, scarcely changed the attitudes of leading union officials. As legal sanctions were applied against the unions, they swelled the membership lists of the party for the purpose of exerting pressure to have them reversed. Nothing was further from their minds than an attack on the foundations of the social order. Their reticence arose from conditioned as much as tactical reflexes. They wanted above all to gain a reasonable share of the national income for their members, and they believed they could do so as a pressure group both within the Labour party and through their uninterrupted contacts with the Liberals. In these calculations, they met no real opposition from the leadership of the Labourites whose caution equaled their own. Since the impact of the "new unionism," the unions certainly had their share of Socialists, and some of them were consequently not unsympathetic to declarations of class war, but other unions exploited such slogans without attaching themselves to socialism. For the first time on a significant scale, the accepted modes of labor behavior were modified in the half-decade before the war. A truly unprecedented series of strikes prompted by social and economic grievances was endowed with an ideology strongly influenced by the aggressive tactics and long-term objectives of French syndicalism, as well as other critiques of industrial society, some native to Britain, and others adopted from the United States.

It is noteworthy that the strikes in Britain at this time were not paralleled in France or Germany either in frequency or violence. Apart from some exceptions in unusually favored industries, and then most notably in Germany, all three industrial societies were experiencing rising living costs without a corresponding increase in wage rates. Why did industrial violence flare so dramatically only in Britain? For a brief time Germany also witnessed bitter strike action induced by a combination of economic and political grievances, but trade union and S.P.D. leadership did their utmost to dampen the agitation. Moreover, the sense of industrial achievement which communicated itself to the German working classes was greater than in Britain where by contrast many workers felt less confident about the country's capacity to expand and ensure rising living standards. A sense of *malaise* swept great sections of the British working class, and the strikes that expressed it while disconcerting to union leadership were nevertheless endorsed by it and hence accounted for their duration. Spectacular strike action in France had spent itself before this time owing to spotty organization, lack of union funds, armed government intervention, and even criticism from within the S.F.I.O. The German leadership desperately wanted to avoid a prolonged clash with the state; the French leadership, despite its philosophy of direct action doubted after the disastrous strikes in 1909 and 1910 that it possessed the resources for such an encounter; the British leadership also had qualms and reservations, but could not set their face against success. Besides, it had managed in previous years to exercise restraint upon the more vociferous labor agitators and gambled that it would be able to do so again.

In large measure, ideology had become an excrescence in the German movement despite the avowed Marxist orientation of the S.P.D. More than in any other major European industrial society, the integration of the Socialist movement within the capitalist state was most pronounced in Germany. The S.P.D. and the unions represented and spoke for the advantaged sections of labor; in time the large masses of unorganized labor would, it was felt, also take their place in the movement. No heroic and vain revolutionary slogans would accomplish this; rather self-interest would see to it. This was also the expectation of the leaders of British labor. Shorn of its ideological content, the pre-1914 industrial violence was seen by them as adding to the strength of the organized labor movement. If they thought at all about the kinds of questions industrial unionists, syndicalists and Guild Socialists were raising—workers' control and decentralization, for example—they believed that the power of numbers necessarily preceded any concern for the quality of life encountered by the worker either in the factory or outside it. The tasks facing the French syndicalists were even greater. French labor was far less an organized force than its counterparts in the other industrial states. But the ideological dilemma confronting it was greater. Priding itself on its revolutionary goals, the C.G.T. refused to contemplate its subordination to the demands of organization and efficiency, yet knew that the newer forms of industrial concentration could be fought only by an equally powerful concentration of organized labor. It might be said that already by 1914 the policymakers in the labor and Socialist movements were beginning to take their place within their national corporate and power structures. Some did this more consciously and less reluctantly than the others. In all there were voices of alarm and disillusionment momentarily drowned by their own appeals for revolutionary change.

NOTES

CHAPTER 1.

1. Support for this view may be found in the writings of a large number of specialists investigating labor's responses to the demands of

industrialism. One of the most convincing recent expositions is given by Jean D. Reynaud, *Les Syndicats en France* (Paris, 1963). He writes, "The level of economic development, the processes utilized for this development, the nature of the prevailing activities, the political history, and traditions make [it necessary to look at] each national [form of] trade society or trade union [syndicalisme] as a separate problem, because the societies where they emerge are different," 19. For similar observations, see Clark Kerr, F. H. Harbison, J. T. Dunlop and C. A. Myers, "The Labour Problem in Economic Development, Framework for a Reappraisal," *International Labour Review*, LXXI (Jan.–June 1955), 227–28.

2. Joseph A. Schumpeter, *Capitalism, Socialism, and Democracy* (2nd ed., New York and London, 1947), 167. Although Schumpeter makes it clear that this description is more fitting for what he terms "commercial society," and that other elements, such as credit and financial institutions must be included in a description of capitalism, he writes that "commercial society, as an alternative to socialism, in practice always appears in a particular form of capitalism. . . ."

3. Ralf Dahrendorf, *Class and Class Conflict in Industrial Society* (Stanford, 1959), 40.

4. We owe to Walt W. Rostow, *The Stages of Economic Growth* (Cambridge, Mass., 1960), the term *take-off* by which he means the "take-off into self-sufficient growth," one of the five stages of economic growth he discusses. Take-off is the acceleration of trends in the economy conducive to industrialization.

5. Alexander Gerschenkron, *Economic Backwardness in Historical Perspective* (Cambridge, Mass., 1962), cited in David S. Landes, *The Rise of Capitalism* (New York, 1966), 115.

6. See Charles P. Kindleberger, *Economic Growth in France and Britain 1851–1950* (Cambridge, Mass., 1964), 227. After reviewing the various theories about the cheapness or dearness of labor, Kindleberger writes: "When the rhetoric of these statements is dismissed, the argument has shifted, at least part way, from the price of labor in industry to the labor cost of production."

7. David S. Landes, "Technological Change and Development in Western Europe, 1750–1914," in *The Cambridge Economic History of Europe,* eds. H. J. Habakkuk and M. Postan (Cambridge, 1965), VI, 462.

8. *Ibid.*, 463.

9. *Ibid.*

10. See Wolfram Fischer, "Some Tensions at Early Stages of Industrialization," *Comparative Studies in Society and History*, IX (1966), 64–83.

11. I am indebted to the observations of Val R. Lorwin, "Working-Class Politics and Economic Development in Western Europe," *Amer-*

ican Historical Review, LXIII (1958), 338–51, especially 349, for these remarks.

12. Gerhard W. Ditz, "Utopian Symbols in the History of the British Labour Party," *British Journal of Sociology,* XVII (1966), 146.

CHAPTER 2.

1. See for example, William Ashworth, *An Economic History of England 1870–1939* (London, 1960), 250–52.

2. See L. G. Chiozza, *Money, Riches and Poverty* (2nd ed., London, 1906), Chap. iii.

3. J. H. Clapham, *An Economic History of England* (3 vols., Cambridge, 1926–38), III, 369.

4. Phyllis Deane and W. A. Cole, *British Economic Growth 1688–1959. Trends and Structure* (2nd ed., Cambridge, 1967), 28.

5. See Paul R. Thompson, *Socialists, Liberals and Labour. The Struggle for London 1885–1914* (London, 1967) for an analysis of the Liberals' renewed strength after 1900.

6. In view of the evidence which has been accumulated of Socialist influence in the "new unionism," it is curious to find that the authors of the most recent history of British trade unionism claim that it has probably been exaggerated. See H. A. Clegg, Alan Fox and A. F. Thompson, *A History of British Trade Unions Since 1889* (Oxford, 1964), I, 90–95. Their study should be contrasted with Eric J. Hobsbawm, *Labouring Men. Studies in the History of Labour* (London, 1964).

7. They also aimed their appeal at skilled workers who felt insecure under the pressure of technological innovations, the introduction of piecework, and the recruitment by industries of semiskilled workers. See A. E. P. Duffy, "New Unionism in Britain, 1889–1890: A Reappraisal," *Economic History Review,* XIV (1961–62), 311.

8. From *A Speech by John Burns on the Liverpool Congress* (London, 1890), 6.

9. See the Preamble to the National Union of Gasworkers and General Labourers in *Labour's Turning Point,* ed. Eric J. Hobsbawm (London, 1948), 100–1.

10. From T. Mann and Ben Tillett, *The "New" Trades Unionism,* in *ibid.,* 105.

11. *Ibid.,* 98.

12. See *Strikes and the Labour Struggle,* issued by the Strike Committee of the Socialist League, 1886, cited in E. P. Thompson, *William Morris, Romantic to Revolutionary* (London, 1955), 513.

13. This is the point made by Eric J. Hobsbawm in a lengthy review of Clegg, Fox and Thompson, *A History. . . .* See "Trade Union

History," *Economic History Review*, XX (Aug. 1967), 358–64, especially, 363.

14. See Table 2 in Clegg, Fox and Thompson, *A History* . . . , 83.

15. See "The New Age," *Times Literary Supplement* (Apr. 25, 1968), 436.

16. George Lichtheim, *Marxism: An Historical and Critical Study* (New York, 1961), 280.

17. Paul Thompson, *Socialists* . . . , 31.

18. The case for the S.D.F.'s influence is made most convincingly by Paul Thompson, *Socialists.* . . . His views should be compared with C. Tsuzuki, *H. M. Hyndman and British Socialism* (Oxford, 1961). A new study by the latter, *The Life of Eleanor Marx 1855–1898, A Socialist Tragedy* (Oxford, 1967), tells of her connections with the S.D.F.

19. Beatrice Webb, *Our Partnership*, eds. Barbara Drake and Margaret I. Cole (London, 1948), 106–7.

20. The new study, Kitty Muggeridge and Ruth Adam, *Beatrice Webb: A Life 1858–1943* (London, 1967), reveals how a stern morality permeated Beatrice Webb's social philosophy, particularly in her attitudes toward the poor whom she felt needed discipline and self-reform.

21. A. M. McBriar, *Fabian Socialism and English Politics 1884–1918* (Cambridge, 1962).

22. E. P. Thompson, "Homage to Tom Maguire," in *Essays in Labour History*, eds. Asa Briggs and John Saville (rev. ed. London, 1967), 287.

23. K. S. Inglis, *Churches and the Working Classes in Victorian England* (London, 1963), 227.

24. For an account of Socialist infiltration in the unions, see Clegg, Fox and Thompson, *A History* . . . , 294–302.

25. These calculations are based on the figures supplied in Appendix B of Henry Pelling's *The Origins of the Labour Party 1880–1900* (paperback ed., Oxford, 1966), 230.

26. Clegg, Fox and Thompson, *A History* . . . , 318. Cf. Sidney and Beatrice Webb, *History of Trade Unionism* (rev. ed., London, 1920), 607–8, for their opinion that the unions should have asked for a reform of the law in which the unions would have been "subject in the same way as any other associations."

27. By February 1903 union affiliation had increased to 56 percent of T.U.C. membership. The figures are in Clegg, Fox and Thompson, *A History* . . . , 375.

28. For the various ways in which the results have been computed, see Philip P. Poirier, *The Advent of the Labour Party* (London, 1958), 247–48; Frank Bealey and Henry Pelling, *Labour and Politics 1900–*

1906: A History of the Labour Representation Committee (London, 1958), 274; Carl F. Brand, *The British Labour Party: A Short History* (Stanford, 1964), 19; and Clegg, Fox and Thompson, *A History . . .* , 387–88.

29. Bealey and Pelling, *Labour and Politics . . .* , 276–77.

30. See *Is the Parliamentary Labour Party a Failure?* (London, 1908). On the distinction that can be made between the theories of industrial unionism and the hard facts of economic life, see Ronald V. Sires, "Labor Unrest in England, 1910–1914," *Journal of Economic History,* XV (1955), 246–66.

31. Ralph Miliband, *Parliamentary Socialism: A Study in the Politics of Labour* (London, 1961), 36. See V. L. Allan, "The Ethics of Trade Union Leaders," *British Journal of Sociology,* VII (1956), 314–36, for a discussion of the mental framework of union leaders.

CHAPTER 3.

1. According to François Simiand, such economic conditions are productive of social struggle because the problems of profits and wages and their relationship are posed more dramatically. See his large-scale study, *Le Salaire, l'évolution sociale et la monnaie* (3 vols., Paris, 1932).

2. Unfortunately the study by J. Néré, *La Crise industrielle de 1882 et le mouvement boulangiste,* which deals with the Boulangist appeal for the hundreds of thousands who were out of work, has not been published. References to some of Néré's findings may be found in Claude Willard, *Les Guesdistes. Le Mouvement socialiste en France (1893–1905)* (Paris, 1965).

3. For a rare and revealing view of Guesde's and Lafargue's optimism during the Boulangist episode, see *Correspondance Friedrich Engels–Paul et Laura Lafargue, 1886–1895* (3 vols., Paris, 1956–59).

4. See Jean Lhomme, "Les Enseignements théoriques à retirer d'une étude sur les salaires dans la longue période," *Revue économique* (No. 1, 1965), 18–61. Lhomme's more recent article on the purchasing power of the working classes for the period 1840–1940 substantiates his earlier findings in "Le Pouvoir d'achat de l'ouvrier français au salaires à Paris au XIXe siècle," *Le Mouvement social* (No. 63, Apr.–June 1968), 41–69.

5. The subject is fraught with difficulties, some of which have been recently examined by Jacques Rougerie, "Remarques sur l'histoire des salaires à Paris au XIXe siècle," *Le Mouvement social* (No. 63, Apr.–June 1968), 71–108. The real breakthrough in Parisian working-class living standards, he suggests, came during the Second Empire, while they began to deteriorate on the whole at the beginning of the twentieth century. Similar conclusions are suggested in the regional

study of the Isère by P. Barral, *Le Département de l'Isère sous la Troisième République* (*1870–1940*) (Paris, 1962).

6. Such is the opinion of Michelle Perrot, *Les Socialistes français et les problèmes du pouvoir* (*1871–1914*), in Michelle Perrot and Annie Kriegel, *Le Socialisme français et le pouvoir* (Paris, 1966), 89.

7. There is a good but hardly full treatment of the Socialist sects before 1893 in Aaron Noland, *The Founding of the French Socialist Party 1893–1905* (Cambridge, Mass., 1956), 1–33.

8. Willard, *Les Guesdistes* . . . , Chap. ix.

9. Michelle Perrot, "Les Guesdistes: controverse sur l'introduction du marxisme en France," *Annales. E.S.C.*, 22nd year (May–June 1967), 707–8. For an intelligent and highly sophisticated dissection of French Marxism, see George Lichtheim, *Marxism in Modern France* (New York, 1966).

10. The statistics on party strength are derived from Willard's exhaustive analysis supplemented by instructive tables, *Les Guesdistes*. . . .

11. The best account of Vaillant is to be found in Maurice Dommanget, *Edouard Vaillant, un grand socialiste* (*1840–1915*) (Paris, 1956).

12. See Louis Lévy, *Vielles histoires socialistes* (Paris, 1933), 29. A more accurate account is given by Claude Willard, *Socialisme et communisme français* (Paris, 1967), 58–59.

13. On the Broussists, see Sylvain Humbert, *Les Possibilistes* (Paris, 1911), IV of *Histoire des partis socialistes en France*, ed. Alexandre Zévaès. A more satisfactory, because less partial, treatment is offered by Daniel Ligou, *Histoire du socialisme en France 1871–1961* (Paris, 1962), 67–78.

14. Maurice Charnay's *Les Allemanistes* (Paris, 1912), V of *Histoire des partis socialistes en France*, ed. Alexandre Zévaès, is still useful. It should be supplemented by Ligou, *Histoire* . . . , 78–85; Paul Louis, *Histoire du socialisme en France: les faits, les idées, les partis ouvriers de la Révolution à nos jours* (Paris, 1950), 253; Noland, *The Founding*. . . . A valuable source for the various Socialist groups is also to be found in Daniel Halévy, *Essais sur le mouvement ouvrier en France* (Paris, 1901). Halévy is sympathetic without being sentimental; his insights, moreover, are not easily matched.

15. The most thorough analysis of French anarchism is Jean Maitron's *Histoire du mouvement anarchiste en France 1880–1914* (2nd rev. ed., Paris, 1955). George Woodcock's chapter on French anarchism may be read with profit in *Anarchism. A History of Libertarian Ideas and Movements* (Cleveland, 1962). Nor should one neglect the fine study by James Joll, *The Anarchists* (paperback ed., New York, 1966).

16. The Independent Socialists are discussed in Albert Orry, *Les Socialistes Indépendants* (Paris, 1911), VIII *of Histoire des partis*

socialistes en France, ed. Alexandre Zévaès. Cf. Ligou, *Histoire* . . . , 93–97.

17. On Malon, see François Simon, *Une belle Figure du peuple: Benoît Malon, sa vie, son oeuvre* (Courbevoie, 1926).

18. The literature on Jaurès is immense. The best and most reliable study is Harvey Goldberg, *The Life of Jean Jaurès* (Madison, 1962).

19. Perrot, *Les Socialistes français* . . . , 50.

20. *Ibid.,* 52.

21. Leslie Derfler has written two closely reasoned articles on Guesde's political maneuvers during the discussions on party unity and at the height of the crisis occasioned by Millerand's defection. See "Le 'cas Millerand': nouvelle interpretation," *Revue d'histoire moderne et contemporaine,* X (Apr.–June 1963), 81–104 and "Reformism and Jules Guesde: 1891–1904" *International Review of Social History,* XI (1967), 66–80. Derfler places too much stress on Guesde's jealousy of Jaurès.

22. A brief but perceptive assessment of their importance is provided by Gilbert Ziebura, *Léon Blum et le parti socialiste 1872–1934* (Paris, 1967), 63–67. Translated from the German, *Léon Blum, Theorie und Praxis einer sozialistischen Politik. I. 1872 bis 1934* (Berlin, 1963). Blum's own role in this connection is given more extended treatment.

23. Georges Haupt, "Jaurès et l'Internationale," *Actes du colloque Jaurès et la nation* (Toulouse, 1965), 31–64.

24. The bibliography on the French unions is vast. Still useful is Lewis Lorwin, *Syndicalism in France* (2nd ed., New York, 1914). Edouard Dolléans, *Histoire du mouvement ouvrier. II. 1871–1920* (5th ed., Paris, 1957) cannot be neglected. Val R. Lorwin, *The French Labor Movement* (Cambridge, Mass., 1954) devotes more space to the pre-1914 movement than is usually found in general accounts. Robert Goetz-Girey, *La Pensée syndicale française* (Paris, 1948) is excellent for its understanding of syndicalist ideas.

25. The 1901 figures are taken from Reynaud, *Les Syndicats* . . . , 60.

26. See Robert Brécy, *Le Mouvement syndical en France, 1871–1921. Essai bibliographique* (Paris and The Hague, 1963), xxx. Cf. François Gaucher, *Contribution à l'histoire du socialisme français (1905–1933)* (Paris, 1934), 30.

27. Pelloutier's *Histoire des Bourses du travail* (Paris, 1902) is the best summary of his thought and action. Alan Spitzer, "Anarchy and Culture: Fernand Pelloutier and the Dilemma of Revolutionary Syndicalism," *International Review of Social History,* VIII (1963), 379–88 offers a good analysis. For a thoughtful study of another revolutionary syndicalist, see Jean Maitron, *Le Syndicalisme révolutionnaire: Paul Delesalle* (Paris, 1952).

28. Pelloutier, *Histoire des Bourses* . . . , 26.

29. See Bernard Georges, Denise Tintant and Marie-Anne Renauld, *Léon Jouhaux, Cinquante ans de syndicalisme. I. Des origines à 1921* (Paris, 1962), 11–12.

30. On the Amiens Congress, see *ibid.*, 16–19.

31. Victor Griffuelhes, *L'Action syndicaliste* (Paris, 1908), 21.

32. See the observations by Serge Mallet, "L'Audience politique de syndicats," in *Nouveaux comportements politiques de la classe ouvrière*, ed. Léo Hamon (Paris, 1962), 152–54.

33. See Madeleine Rebérioux, "Jaurès et l'unité ouvrière (1904–1914)," *La Pensée* (No. 120, 1965), 69–70.

34. For these statistics, see Perrot, *Les Socialistes français* . . . , 85.

35. On the *embourgeoisement* of the party, see the views expressed by Georges Lefranc, *Le Mouvement socialiste sous la Troisième République* (Paris, 1963), 189. François Goguel, *Géographie des élections françaises de 1870 à 1951* (Paris, 1951), 55–64, should be consulted for a brief analysis of voting patterns. See also the electoral map for the 1914 elections in Alain Lancelot, *Atlas historique de la France contemporaine 1800–1965* (Paris, 1966).

36. *La Bataille syndicaliste*, Sept. 29, 1912.

37. See the article by Crater (Francis Delaisi), "Dans le camp patronal. Comment connaître la situation d'un industriel," *La Vie ouvrière* (No. 25, Oct. 5, 1910), 400–14.

38. *La Bataille syndicaliste*, July 15, 1913. On the subject of labor's growing awareness of the new tactics that required formulation, see the suggestive article by Jean Bouvier, "Mouvement ouvrier et conjonctures économiques," *Le Mouvement social* (No. 48, July–Sept. 1964), 3–30. This may be supplemented by two others, Michelle Perrot, "Grèves, grévistes et conjoncture. Vieux problème, travaux neufs," *ibid.* (No. 63, Apr.–June 1968), 109–24 and Christian Gras, "Merrheim et le capitalisme," *ibid.*, 143–63.

CHAPTER 4.

1. Gerhard A. Ritter, *Das deutsche Problem* (Munich, 1962), 40.

2. Barrington Moore Jr., *Social Origins of Dictatorship and Democracy: Lord and Peasant in the Making of the Modern World* (Boston, 1966), 437.

3. Thorstein Veblen *Imperial Germany and the Industrial Revolution* (paperback ed. Ann Arbor, Mich., 1966), 249.

4. Moore, *Social Origins* . . . , 438.

5. Vernon L. Lidtke, *The Outlawed Party. Social Democracy in Germany, 1878–1890* (Princeton, N.J., 1966), 6.

6. Ralf Dahrendorf, *Society and Democracy in Germany* (New York,

1967), 43. Translated from the German, *Gesellschaft und Demokratie in Deutschland in 1965* (Munich, 1965).

7. On the background to the fusion, see Roger Morgan, *The German Social Democrats and the First International 1864–1872* (Cambridge, 1965); Lidtke, *The Outlawed Party* . . . , 18–42; Carl Landauer, *European Socialism* (2 vols., Berkeley and Los Angeles, 1959), I, 239–50; Guenther Roth, *The Social Democrats in Imperial Germany* (Totowa, N.J., 1963), 42–57.

8. For a stimulating analysis of the Gotha Program see Lidtke, *The Outlawed Party* . . . , 43–52. Brief but cogent are the observations of Henri Lefebvre, *The Sociology of Marx* (New York, 1968), 182–85. Translated from the French, *Sociologie de Marx* (Paris, 1966).

9. Karl Frohme, *Friedliche Entwicklung oder Gewaltsammer Umsturz? Ein Mahnwort an alle Gesellschaftsklassen* (Nürnberg, 1885), 13. Cited in Lidtke, *The Outlawed Party* . . . , 140.

10. Bebel's autobiography is an indispensable source for this period of his political activities, *Aus meinem Leben* (3 vols., Berlin, 1946).

11. Kautsky's early memoirs became available a few years ago, *Erinnerungen und Erörterungen,* ed. Benedikt Kautsky (The Hague, 1960).

12. See E. Engelbert, *Revolutionäre Politik und Rote Feldpost 1878–1890* (Berlin, 1959).

13. On the Erfurt program, see Lidtke, *The Outlawed Party* . . . , 323–26, whose analysis informs my own.

14. See J. Peter Nettl, "The German Social Democratic Party as a Political Model," *Past and Present* (No. 30, April 1965), 65–95.

15. On Vollmar, see R. Jansen, *Georg von Vollmar. Eine politische Biographie* (Düsseldorf, 1958).

16. "Die deutsche Sozialdemokratie. Parteimitgliedschaft und soziale Zusammensetzung" *Archiv für Sozialwissenschaft und Sozialpolitik,* XXIII (1906), 482.

17. For an analysis of the 1903 elections see Gerhard A. Ritter, *Die Arbeiterbewegung im wilhelminischen Reich 1890–1900* (Berlin, 1959), 69–77.

18. See Lidtke, *The Outlawed Party* . . . , 292.

19. On the Free Trade Unions, see Heinz-Josef Varain, *Freie Gewerkschaften, Sozialdemokratie und Staat* (Düsseldorf, 1956).

20. Gerhard Bry, *Wages in Germany 1871–1945* (Princeton, N.J. 1960), 32.

21. See Jürgen Kuczynski, *Die Geschichte der Lage der Arbeiter in Deutschland von 1789 bis zur Gegenwart.* Teil I. Band 3: *Darstellung der Lage der Arbeiter in Deutschland von 1871 bis 1900* (Berlin, 1962), 205.

22. *Annuaire statistique de la France* (Paris, 1966), 120.

23. The two most valuable studies on Bernstein are Peter Gay, *The Dilemma of Democratic Socialism: Eduard Bernstein's Challenge to Marx* (New York, 1952) and Pierre Angel, *Eduard Bernstein et l'évolution du Socialisme allemand* (Paris, 1961). For additional studies on revisionism, see Erika Rikli, *Der Revisionismus. Ein Revisionsversuch der deutschen marxistischen Theorie, 1890–1914* (Zurich, 1935) and Harry J. Marks, "The Sources of Reformism in the Social Democratic Party of Germany 1890–1914," *Journal of Modern History*, XI (1939), 334–56.

24. See Z. A. B. Zeman and W. B. Scharlau, *The Merchant of Revolution. The Life of Alexander Israel Helphand (Parvus) 1867–1924* (London, 1965).

25. The two-volume biography, *Rosa Luxemburg* (London, 1966), by J. Peter Nettl is an extraordinary work of scholarship, erudition, and brilliance. In most respects, it supersedes Paul Frölich, *Rosa Luxemburg* (London, 1940). Translated from the German, *Rosa Luxemburg. Gedanke und Tat* (Paris, 1939).

26. Quoted in *ibid.*, 217.

27. See Carl E. Schorske, *German Social Democracy 1905–1917* (Cambridge, Mass., 1955), 31.

28. On the Ruhr strike, see Dieter Fricke, *Der Ruhrbergarbeiterstreik von 1905* (Berlin, 1955).

29. For the impact of the 1905 Russian Revolution on the German labor movement see Richard W. Reichard, "The German Working Class and the Russian Revolution of 1905," *Journal of Central European Affairs*, V (1953), 136–53.

30. See Ursula Hermann, "Der Kampf der Sozialdemokratie gegen das Dreiklassenwahlrecht in Sachsen in den Jahren 1905–6," *Zeitschrift für Geschichtswissenschaft*, III (1955), 856–83.

31. On the Hamburg demonstrations, see Reichard, "The German Working Class . . . ," 145–46.

32. Rosa Luxemburg, *Mass Strike, Party and Trade Unions* (Colombo, 1953), 23.

33. *Ibid.*, 48.

34. The best view of Ebert is to be found in the collection of his writings and speeches, *Schriften, Aufzeichnungen, Reden* (2 vols., Dresden, 1926).

35. Schorske, *German Social Democracy . . .* , 116–36, offers an excellent discussion of the party's structure. See also, Marks, "The Sources of Reformism . . . ," 347–50; Julius Braunthal, *History of the International. I. 1864–1914* (New York, Washington, 1967), 30. Translated from the German, *Geschichte der Internationale. I.* Robert Michels, *Political Parties* (paperback ed., New York, 1962), should be consulted for the now-famous theory of the bureaucratization of the

labor movement. Roth, *The Social Democrats* . . . , has many stimulating observations to make on Michels, Max Weber, and others, *passim*.

36. Two articles by Abraham Ascher are the best guides to the party's imperialists, "Imperialists within the German Social Democratic Party to 1914," *Journal of Central European Affairs*, XX (1961), 397–422; "Radical Imperialists within German Social Democracy, 1912–1918," *Political Science Quarterly*, LXXVI (1961), 555–75.

37. A fine assessment of S.P.D. timidity is Dieter Groh's, "The 'Unpatriotic Socialists' and the State," *Journal of Contemporary History*, I (No. 4, 1966), 151–77.

CHAPTER 5.

1. Braunthal, *History* . . . , 356.

WORKERS & PROTEST

The European Labor

and the

Movement

Working Classes, 1890–1914

by Peter N. Stearns

A mood of increasing unrest spread among workingmen in all areas of Europe in the decades before World War I. It took many forms—Socialist parties arose wherever they legally could and Socialist agitation extended to the authoritarian states of eastern and southern Europe. Unions grew with particular rapidity from 1890 onward. Union membership, previously a matter of thousands of workers, now rose to the millions. Strikes spread as well. Bloody but infrequent before the 1890s, they now became almost commonplace, calling forth several hundred thousand workers a year in the major countries.

Considering all its various facets, this was a mighty wave of protest, forcing changes in political structure from Russia to Britain. In all the states of western and central Europe, workers were given more political voice and all existing parties began to heed their demands, resulting among other things in the beginning of social insurance and other trappings of the welfare state —major innovations in the activities of governments. Relations within industry changed just as drastically. Faced with powerful unions and strike movements, manufacturers either had to tighten their hold over workers or allow labor to share in decision-making about industrial conditions. Manufacturers' whole image of workers as inferior, docile if worthy creatures, had to change. Workers now were viewed as active enemies or reluctantly perhaps as partial collaborators; devices ranging from company police to collective bargaining resulted from the new framework of industrial relations. The workers never seized control. No government became their creature and even politically advanced states like England and France still served frequently as agents of repression against the labor movement. Manufacturers, even when they granted collective bargaining, still ruled their industrial empire. Profits continued to rise faster than wages and despite the growing power of labor movements, living conditions for many workers deteriorated after 1900. Yet even in failing to reach its most basic goals the labor movement had an increasing impact. The social question—the question of what to do for, with, or against workers—became the leading issue of the day.

As befits its importance, the labor movement has been studied intensively and from many angles. It is however quite difficult to come to grips with the phenomenon as a whole. The basic problem is this: should the organized features of the movement, that is, the formal ideas and top leadership, be stressed above all; or should the movement be approached from the bottom up, from its social base? Which explains the labor movement more fully, the proclamations of union and Socialist congresses or the interests and activities of ordinary workingmen?

Similar problems of approach exist for any modern political movement. Each movement is composed of formal leaders and key ideas combined with a vast array of secondary leadership and ordinary constituents. Both aspects require study; an understanding of why key ideas catch on with constituents and what they are taken to mean is necessary in order to grasp the probable direction of any broad political current.

For the labor movement in these decades, however, the need for attention to the constituency is particularly acute for three reasons. In the first place, almost all elements in the movement were sincerely and self-consciously democratic. Local union and Socialist organizations took votes on many issues, so what ordinary members thought or were encouraged to think played a major role in shaping formal decisions. Increasing centralization in both parties and unions did tend to reduce direct democracy and this disturbed many workers; but even by 1914 the labor organizations remained unusually responsive to the mood of their membership. The almost unanimous decision to support the war effort in that year resulted in part from the accurate realization that ordinary workers expected such a policy.

The second reason to approach the labor movement from the bottom up is that local organizations and leaders, closest to the constituents in any event, were faced with decisions about the relationship between ideas and practical policy considerably before the top-level leadership. It is well known that, in the period as a whole, Socialist and even revolutionary-syndicalist leaders had to come to grips with the problems of relating a revolutionary ideology to practical activities in parliament and in collective bargaining. Local leaders encountered these problems earlier and more intensely. What was the Socialist municipal councilman to do in Germany when dealing with prosaic matters like sewage systems and the real but limited opportunities for improving living conditions in the cities? How would the leader of a revolutionary-syndicalist local in the French building trades respond to a chance for a collective contract with theoretically evil employers or to a new code of job conditions on public works to be promulgated by an equally tainted city administration? It was here that the first compromises with theory were made in response to practical problems and opportunities and to the wishes of the ordinary participants in the labor movement. Here were developments at least as important as the ideological debates of the national leaders.

The final reason to stress the constituency of the labor movement lies in the newness of the movement itself. Two characteristics of the labor movement have tempted many historians to assume a greater maturity in the movement as a whole than in fact existed. An elaborate doctrine antedated significant labor agitation in most countries. And many branches of the labor movement stressed strong leadership and organization from the first; in countries like Italy and France, for example, Socialists produced the first formal political parties in the later nineteenth century despite the fact that they were much weaker and newer than liberal and conservative groups. It is easy to translate elaborate philosophy and extensive organization into a fully developed, though not unchanging, political movement. Yet with some qualifications for Great Britain the movement gained a significant constituency only in the 1880s and 1890s. As with any new political current it would take decades for the impulses of the principal leaders to mesh with the interests of ordinary voters and participants. Moreover in this case working people, the main constituency of the labor movement, were new not only to socialism and unions, but to all organized and political activity. They had only recently received a vote; many of them had only recently become literate. It was not easy for them to express demands and grievances or even to formulate them, and it was difficult to persist in any effort. Symptomatic of this was the radical fluctuation of union and party membership during the years we are discussing. If we look at the participants in the labor movement in addition to formal doctrines and leadership we must view the prewar period as a formative one in which the whole tone of the movement was still uncertain. The principal leaders naturally played a great role in maturing the movement but only insofar as they persuaded workers to accept their ideas and linked them to their institutions. At the same time workers though in most cases politically immature were not ciphers. They might adopt an organization for reasons quite different from those its leaders intended and they might force changes in both methods and ideology. In the prewar years the labor movement was just beginning to acquire a constituency; the constituency remained separate from the movement in many ways and it must be studied directly.

Needless to say the labor movement has usually been studied from the top down. The focus has been on doctrines and leadership. These topics are undeniably important. It must also be noted that they are easier to study than the activities of local leaders or the interests of ordinary workers. Ideas were conveniently written down and leaders made reasonably clear pronouncements. Historians are usually intellectuals and they are politically conscious; furthermore many of the historians who deal with the labor movement have been sympathetic to one or another of the doctrines of the movement. It has been natural, appropriate, and in many ways useful to focus on the formal aspects of labor organizations. At the least however this approach has almost exhausted itself; now it risks becoming dull. For the industrial countries (and also Russia) we need only a few more descriptions of formal labor organizations. The structure and doctrinal evolution of Belgian socialism still need comment; a survey of German unionism would be useful. But no student of French labor needs another catalogue of the biennial resolutions of the C.G.T.; no student of German socialism needs another account of the debates between the factions of Rosa Luxemburg and Karl Kautsky. It is partly because the surveys of doctrinal developments have been so thorough that we can turn to other matters. (1)

But there is more to it than this. The standard approach to labor history has not simply fulfilled its mission, or nearly so; it has also been incomplete and often misleading—incomplete, in the sense that it has largely neglected the role of local leaders and ordinary constituents in shaping the labor movement; misleading, in that it has assumed that these constituents can be described in terms of ideological commitments. To be sure, the better histories have given ordinary participants a modicum of attention; they have discussed working conditions a bit and have noted that some workers were likely to head toward one type of labor organization, others to another, and some to none at all. My statement that a new approach to labor history is needed should, like all promptings to innovation in history, be taken with a grain of salt; for traditional labor historians have done some of the necessary work and the conclusions drawn from a new approach will not be totally unfamiliar. Still there is need for more explicit and detailed attention to the contributions of ordinary participants to the labor movement. Finally for the sake not just of completeness but of accuracy we must get away from the tendency to discuss the working classes in this period solely in terms of formal labor movements. Too often it has been assumed that the topics are identical with the result that we do not know about workers who resisted the labor movement or who participated in it only sporadically (yet both these groups influenced the labor movement) and we know little about the reasons and intentions of those who were active.

One obvious result of the tendency to view the working classes simply in terms of the labor movement is that the literature on working-class life is surprisingly limited. A great deal has been written about workers in the early stages of industrialization, particularly in Britain. We know something of their family life, personal expectations, and material conditions. For the later nineteenth century however most of these topics have been neglected in favor of the concentration on unions and political parties. A few historians have dealt with real wages in the period; and fortunately many contemporary social scientists investigated various facets of working-class life. (2) This provides some basis for a discussion of the causes and direction of the labor movement from the workers' standpoint.

What can we hope to gain from an approach that deals with the grassroots of the labor movement before it touches the grass? First we can try to determine what a political commitment meant to workers and others who participated in the labor movement. This is a dimension of labor history which is often evoked but rarely investigated. Socialism has been called a new religion, with a bible (the gospel according to Saint Marx), a heaven, and martyrs. The image is appealing but is it useful in describing historical reality? It implies an important change in the life of a worker who became Socialist, so we must study the sort of commitment involved. We must see why workers were drawn to the labor movement, what they hoped to gain from it, and what it did for and to them. We must see the role of labor doctrines in the life and interests of various kinds of workers.

Beyond this as has already been suggested it is important to view the development of the labor movement in terms of an interaction between ideologically committed leaders and ordinary participants. This essay contends that, broadly speaking, the leadership of the most formal labor movements did not initially represent ordinary working-class interests; indeed, it often came from outside the working class altogether. Even as workers were drawn to the movements their interests often remained distinct. Most basically, the factors that influenced leaders directly—largely political and cultural—differed from those that shaped direct worker action, for these were largely economic and personal. Leaders were moved to anger by inadequacies in the political system and by their theoretically derived view of the nature of the economy. Workers, at least where they had basic political rights, were stirred by economic grievances (which they perceived somewhat differently from their presumed mentors) and by personal relations, amicable or hostile, with fellow workers and supervisors. In some cases, notably with French revolutionary syndicalism, the gap between participants and leaders remained unfilled; few members of syndicalist organizations wanted what their leaders thought they wanted or ought to want. Ultimately, as a result, revolutionary syndicalism collapsed but two decades elapsed before workers and leaders alike realized how different their interests were. More commonly the two strands of the labor movement drew together, as leaders adapted their programs and as increasing numbers of workers were convinced by some of their leaders' arguments. The result, most apparent in German socialism by 1914, was a solidly developed labor movement. Until this point however the ingredients of the labor movement must be viewed separately at least in part. Even if it ultimately appears that leaders and doctrines played the most decisive roles, a distinct treatment of the participants is essential to complete the picture.

This basic conception of a distinction between leaders and leading ideas and ordinary workers is open to many challenges. Can it apply equally to unions and political parties? Unions were often led by genuine workers; were they therefore closer to what other workers really wanted? Can it apply to different national patterns, to Britain where the labor movement did evolve largely from the bottom up, from strikes to unions to politics and ideology, as well as to Germany where leadership from above started the movement and continued to dominate it in many ways? We must deal with these and many other questions and we will be subjecting the thesis to examination and qualification in the course of this essay. Nevertheless it is useful to state the thesis outright at the beginning in order to explain where we are heading and why the stress on the constituency of the labor movement is so important.

Following from this thesis another crucial preliminary point must be made. Because of the focus on doctrines and formal leadership most histories of the labor movement have exaggerated national differences. With regard to national boundaries socialism raises a classic problem of historical interpretation comparable to the difficulties of discussing liberalism or nationalism or the revolutions of 1848. The fact of a wave of protest in many countries at the same time and by comparable if not identical methods creates a presumption that there must have been some common fund of grievance and expectation among the participants regardless of their nationality. But the movement was not internationally organized—there was of course during most of the prewar period a Second International but no one claims that it affected national parties or unions significantly. And as soon as one tries to study a labor movement in any detail, national differences seem to be overwhelming, so the only thing to do is to trace each national pattern or as many as one has the energy to complete one by one.

Hence most studies have focused on a single nation; even general surveys of socialism or trade unionism are usually divided into chapters by nation. This is partly a matter of convenience of course, for each nation did have its own nationally based labor movement and so the publications and archives that each movement produced apply to a single country. Moreover each nation had a distinctive political structure, so that labor parties inevitably varied; each nation had distinctive laws on unions and strikes and a somewhat distinctive industrial structure, so that unions naturally took on different forms. But most of the leading studies have pointed out or assumed more basic national peculiarities. England emerges as the country of pragmatic trade unionism *par excellence,* with a labor party developing belatedly and slowly and taking on the same practical, compromising tone as its trade-union antecedents. Germany is the headquarters of Socialist theory and disciplined party activity; the union movement, long a weak appendage to the party, is seldom mentioned until after 1900. France, for the lover of national characters, is most conveniently summed up through revolutionary syndicalism. Here was a badly organized, individualistic movement with roots in France's revolutionary tradition, based in unions primarily but with political, or one should say antipolitical, overtones. If one adds to this a Socialist movement that was often divided and organized to an extent around personalities (like most French political groupings at the time), another distinctive though not unified national labor movement seems clear. The list can be extended to include calm, pragmatic Danes and excitable, anarchistic Spaniards; if it is difficult to talk about an overall tone in the Belgian labor movement, reflecting the problem of defining Belgian national character in any sphere, one can certainly divide the ardent, Socialist Walloons from the phlegmatic Flemings who either stayed out of the labor movement or formed rather conservative unions. With so many divisions the historian who risks more than a prefatory note on the European scope of labor agitation before getting down to national cases would seem foolhardy indeed.

No historical approach so sanctified by usage as the national studies of labor movements is likely to be entirely or even mostly wrong. National differences, including the basic ones already suggested, were real and important, and this essay will touch on them at many points. Too much attention to a national framework however raises real problems. There is always the forest-trees dilemma. One has to choose the level of historical truth that is most important. Even granting many objections to any generalization beyond the national units, it is still possible that the labor movements had some elemental features in common, hard to assess and prove but basic to the sweep of the movement and too often ignored in purely national studies. Certainly many national studies need a firmer comparative base; some of the national features have become commonplace, no longer subject to comparison with other labor movements, if indeed they ever were. As a result many national distinctions have been exaggerated and a few cannot stand up to empirical examination at all. At the other pole, many national studies distort the huge differences between smaller regions, as between Paris and northern France or Saxony and the Ruhr, which call a national approach into question.

National differences are clearest at the level of ideology and formal leadership. There were vital distinctions between the ideas of Marxists, revolutionary syndicalists, or Fabians, and these follow national lines to some extent. The top leaders of the labor movement depended on these ideologies rather closely; even in Britain, where admittedly some union chiefs had no ideological commitment, a moderate, gradualist socialism gained increasing ground. Partly because of ideological differences, partly because of the important distinctions in national political setting, the methods as well as the goals of labor leaders differed greatly from country to country. No major English labor politician or union official devoted much attention to defining and defending a comprehensive ideology, yet this was a central concern of German Socialists like Kautsky and so dominated many party meetings. Not only the ideology but also the lack of concern with firm organization, with funding and staffing the labor movement, make a French revolutionary-syndicalist leader like Victor Griffuelhes inconceivable in Germany or Britain. Nor can one easily find counterparts to Jean Jaurès outside France for Jaurès drew heavily on French democratic and anticlerical traditions that antedated socialism.

Again, however, formal leadership was not the whole story of the labor movements. The causes that operated on labor leaders were national in scope. They included somewhat distinctive national cultures, so that Marxism took roots in Germany that it never developed in this period in western Europe; the ideological shallowness of French Marxism can be taken as proof that the individualistic national culture could not easily assimilate Marxism. Political leaders were naturally influenced by national political structures and traditions. French revolutionary syndicalism undeniably called upon the distinctive revolutionary tradition in France, as well as more recent developments such as the conservatism of French republicanism that disillusioned many people with politics altogether. German leaders derived their organizational bent from the power of the German state as well as from the Marxist ideology.

The factors that shaped ordinary workers were less uniformly national in scope. Workers had only a limited share in national political traditions, for their political rights and probably their political consciousness were quite recent. Perhaps they shared more in national culture; but again, the national educational systems that sought to implant such culture had only recently been extended to them. Insofar as their lives or at least their protest activities were shaped by economic factors above all, they were less exposed to purely national influences. To be sure, each nation did have a distinctive economy. Students of the French labor movement have long stressed the relationship between the artisanal character of much French manufacturing and revolutionary syndicalism, while German historians point to the dominance of big business in fathering a centralized labor movement. There is truth in this, as in many of the national characterizations of labor, but the picture is incomplete. Each industrial nation was subject to many supranational economic currents, ranging from periodic crises to roughly parallel innovations in technology and business organization. It is more important for example to see the common spread of automatic composing machines in printing than to lump each printing industry in a broad national category; printers, as we shall see, behaved much more like printers than like Germans or Englishmen. Relatedly, the national economies are statistical abstractions; their reality is questionable. It is true that on the average Germany was the land of big companies. But the average conceals a vast gulf between a few modernized sectors of German industry, notably metallurgy, and a persistent artisanal sector that was in some cases technologically behind France. Similarly the presumed artisanal tone of French industry does not describe industries like mining that played a great role in the labor movement. The factors that shaped workers and their protest were not primarily national though national elements played a role. Here is another reason to stress the gap between formal leadership and the constituency of labor movements.

A few illustrations of these general points are in order now. Historians of British labor correctly note that the Labour party began to win support when union leaders, shocked by the Taff Vale decision that virtually banned picketing on pain of damage suits against participating unions, realized that they needed a special political arm and turned to the fledgling Labour party for help. Here is good old British pragmatism; the contrast between this and German labor politics, which began so clearly on a theoretical basis of Marxism or Lassalleanism, seems obvious. But dig a little deeper, look at some second-level leaders, like the general secretaries of most metalworkers' and construction workers' unions. Here, as evidenced by union publications, there was by the early 1900s a rising fervor for a Socialist, albeit not Marxist, society. These men did not see their new politics as a matter of legal aid to unions alone. German unions, admittedly less strong in party councils than their British counterparts, were appealing for legal aid (among other things against a proposed legal ban on picketing around 1900) at precisely the same time. Here the national distinctions drawn on the basis of formal ideologies and top-level leadership cannot be discounted but they have often been overdrawn. They conceal pragmatic impulses in Germany and idealistic ones in Britain that need further investigation before national differences can be stated precisely.

In other cases stereotypes about a national labor movement have not just oversimplified a comparative approach—they have led to outright error because of the common failure to go much beyond what labor's leadership was saying. Who could doubt in looking at French and British labor agitation between 1895 and 1914 that the French were more violent? Anarchist leaders poured into every major French strike center around 1900. The principal segment of French unionism was revolutionary syndicalist and many union organizers urged violence and sabotage, in pamphlets and in actual strike meetings. In contrast through most of the period British leaders counseled against any violations of the law. For them, strikes were at best regrettable necessities in bargaining with employers whereas for ardent French revolutionary syndicalists, they were a training ground for the violent upheaval that would overturn society. These differences were important. They may have influenced later generations of workers and their leaders. They certainly affected people at the time who were outside the labor movement. The vocabulary of French revolutionary syndicalism helped keep timid workers out of unions (whereas in Britain they could easily join without being bold) and frightened businessmen and government officials. However, different language did not produce comparable differences in actual agitation. Violence is of course hard to measure; and since there were more workers and strikers in Britain, a direct comparison would be unfair. But though French leaders were more likely to urge violent measures against blacklegs than British leaders were, attacks on renegades and strikebreakers were equally frequent in the two countries, particularly in agitation by maritime and construction workers. The small numbers of deaths in strikes, almost all due to clashes with police, were about the same. British workers carried guns less frequently but they were more likely to attack property, steal, and commit arson during a strike. Few strikes brought major violence in either country. It was not uncommon however and the key point is that its incidence had little to do with the presumed tone of a national labor movement. What national differences there were stemmed perhaps from different traditions of how violence should be expressed; British efforts at arson, a part of several dock and mine strikes, may have some relation to a far older tradition of burning in protest, notable in British rural agitation in the eighteenth and early nineteenth centuries. Far more important were the common features: violence accompanied strikes in which there were serious problems of blacklegging particularly among lesser-skilled workers, or in which there was an unusually intense feeling of grievance. The most violent outburst of the period came not in syndicalist France but in Wales in 1910–11 where mining and railroad strikes were accompanied not only by attacks on blacklegs but by efforts to burn power stations and trains, the sacking of Jewish shops (resented because of price rises and expensive credit) and even assaults on local magistrates.

To offer a final example, if one looked only at statements of ideology and the resolutions of national congresses one would conclude that English labor always favored collective bargaining where possible, that leading French unions almost always opposed it, and that German labor made a rather formal about-face on the question as Marxism gave way to reformism in practice. A more realistic approach would recognize that workers and their local leaders almost always bargained collectively when they could in France as well as in England; that everywhere there was a minority afraid that collective bargains tied them to an unacceptable existing order; but that only in Britain, in the agitation after 1910, was the principle of collective bargaining widely challenged in practice.

These brief examples at least suggest the problem of judging a labor movement by its stated doctrines and, relatedly, of relying too much on its national divisions. This essay is intended to amplify this problem and to suggest some alternative approaches. We will do this by looking first of all at the social composition of labor movements and the demands of workers independent of much formal leadership. We can then turn to the introduction of formal ideas and organizations. We must ask how much the familiar doctrinal disputes and evolution had to do with the development of the labor movement from the workers' standpoint. Did the divisions in the French labor movement reflect or further divisions in the working class? What echo did the arguments between Kautsky and Luxemburg have among German workers? We can judge this only when we know what ideology meant to the workers themselves and what they intended by it. Finally, how deep did the national differences in the labor movements run? Did workers want roughly the same things while necessarily using different doctrines because these had developed independently, in response to different causes? Or did the doctrines correspond to national characteristics of workers and to different types of industrial development?

A few final preliminaries. We must stress again that the approach that tests the nature of socialism and trade unions by their relationship with their participants will by no means overturn all the usual judgments about the labor movement. On specific questions it can produce quite novel conclusions, as in the examination of labor violence or collective bargaining. But on bigger issues it may simply shade or modify the common generalizations. For example historians have long recognized that the labor movement was becoming more reformist by 1914, except to an extent in Britain, and that this was due in large part to a growing pragmatism among workers. We shall simply add that worker pragmatism was not new and that the big change was that leaders now recognized it clearly.

We must guard against oversimplification, even in this brief essay. National differences will be played down. Among industrial countries similarities of goals and methods override such differences when the working classes rather than the formal labor movements are examined. But we stress working classes, not working class. Within any country there were great disparities among different industries and among different kinds of workers. These disparities, which override national differences, make generalizations about the labor movement difficult just as they impeded the formation of any coherent labor movement in the first place. It is not possible to talk about *the worker,* or even *the Socialist worker.* Here again, doctrines and organizations must be studied against the realities of working-class life.

In all this, we are trying to determine what various kinds of workers wanted. This is a risky procedure. We lack much information about matters such as the activities of Socialists in local government or the areas and groups that voted for labor parties. Hopefully, the good new work that is being done on the social basis of labor movements and on the interests of local leadership will continue to expand our knowledge on such points. (3) But there will remain problems that further scholarship cannot solve definitively. We can never be certain about the extent to which an ordinary Socialist worker believed in his party's formal program. I have claimed already that workers were long affected by their newness to the political process and that formal ideology did not penetrate worker ranks quickly or extensively, even where Socialist voting rose rapidly. Later I will offer evidence for this; but the claim can never be made with certainty for we can never know what was in the hearts of people who did not write treatises on the subject. In this sense historians who stick to formal union and party resolutions will always be on safer ground. But even so we must attempt interpretation. The resolutions are hollow unless we know what impact they had. The labor movement drew its character as well as its strength from a mass of working people who saw in it a solution to their problems.

THE CONSTITUENCY OF THE LABOR MOVEMENT

It is or ought to be a truism that no social class even in a single country corresponds to a single political movement. Even at their highest points labor parties have never commanded all working-class votes; there always seems to be at least a quarter of the urban, manual-laborer population that resists labor voting. Before 1914 this group was far larger. In Germany in 1914 where the percentage of workers who voted Socialist was undoubtedly highest, only a minority of male factory workers voted Socialist and probably only a minority of all manufacturing workers did so. The rest were divided between the large number that did not vote at all and those who voted for anti-Socialist parties. Similar patterns hold true for the union movements. The majority of urban workers did not join unions. A minority in most countries joined yellow unions or religious unions that were yellow in effect—that is, unions that specifically resisted all industrial conflict. Clearly we cannot associate lightly the working class with the labor movement in this period. More than this, we must know something of the types of workers who resisted labor agitations for they influenced the labor movement in many ways.

Three widely spread attitudes kept many workers from participating in any aspect of the labor movement—two of them might induce active resistance. Most common, no doubt, was a traditional resignation in adversity. To many workers there was simply nothing to be done about economic hardship—it was a fact of life. Politics were irrelevant. Large numbers of workers simply did not vote, not because they were hostile to the political process but because it had no meaning for them. In Germany only 50 percent of all eligible voters participated in the first national election under universal suffrage, in 1871; undoubtedly there were more rural than urban abstentions, but even so a significant minority of all workers did not vote at all. Politicization did spread; by 1907, 75 percent of the electorate was voting in Germany; by 1912 over 90 percent. But no other country matched these figures. Furthermore, apathy was visible in other spheres. It simply never occurred to many workers to form a union. Government investigations of workers who did manufacturing in their homes (mainly but not exclusively women) revealed enormous hardship and considerable complaint, but an almost complete absence of any feeling that something could be done. Ignorance, isolation from other workers, continued religious belief, and recent contact with rural traditions—any combination of these factors could produce indifference.

Secondly, repression obviously kept many workers from joining the labor movement and it could force some of them into anti-Socialist voting or into yellow unions. Many companies formed their own tame unions and by threats of dismissal forced most of their workers to join. Actual dismissals of agitators, sometimes including hundreds of workers in a major strike, undoubtedly intimidated many workers. Companies also discriminated against workers known to be Socialist voters; even when they could not afford to dismiss them, they tried to give them the more difficult and less rewarding jobs. There was an interesting debate at the time about whether activist workers were more or less diligent and able than the average worker. Employers liked to claim that they were disorderly drones, who were too incompetent to earn a living on their own merits. Workers naturally claimed the reverse. Probably the workers were closer to the truth and aside from entirely unskilled trades it was difficult for employers to be as repressive as they might have liked to be lest they lose essential workers. In addition to employer repression governments inhibited the labor movements in many ways. Strikes and unions were legal in all the industrial countries but they were hedged with restrictions such as the provision that no worker could intimidate another in an effort to induce him to join a strike. So police appeared (and often troops, particularly in France) in most strikes, and arrests of ordinary strikers and of leaders were not uncommon. Here was another reason for the fearful worker to stay away from the labor movement altogether. After 1890 explicit governmental repression of Socialist political activities was less important in the industrial countries; but even here police presence at a speech could intimidate.

Finally there were workers who were content. (4) They benefited from a rising standard of living during much of the period, occasionally when certain other groups were suffering. Sometimes they looked to individual advancement for themselves or their children; and social mobility was extensive for the working classes in this period as employers recruited new foremen from the ranks of skilled workers and new semiskilled workers from among the unskilled. It was not hard for workers who had middle-class expectations to feel satisfied with increasing material well-being and opportunities for the future. This same outlook would lead them to shun disorder. Other workers sought stability above all and were content so long as they found it. In most industrial countries, England being the only major exception, railroad workers were in this category. Railroad work encouraged an appreciation of stability. Many railroad workers, particularly signalmen, worked alone or in small groups and their residences were scattered throughout the countryside; they had more contact with nonworking-class elements, often conservative, than they did with their fellows. At the same time railroad companies (including the state as an employer) granted benefits ranging from distinctive uniforms to pensions that encouraged a conservative attitude; and there was very little unemployment. All this meant not only that the type of work promoted a sense of contentment but that workers who sought a stable work situation above all (as opposed for example to very high earnings) were drawn to railroad work in unusual numbers. Another combination of distinctive goals and a distinctive work situation encouraged contentment. Many workers had highly traditional expectations that were easily satisfied in the industrial world at the turn of the century. Immigrants from eastern Germany, including many Poles, were willing to work long hours in the mines of the Ruhr for relatively low pay because the wages were much higher than they were accustomed to receiving and because, through hard work and low expenditures, they could hope to return home and buy a plot of land. Many barbers and bakers in France despite low pay and fifteen-hour days were satisfied by the friendly relationship they had with their employers which included board and room in the employer's shop and by the prospect of rising some day to an independent status in the traditional manner of artisans. There were many reasons to be content and many types of workers who were.

Obviously many workers shunned the labor movement for a variety of reasons; we cannot say how many workers actively feared repression or how many felt positively satisfied. Outside England, metallurgical workers rarely joined in protest in this period; even in England where they did belong to unions they were not aggressive. Metallurgical employers were repressive in blacklisting agitators and compelling participation in company unions. On the other hand they offered high wages and many company benefit programs; there were many reasons for contentment. My own impression is that fear was less important than traditional resignation and active satisfaction in inhibiting the labor movement but for our purposes it is not necessary to guess how many workers were influenced by any one motive. What is important is that many individual workers and some whole industries and regions were not open to the labor movement in this period and that many others were penetrated only with difficulty. Most female workers, except in the textile industry, shunned all aspects of the labor movement; and to union and strike leaders, the housewife was a vigorous and often successful opponent. State-run operations such as railroads in Belgium and Germany were largely immune. Workers in the home, clothing workers, waiters, and many others were seldom found in the labor movement. Regions with relatively scattered industry and often considerable traditional piety were hard to penetrate yet there were many manufacturing workers involved. A contemporary novel by a disenchanted labor militant describes the indifference of workers in southern England to all efforts to rouse them. (5) One of his characters resists political discussion: "Much better left alone . . . argufying about politics generally ends up with a bloody row an' does no good to anybody." Outside of Ghent, Flemish workers stayed out of the labor movement or joined a Catholic union that was highly conservative and was in fact subsidized by the government. Silesia and much of western France were other no-man's-lands for the labor movement.

Of course the labor organizations steadily cut into new areas. Indifferent workers could be converted; fearful workers could burst forth in anger at too much repression; even satisfied workers might lose the reasons for their satisfaction or alter their criteria of judgment. This is how the labor movement spread. But to extend agitation in this environment required great care and many compromises with doctrine. Traditionally resigned workers could be led only gradually into positive action. Traces of their ignorance long remained; it was after months of vigorous striking and exposure to scores of union and political agitators that metallurgical workers in one French city noted rather plaintively: "We wondered what the word 'solidarity' meant, which appeared on the cards we received from other areas." Fearful workers had to be assured that the labor movement would not involve them with needless repression; so revolutionary syndicalists and Socialists increasingly sought to avoid clashes with the police. And always limitations remained, in the many workers that had not yet been roused at all, to remind leaders that they had not yet won the full strength of the working class and to suggest that perhaps a bit more caution and subtlety were necessary. Citation of the workers who resisted or avoided the labor movement is necessary not simply to correct the exaggerated implications of terms like *working-class politics;* it also helps explain the pragmatic evolution of the labor movement itself. Socialism and revolutionary syndicalism in theory recognized the preeminent importance of an active, alert minority of workers. In practice however the mass could not be ignored. Its votes and its assistance in strikes could be vital; and its suffering in many cases cried out for redress.

Finally much of the constituency that the labor movement was able to carve out of the more aloof and recalcitrant workers remained only loosely won, ready to slip back at any moment into older habits. One of the enduring characteristics of the labor movement until long after World War I was the extreme volatility of interest and participation. Until the war many German unions underwent 100 percent shifts in membership each year. That is, as many workers would quit the organization as belonged to it at the beginning of the year though an even greater number newly joined. These figures conceal the fact that a core of workers remained true for years and even decades; but this means that many members joined and quit during the same year. French unions suffered fluctuations only a bit less great. The growth of unions in both cases was fairly steady; but this involved a proliferation of fleeting contacts with the organizations more than steady additions to an expanding nucleus of loyal participants. Fluctuations in Socialist voting were less great though years of regression like 1907 in Germany suggest that many voters were not firmly committed to socialism. And we cannot know how many workers voted Socialist one time and not the next, to be replaced by other

workers voting Socialist for the first time. For the labor movement
as a whole the problem of fluctuation was acute. It meant that
many workers who ventured a commitment once were then subject to intimidation or punishment by their employers and had to
withdraw. It meant that many after a moment of excitement
drifted back into indifference, feeling that it was no longer worth
paying dues to a labor organization. It meant also that many
workers remained easily satisfied. Union leaders often noted that
their membership declined not only after abortive strikes in which
workers lost faith in the organization but after successful ones
when workers felt that no further efforts were necessary. Labor
organizations of all sorts fought the volatility of workers with
some success; but many compromises with indifference and contentment were necessary in the process.

The active constituency of the labor movement was drawn
from many groups and many types of people. As the movement
expanded and drew in more workers who had until recently been
resigned or contented, the diversity of the constituency naturally
increased. But there were some types of people who joined the
labor movement early and stayed with it rather faithfully. In some
cases workers who did not stay in their party or union because
it was a bit too much trouble or too expensive were effectively
loyal and would obey directives from their leaders; this was true
of many miners for example. It was on the active supporters that
the solidity if not the massive numbers of the labor movement
depended; and these supporters require a close analysis. Two
points must be made: the working-class support was varied, sometimes almost contradictory, in its needs and goals; and Socialist
politics drew many people who were not workers at all.

Workers could turn to the labor movement for a number of
reasons. Some did so in desperation because their material conditions were such that subsistence itself was difficult. Others resented
not just misery but the whole industrial order that seemed to
be eliminating human skills and values that they held dear. Some
used the labor movement to defend what they had; some used it
to win new but pragmatic gains; some used it as a vehicle to express essentially middle-class aspirations which had been thwarted
by the established order. The working class, even the active mi-

nority of the working class, was not united. It is easy to ignore the newness of that which people in the later nineteenth-century and subsequent historians have called *the working class*. Even in Britain where working-class unity was greatest the class was barely a hundred years old. It is easy enough to define it by economic criteria—workers were wage earners, they earned less than the middle classes, they had no property and so on. But they had diverse origins, diverse professions, and diverse personalities. They did not share many values or attitudes. The labor movement tried to increase the common bonds but it had nowhere completed the process by 1914, if indeed it ever has. Correspondingly many of the problems that labor leaders faced related to the need to find common denominators among diverse elements while many of the variations in the labor movement derived from differences among the participants.

There are many ways to try to define the varieties within the active working-class constituency. Later we shall have to fall back on some vague divisions such as militants versus supporters or revolutionaries versus reformers. It is important to refer to the gap in almost any industry between skilled and unskilled workers. It is sometimes contended that the unskilled form the clearest support for a revolutionary labor movement but that was not usually true before World War I; more important was the greater education and political consciousness and also growing uneasiness of the skilled workers. Young and old workers behaved differently; the young in many industries played a vital role not only in introducing vigorous and sometimes violent methods of agitation but in raising the expectations of their older colleagues. Workers in big cities, unusually politically conscious but hampered by large numbers of unemployed, differed from workers in more homogeneous factory centers. And in any category of workers there were great variations from individual to individual; some people are timid, some people are bold in any social grouping.

The most realistic way to suggest the divisions within the active element of the working class is to point to the leading industries in which the labor movement took root. (6) Without denying many other variables it is true that each of these industries created a distinctive environment and also attracted people of a somewhat comparable background and personality type. The key worker support for all aspects of the labor movement came from unskilled male workers (particularly dockers), miners, textile and leatherworkers, metalworkers, and artisans. These workers were the most likely to strike, to form large and solid unions, and to vote Socialist or labor. Yet each of the groups joined the labor movement for rather different reasons and in different ways.

In many of the industrial countries an explosion of anger by dockers opened a new period of labor agitation. The London dock strike of 1889 clearly did so; the Hamburg strike of 1896 and the Marseilles strike of 1900 played a somewhat similar role. (7) Dockers showed that a strike by unskilled labor was possible and they had direct contact with other unskilled workers such as truckers and warehousemen who soon imitated them. Tram workers, construction laborers, garbagemen and railroad maintenance men followed soon in many cases. Unskilled workers contributed much of the violence to the labor movement in the period for they were rough men and they were angry. They raised important demands in their strikes, asking for big raises and reductions of hours. With some local exceptions however they had trouble forming permanent organizations and it is not clear that they readily turned to labor politics. Their activities were hampered by substantial unemployment which made it easy for employers to resist them after some initial confusion. British dockers were beaten by 1893 though they rose again just before the war; Marseilles dockers beaten by 1904 only cautiously reemerged around 1910. Many unskilled workers were also easily satisfied with initial gains or a promise of more regular employment. Their expectations were not persistently high. And some of them preferred a life of irregular work—a few days of strenuous exertion and then some time off—or of wandering from city to city to any disciplined labor movement. Broadly speaking unskilled labor of this sort was just being brought into the industrial proletariat at this time as employment became somewhat more regular, the pace of work greater, and as machines like loading cranes were introduced for the first time. The labor movement was itself part of this introduction of industrial conditions to the unskilled for it too involved discipline and assiduity; but the unskilled were not fully ready for this yet.

Miners were the backbone of the labor movement in most industrial countries. Only in Germany did they lag somewhat, in large part because of the use of immigrant and Catholic labor, with decisive results for the tone of the German labor movement as a whole. Miners gave great numbers to the labor movement; theirs were the largest unions and the largest strikes. They turned to politics as well. The Belgian Socialist party rested on the miners' support; the great strikes for universal suffrage in Belgium were miners' strikes above all. In France miners led in the support of reformist socialism; in Britain they turned to the Labour party a bit more slowly. In most countries miners had a long tradition of protest. They could be violent, though after 1890 their violence was almost always restrained and directed mainly against more conservative colleagues. They fought for solid improvements; they wanted higher pay and shorter hours by collective agreement or by law. They resented the high-handedness of owners and managers in the mines. But their protest seldom had a sweeping or doctrinaire quality to it. They wanted specific improvements above all. Their politics were pragmatic as well, designed to promote reform legislation. It was typical that in France the first major strike on behalf of welfare legislation came from the miners, in 1912. Miners had many of the classic ingredients for a labor-protest movement. Their work was dangerous; they lived with their fellow workers without much contact with other elements of society. But there was a traditionalism in miners' life that limited their vision of the future. They were proud of their work and were quick to protest major changes in it. They were devoted to their families and often religious. They benefited from full employment and their wages often rose even when those of other workers were falling. They also had gardens which in my opinion, obviously open to challenge, is a likely index or cause of a certain basic conservatism. Finally they were isolated from other workers. Even when they joined them in labor politics they acted as miners not as workers. One of the reasons that Welsh miners were slow to accept the Labour party was that the Liberals gave them candidates who were miners to vote for, wheras Labour offered them other workers or, even worse, intellectuals. Many notable radicals came from the ranks of miners. Some German miners penned knowledgeable pamphlets on revolutionary socialism while the young Welsh miners that went to Ruskin College in the 1900s led the attack on older British labor leaders. Still, miners generally were a vigorous but moderate force in the labor movement.

Textile and leatherworkers were less solidly united partly because their factories were smaller and more dispersed and partly because of the many women in their ranks. Important textile regions like Flanders and eastern France avoided the labor movement almost completely. And textile workers did not blend all aspects of their protest activities as coherently as the miners did. With the exception of Lancashire, where cotton workers combined strong unions with pragmatic votes for the Conservative party in return for factory legislation, textile workers acted on two fronts. They struck frequently, but in disorganized fashion and for very limited goals; typically in fact they simply sought to defend what they had against wage cuts and technical innovations. At the same time they were often enthusiastic Socialists, believing in a Socialist Utopia perhaps more fervently than did any other large group of workers. They backed the doctrinaire policies of Jules Guesde in northern France; they were eager Marxists in Saxony and in Walloon Belgium. Textile workers suffered from low and stagnant pay. Wives and children had to work which put a strain on health and on family structure. They were not an aggressive bunch; their strikes were feeble and usually without violence. But some of them at least had a dream of the future perhaps because they seemed able to do so little about the present.

Finally, the artisans had a fourth pattern of protest and of expectation. Along with the miners they were the leading participants in the labor movement as a whole and undoubtedly contributed more support to labor politics than any other group. This should immediately make us pause in judging the labor movement. The artisans' lead in political awareness had been visible much earlier, with the Chartists in Britain for example. Their continued special importance suggests again that the motives involved in the labor movement were not so new as might be assumed and that the working class if it was a class at all remained extraordinarily diverse. The labor movement did result from a partial convergence in the position and attitudes of artisans and factory workers. An increasing number of artisans did work on power machinery and in relatively large units of employment, but even these workers retained special craft traditions.

Artisans were still the most numerous of all manufacturing workers. In Germany, to use a rough measure, most manufacturing workers were employed in units with less than five employees —the typical artisan shop. And many skilled factory workers, particularly in the machine trades, had been trained in such shops and looked back on them fondly. The German labor movement, so often wrongly attributed to the direct impact of big business, owed many of its basic characteristics, including perhaps its ultimate conservatism, to men in the crafts. To understand labor protest in Germany and elsewhere we must avoid the confusion implicit in terms like *the* labor movement and *proletariat*. Many artisans joined the labor movement precisely because they feared they were sinking into the proletariat in which their independence and special skills and indeed their relatively privileged social status would be lost.

No group as numerous as the artisans could be unified of course. Craftsmen ranged from the metalworkers recently drawn into factory life through masons and bricklayers whose contacts with unskilled laborers sometimes involved them in violence, to printers, the conservative elite of the artisanal trades.

Some artisans, like the French bakers who would not unionize or strike or the many German bakers who joined a patriotic union, were conservative. They hoped to maintain the traditions of the crafts—many German bakers still lived contentedly in the homes of their masters and belonged to modified guilds—or aspired to respectable lower middle-class status.

Others were revolutionary—they wanted not simply an overturn of the government and capitalism but a rebellion against the whole industrial order. Revolutionary syndicalism in France captured much of this mood. Artisans in many countries feared the extension of machinery to their craft and attendant unemployment and decline of skill. Many would have agreed with the

Parisian shoemaker who proclaimed: "If I want the revolution, it's not to do any harm to people, but to be able to destroy all these machines." An important group of artisans, then, consisted of social reactionaries. This does not mean that they were wrong or evil or that their politics at this point were reactionary, but they wanted society to turn the clock back. This gave them their special fervor, for popular participation in revolutions even in modern times has more often been based on reactionary than on progressive sentiment. For the reactionary has clear though idealized standards of the past to apply to his situation; he knows the world is going to the dogs and that only a complete reversal will stop it. However the definitively reactionary artisan was now in a minority, probably most commonly found among groups like shoemakers whose trades really had been taken over by the factories. And the labor movement except for revolutionary syndicalism to an extent did not cater to reactionary sentiments, for it accepted the industrial order if not its governance.

The most characteristic artisanal contribution to the labor movement combined a verbal vigor and an interest in doctrine with a rather cautious pragmatism. Artisans still differed from factory workers in many ways. They were usually better educated and in the bigger cities had contacts with all sorts of people and ideas that would seem foreign to the factory centers. From the standpoint of doctrinal fervor and division the most lively cities involved in the labor movement were always substantially artisanal—Paris, Amsterdam, and Berlin. At the same time, artisans had many habits and expectations that were rather middle class. They had a low birthrate, about half that of miners or unskilled workers. This suggests that they were relatively free from tradition and strict religion, and relates to their interests in Socialist or revolutionary-syndicalist doctrine. But birth control of this sort also suggests an attachment to material acquisition and to social mobility that could link artisans to the existing order; that is, artisans limited their birthrate to promote the material well-being of themselves and their children. In essence most artisans had made a bargain with the industrial economy. They might bemoan the advent of new equipment or the decline of traditional apprenticeship and skill and they might try to retard these developments a bit but there was little frontal resistance. In return artisans wanted higher pay and they often hoped for personal advancement. Often they were successful. Contemporary studies of German printers showed that in some companies literally all the printers' sons went on to a higher profession. At the same time many artisans had hopes that were not fulfilled. On the basis of other German inquiries, admittedly covering only a tiny sample of workers, it is tempting to say that the typical German Socialist was a locksmith artisanally trained but now working in a machine factory who was fervently Marxist while personally hoping for a chance to set up a bicycle—or automobile—repair shop on his own, thereby becoming a good bourgeois whether he admitted this or not. (8) Socialism for such a person must have combined an interest in doctrine and resentments against the existing order with continued hopes for progress in middle-class terms, including advancement in status which labor organizations could provide in their own hierarchies. Artisanal unions, though often more interested than any other type in ideology, worked vigorously for immediate gains particularly in wages and led the way in collective bargaining. Here too was an artisanal characteristic: however class-conscious artisans might be now in theory, they had rather close contacts with their small employers and were accustomed to dealing with them.

To spare both author and reader we can stop the proliferation of industrial and professional types at this point. The conclusion is clear. Even if we look at those workers most likely to be drawn into the labor movement the diversity is overwhelming. Some workers yearned for a Utopia, others did not. Some were prone to violence while most were calm. They could and did join common movements particularly in politics but their intentions still differed. Some were quite religious and attached to a traditional family structure; even in big-city factories there were still workers who did not know of birth-control devices. Could such people view either politics or union activity as did de-Christianized family planners? The differences among types of workers were profound. For the historian they raise acute question about the utility of accepting the concept of a working class.

For the contemporary labor leader they necessitated great efforts to find, if not common denominators, at least common slogans.

To confound both historians and labor leaders the labor movement drew many people who were not workers. Peasants formed unions and particularly in France conducted important strikes. Many white-collar workers unionized as well. The leading white-collar unions in central Europe were anti-Socialist and conservative and need not concern us here. But it is important to note the beginnings of unionization among postal workers, teachers, and the like often along Socialist lines. In France strikes by postal workers roused considerable excitement in the labor movement. However, before World War I, nonworking-class participation in strikes and unions did not force major modifications in the generalizations about the labor movement; after the war when 400,000 white-collar workers were in Socialist unions in Germany and the teachers' union in France played a great role in setting up the Communist union organization, the situation was different. For our period nonworker unions did not have a great voice and their strikes were relatively isolated. Far more important was the question of peasant and middle-class participation in labor politics.

Most of the early Socialist leaders came from the middle classes. Liebknecht, Kautsky, Jaurès, Turati and many others were trained professional people, usually lawyers. Leading anarchists such as Bakunin were drawn from similar groups. Even some union leaders particularly in the more doctrine-oriented movements came from outside the working class. Fernand Pelloutier, who more than anyone else established French revolutionary syndicalism came from a conservative, upper-class background and was himself a journalist. How significant were these nonworker origins? Middle-class labor leaders were clearly rebels against their class; social origins in no sense predetermine political outlook. And most Socialist theory, particularly Marxist theory, easily justified the combination of intellectuals and labor, workers of the mind and workers with the hands. Yet it may be more than coincidence that the artisan August Bebel, the only worker among the top German Socialist leaders, was among the most pragmatic, particularly with regard to the importance of an active, reformist trade-union movement; or that the British labor movement that sprang largely from workers themselves was undoctrinaire. Middle-class labor leaders were spurred by doctrine; even their rebellion against their own class set them apart from workers, who seldom had such a sweeping sense of the evils of the capitalist order. Here as we have seen already is a principal source of the difficulty of reasoning from the pronouncements of leaders to the interests of ordinary workers.

Equally important, elements of the middle classes helped fill the ranks of the labor movement's political constituents. In so doing they often carried forward the doctrinal interests of the middle-class leaders. In France until 1890 Socialist voters probably came more from the middle than the working classes. Long after this observers noted that typical Socialist meetings in many French cities drew mainly lawyers, doctors, students, and the like with just a smattering of workers. One of the three main centers of the Guesdist party, the most orthodox Marxist wing of French socialism, was in southern France where support lay primarily among the middle classes and the peasantry accustomed to a radical political stance. In France also shopkeepers and other middle-class people frequently contributed to strikes and other aspects of the labor movement. Middle-class support was equally important for Italian socialism where suffrage restrictions kept most workers from the polls until 1912, but where nevertheless the Socialist party piled up increasing numbers of votes even before 1900. Even in Germany where the middle class was more conservative and where the Socialist party's constituency was more solidly working class, middle-class voters played an important role. Many in the middle classes resented the class voting systems of states like Prussia or the new suffrage restrictions introduced in Hesse and elsewhere after 1900; they drifted to the Socialist party in protest and stuck to it thereafter.

We cannot of course know how many in the middle classes turned to socialism; undoubtedly even in France it was only a minority. Nor can we know what percentage of Socialist votes came from outside the working class. Everywhere on the continent however it was an important phenomenon and everywhere it had a potential impact on the nature of socialism.

Economic grievances drove many in the middle classes toward socialism just as they drove others toward some sort of radical rightist or antisemitic protest in the same period. Like the workers many small shopkeepers and clerks suffered in economic crises and had problems simply making ends meet. But for some the economic grievances were more sweeping than most workers shared. Through socialism many professional people (such as teachers in France) and shopkeepers sought to protest the whole capitalist orientation of the economy with its emphasis on material gain and economic concentration. They disliked big companies and the prestige of businessmen which threatened to eclipse their own status and economic forms. In these respects the middle-class elements could be more radical than many workers, more open to Socialist doctrine; and their higher levels of education prepared them for an interest in ideology anyway. On the other hand many in the middle classes were drawn to socialism for purely political reasons because they wanted more complete suffrage (as in Germany) or more complete protection of freedom of expression (as in Italy in the 1890s during the years of repression of political dissent). Many, particularly in France and Italy, drifted to socialism because they had long been accustomed to being farthest to the left politically and socialism was farthest left; for them socialism meant above all a defense of democracy, anticlericalism, and equality under the law. Finally, some important middle-class Socialists had been workers originally and simply brought their socialism with them to their new estate. This was true for example of many tavern owners, some of whom had been fired as workers for their radicalism but continued to play a leading role in the labor movement.

In sum, elements of the middle class came to socialism for various reasons which were partially distinct from those of workers. They might be more radical than workers at least in theory. In France it was long to be characteristic that the middle-class Socialist constituency, particularly teachers, was more vigorous in its demands for Socialist purity than were either working-class supporters or the parliamentary leaders; and there were signs of this in some Socialist groups before 1914. Middle-class socialism was by no means necessarily reformist. On the other hand the many middle-class voters who saw socialism as a periodic outlet for a somewhat ritualistic proclamation of devotion to the left and who committed themselves to no other participation in the labor movement undoubtedly weakened Socialist fervor and might actually have repelled workers who sought something more relevant and vital. This may have been the case for example in southern France at this time. There was no general pattern. What was uniformly true however was that middle-class participation in the labor movement helped turn it ever more intensely toward politics; even economic grievances for the middle class were to receive political solution. The middle class gained political consciousness far earlier and more completely than did most workers. This is why the support from middle-class elements was vital to much early socialism. Yet in the long run the politicization of the labor movement helped attach it to the existing order, helped turn it away from revolution; in this sense even middle-class radicals may have helped tame the working class. It is relevant to note the role of the labor movement in inculcating among the workers other essentially middle-class values: temperance and sobriety; regularity of work and savings; even better treatment of women and children in the family. From a variety of vantage points the role of the middle-class elements in socialism cannot be ignored.

Like any major political movement socialism drew support from a wide variety of groups who turned to it for a great variety of reasons. Like any major movement it failed to draw unanimous support from the groups for which it was in principle particularly designed and it attracted important elements from groups to which it was theoretically hostile. Earlier in the nineteenth century liberalism had similarly won only a portion of the middle class whose interests it presumably represented and had drawn many aristocrats whose position in many ways it attacked. This is simply to say that the social composition of any political constituency is highly complex and often seemingly contradictory.

Have we then advanced our understanding of the labor movement by this brief glance at its social ingredients, or have we simply muddled the whole situation? First it is clear that socialism was not simply a working-class product. It derived from middle-class leadership and had important middle-class support. It derived in fact from what may be called a fundamentally middle-class philosophical tradition—the ideas of the Enlightenment that held that men are rational and will behave rationally if their environment is properly arranged and that progress on this earth is possible and desirable. As we turn now to working-class conditions and action the nonworking-class elements in socialism must not be forgotten; we must return later to assess their relationship with more purely worker interests. Socialism did help spread to workers many values already developed in middle-class culture albeit in different form. It stressed progress, the importance of politics, even the acceptability of industrial (though not capitalist) society, a society open to technological change and steadily increasing production and prosperity. Along with its message of class consciousness it may ultimately have helped integrate workers with modern industrial life.

The working-class constituency for the labor movement was highly complex even by itself. It included reactionaries and progressives, utopians and piecemeal reformers. Diversity within the ranks of labor ran through all aspects of the labor movement. And always around the islands of activist workers were masses of laborers who were indifferent or at best occasionally aroused.

CONDITIONS AND EXPECTATIONS OF WORKERS

So far we have indulged in the luxury of analysis without much attention to chronology or geography; let us continue the indulgence for another section. Developments in broad social groups like the working classes can seldom be pinned to precise dates. Just as it is more important to know the principal types of workers from whom support for the labor movement developed than to know exactly when they turned to it so we can now discuss certain general trends in working-class life without worrying unduly about their precise dates. And these trends affected all the industrial countries, differing only in degree. We are now seeking the causes of worker commitment to the labor movement and from this something of the nature of this commitment.

Did the labor movement constitute among other things a vigorous demand for progress in material conditions or a protest against deteriorating conditions? There is evidence in both directions. Prior to the late nineteenth century working-class protest particularly its most violent forms was traditionally defensive, directed against increasing hardship. Certainly the great riots and revolutions of the first half of the nineteenth century occurred during economic slumps when the urban lower classes were driven to the edges of misery and beyond. Great Britain, the only western European country in which a substantial labor movement developed during the first phase of industrialization, was also the only country in which material conditions persistently deteriorated for urban workers during this phase. With some exceptions particularly for artisanal groups and miners who sometimes sought positive improvement workers were long spurred to protest by the knowledge that they were losing ground; they found it difficult to formulate progressive demands.

By the late nineteenth century the situation had changed and most historians of protest have clearly distinguished this industrial protest from preindustrial types. Almost all the labor movements pointed to better times in the future, if not under the existing capitalist system at least under some other. Furthermore the movements took root in a basically prosperous period and they depended on prosperity in many ways. Most categories of workers had benefited from a fairly steady increase in real wages in the second half of the nineteenth century. Between 1870 and 1900 alone real wages increased from 30 percent to 100 percent in the industrial countries. This meant that workers were able to improve their diets and health; new physical energy was clearly relevant to the labor movement. They were able to afford union and party dues; some ordinary workers spent up to 5 percent of their budgets on dues and party publications, a figure inconceivable in the earlier, poorer years. Hours of work had fallen too. In the 1890s most urban workers worked ten to twelve hours a day instead of twelve to fourteen; this meant there was free time that could be devoted to the labor movement. Finally these improvements not only permitted labor agitation but also encouraged it

for they gave workers new expectations. Workers now knew that
it was possible for wages to improve and they could easily demand a more rapid improvement than they received.

The correspondence between the labor movement and prosperity showed in many ways. It was in prosperous years that
union membership and strike activity increased, often to fall
back slightly in a slump; for workers in bad times feared the
risk of participating in labor organizations lest they lose their
insecure jobs and pay. In individual countries new bursts of
labor activity were caused by new levels of prosperity, as in
England in the 1890s when workers found their services in peak
demand. It remained true also that the poorest workers were
generally unable to protest; here a more traditional link between
some relative prosperity and agitation was maintained.

Along with rising material well-being great hardship persisted.
We are talking about a stage in working-class history in which
improvements led to new expectations and new vigor not to
increased satisfaction. Workers in this period lost ground in
terms of their share in national income as profits consistently
rose more rapidly than wages. Labor leaders pointed this out in
general terms and some workers could sense it on their own as
they saw their employers build new houses and buy automobiles.
More relevant were the real constrictions in workers' own budgets.
Up to 60 percent of all expenses were for food; this was much
improved over the 70 percent characteristic of the early industrial
years but hardly constituted well-being. Diets now included reasonably regular servings of meat and milk products but bread
and potatoes continued to serve as basic staples. Housing and
clothing took most of what was left over and housing conditions
continued to be bad. In Germany where the situation was worst a
substantial minority of worker families lived in a single room.
Health also remained a major concern; many German unions
reported that over a quarter of their members lost over two
weeks a year because of illness while workers could spend at
most 1 percent of their budget on doctors and medicines.

On the job too many material hazards persisted. Despite regulatory laws dangers to hygiene and safety were great in many
industries. Painters and printers contracted lead poisoning; the

protest zeal of coal miners was in part due to their high rates of accident and death on the job. Hours of work were still long. Groups as diverse as bakers and carters had still to protest fifteen-hour days; dockers often worked around the clock. Even where hours had been reduced to ten or twelve, employers had frequently increased the pace of work and eliminated rest periods so that the net gain in terms of leisure time was slight.

In sum, there was still plenty to protest about. Many aspects of the labor movement suggest a decisive new stage in the history of protest in which common people attacked not outright misery but the lack of sufficient progress. A term like *revolution of expectations* seems to be appropriate for the first time in modern European history.

And yet it would be wrong to suggest too great a change. Much of the force of the labor movement in this period came from vigorous protest against deteriorating conditions. Many of the newly active unskilled workers spoke from the depths of misery. The wages of dockers, construction laborers and quarry workers were often less than half the average national level. Textile workers particularly on the continent faced frequent crises in their industry as the pace of international competition mounted; even in better years, many employers tried to reduce their wages. For workers more generally there were frequent economic slumps as in 1895, 1901–2, and 1908–9, in which unemployment rose massively. They might be unable to protest their hardship during the bad years but they acted as soon thereafter as they could seeking above all a restoration of earlier conditions. Here the sense of timing had become more sophisticated but the goals were still essentially defensive.

Aside from periods of recession two forces threatened to reduce the material well-being of the labor force in this period; both were partially new and help explain the new vigor of a still-defensive reaction. First the pace of work was rising in many industries. New machines spread to crafts; automatic composing machines made printers work faster while new machines for boring and lathing increased the tempo for machine builders. In all industries the supervision of work grew more intense. Employers tried to spread payments by the piece instead of day wages to force workers to step up the pace. At an extreme after 1900 American methods of rationalizing work through time and motion studies were imported. Foremen generally grew more overbearing. Here was a major change in working-class life, as decisive in many ways as the initial advent of the factory system. It roused greater resentment or at least greater expressed resentment than the early factories had. Workers complained of fatigue and nervous tension. They feared unemployment as well and with good reason. In most industrial countries skilled workers like printers and machine builders had to count on high levels of unemployment, up to 5 percent even in good years. In some countries particularly England and France many unskilled workers also faced persistent unemployment because the new machines and systems of work tended to stabilize the demand for their services whereas their number continued to increase.

After 1900 inflation added a second new burden to working-class life. There had been periods of inflation before in the nineteenth century but never so persistent or prolonged. Now the rise in food prices alone added over 12 percent to the average worker's budget in France between 1900 and 1910. Rents and many other costs were soaring as well. Money wages were rising too of course. Many historians have claimed that real wages in France continued to advance though at a slower pace until 1910 when they dropped. My own judgment is that the pattern was reversed, that there was a mild decline in real pay until 1910; hence among other things labor agitation was greatest before this date. In Britain inflation was quite severe and outstripped the advance in wages after 1910; in Germany money wages kept up better. But everywhere inflation was important and everywhere groups of workers could find their standard of living affected in individual years in which their money wages did not change. At an extreme in countries like France many workers had to reduce purchases of meat and other items while others depended increasingly on the earnings of wives and children in order to make ends meet. (9)

Much labor protest could then seek largely to maintain existing standards against change. Formal labor movements always urged more positive gains, but many workers looked largely toward preserving what they had. There were variations within the labor force, naturally, and changes over time. Groups like miners worked persistently for positive improvements while textile workers generally tried to hang onto what they had. National patterns varied also due to different economic trends and different expectations. German workers had the lowest standards of living of any major industrial country but they did not face declining real wages; hence they were probably less discontent than British workers. And everywhere increasing numbers of workers were learning to seek positive gains. Both inflation and the rising pace of work helped induce workers to think in terms of progress instead of the standards of the past. Inflation made advancing wage levels essential and the rising pace of work could be made acceptable to some workers by corresponding improvements in pay. It remains important to determine how many workers thought in traditional and how many in progressive terms. And we must decide how sweeping either type of protest was whether induced by new expectations or by the hostile trends of the economy.

Working-class life was not a matter of material conditions alone. Industrialization had long created psychological strains and limitations on workers' freedom; both were in many ways increasing in this period. The labor movement was not simply a revolt against material hardship but a cry of human freedom. Workers sought new relationships with both employers and governments. Both were to some extent repressive elements. But did workers feel isolated in a hostile environment, treated impersonally as cogs in an increasingly mechanized industrial world? Or were their grievances more limited, their sense of alienation incomplete? The answer will say much about the nature of the labor movement; but it is far harder to provide a picture of the human relationships of working-class life than it is to outline material conditions.

Workers had many reasons to resent the governments of the day. Their political rights were often incomplete. German workers in most states received a far less than equal share of the vote due to the class voting system. Belgian workers were long denied the vote altogether and then given a class voting system. Many

British workers were disenfranchised by provisions that various types of lodgers could not vote and by strict residence requirements that could disqualify up to 30 percent of the mobile urban electorate. Even more important whether they had a vote or not workers could hardly feel that the government was really on their side. All the governments sent numerous police and sometimes troops into both large and small strikes. Arrests and clashes with police were common. The government's purpose was not simply to preserve order; all the industrial countries had laws against intimidation of workers by strikers that could be broadly interpreted so that German strikers were arrested for shouting "Pfui" and French strikers jailed for simply looking hard at their fellows still at work. Government handling of strikes exposed millions of workers to the fact that the police were against them and often directly in league with the employers. Official opposition to labor politics was less important. But German workers could remember the repression under the anti-Socialist laws of the 1880s when many of them had turned to socialism in direct defiance of the government. Police surveillance of Socialist meetings in many countries including the implanting of police spies in political groups served as a reminder that the state was hostile. (10)

On the other hand the industrial states did much that was relevant and favorable to the workers. Most obviously they provided increasing regulatory and welfare services in this period. Many German workers were sympathetic to a state that granted them pension plans and health insurance. Workers in all countries frequently appealed to factory and mine inspectors against employer violations of safety provisions and hours limitations. The government also served as a mediator in many labor disputes. Ministers of state in the chief industrial countries moved in to settle some leading disputes for the first time in this period; and most countries had conciliation procedures for smaller strikes, usually under the auspices of local judges. Workers did not have to feel that the state was totally against them in their quarrels with employers. To be sure all this seems painfully inadequate by modern standards and was judged inadequate by the labor leaders of the time. The social-insurance schemes provided little aid and almost all of it was taken from worker dues; no elderly worker could plan to survive on a state pension alone and there was no redistribution of income through the plans. Many workers were not covered at all especially outside Germany. Regulation of work conditions was similarly incomplete; there were too few factory inspectors and the inspectors frequently seemed allied with the employers. Government-mediation services brought men from the middle classes—the same classes from which employers were drawn—to settle disputes; many workers claimed that such men could not be unbiased. Governments were not doing enough. The continued advance of the labor movement while more and more patchwork reforms were adopted was ample proof of this. A question remains—did workers in the labor movement intend largely to press governments for more immediate reforms or were they against the governments themselves?

Welfare programs were not the only favorable or at least partially favorable contact that workers had with the state. They were educated by the state and often served in its army. Through both services the states (particularly on the continent) tried consciously to instill national and civic loyalties, the Germans through a conservative-religious curriculum in the schools, the French through a secular-republican but equally nationalistic program. What was the worker reaction? Varied of course but probably generally favorable. Some young workers, particularly in Britain where generalized education was newest, resented school discipline. Other workers, especially women, were receptive to a conservative curriculum; even in France many girls in worker families were still sent to religious schools in the 1890s. Similar variations undoubtedly existed in the reaction to military service. But many German workers including vehement Socialists looked back to their military service as the high point of their lives, for it was the most decisively novel and broadening experience they had. Lest this seem a solely German characteristic the eager entry of many young Welsh miners into the army during the Boer War must be cited along with the excitement in mining villages when the soldiers paraded. (11) Education and to some extent military service aided the labor movement by spreading literacy and extending worker horizon, but they created new bridges between state and worker at the same time.

Finally local governments in many cities were far more open to worker influence than national governments were. Men in the labor movement and of worker origin increasingly served on school boards and municipal councils; some of them in cities as important as Marseilles became mayors. These advances, which were particularly notable in France, may have reduced workers' sense of political isolation and they brought concrete benefits in the form of local housing programs and welfare schemes.

Within the factory or shop workers traditionally had no direct voice. If they did not like conditions they might complain individually but many companies had no procedure for receiving complaints and often fired workers who ventured any. Or they could quit. Even in this period workers did change jobs frequently, an attack on employers' unfairness which brought some satisfaction but which was individual and temporary in its effects. Aside from this, decisions about wages and other matters were handed down from the top, from the employer. There was no real discussion. Many workers were not even told what their pay was and were not permitted to be present at the assessment of their work for payment on a piece-rate basis. Similarly fines were levied by mangement without consultation. Even company welfare schemes were autocratically run in most cases. Pension funds which depended on dues that the workers paid were directed by the employer who gave no accounting of his actions. Many workers were required to use company canteens and houses; company health programs typically compelled workers to use whatever doctor the company assigned. Company control could go even further, particularly in isolated factory or mining towns. Employers often required church attendance or at least discriminated against irreligious workers in the assignment of work; there were similar attempts to intimidate worker voting.

At the end of the nineteenth century employer controls were being extended in many ways. The key fact was the growth in the size of companies in every industry. The average metallurgical and mining firms employed hundreds of workers and many employed thousands. The spread of machines and factories to shoemaking and tailoring meant an even more dramatic expansion of company size; producers in these industries previously had worked in units of five or ten workers at most, but now they too were surrounded by hundreds. Construction companies grew; in Paris after 1900 the number of companies with less than twenty workers declined absolutely while firms with over a hundred proliferated. In the large companies traditions of personal treatment and acquaintance could not be maintained. Many workers never saw their firm's owner, and often corporate ownership increased anonymity still further. Workers were bossed by underlings who were often themselves bound by rigid rules and pressures to produce. The human element in industry seemed to be fading and without doubt the labor movement was a major response. Yet the labor movement often accentuated the worker's isolation at first for employers reacted vigorously to the threat to their control. Individually and in the many employer associations that burgeoned in this period they resisted dealings with unions, fired suspected agitators, and shouted loudly about the ingratitude of their labor force. Some big companies spread a network of police spies and sought to use their housing and benefit programs to assure absolute loyalty. Others formed company unions that workers had to join which gave the tiniest of voices to workers on condition of their absolute docility. In sum, the traditional subjection of workers to decisions from above was heightened by the rise of impersonal firms and the initial reaction to the labor movement.

Even here however there are qualifications and variations to be noted. We have described a situation in which workers might feel unfree; they did not necessarily do so. Some were accustomed to a lack of voice; some were contented by high wages or benefit programs. Some of the most authoritarian companies, notably in metallurgy, had very little labor trouble. Some workers were too fearful to complain, others found it natural to be bossed around, and many were grateful for the paternalistic concern that these same companies displayed. Nor were employers and supervisors uniformly harsh. There was great variation from one person to the next. British employers were less peremptory than French and German. Many employers did listen to their workers' complaints at least informally; many, as we shall see, were willing to come to terms rather quickly with the new unions. And we must not see the whole working class subjected to large, impersonal factories. There were many small units still. Many artisans in trades like baking still worked alongside their employers as well as being housed and fed by them. Many metalworkers were hired by small companies and they vastly outnumbered the workers in big metallurgical factories. Textile companies though on the average employing three or four hundred workers were not so large that employers or managers did not know many skilled workers personally. Though the growing impersonality of industrial control was a fact of great importance it should not be exaggerated. Many workers might hesitate before they pitted themselves against employers as class against class when they knew their employer personally or sensed some human concern in paternalistic programs.

Finally, did workers feel alone in their broader society? Some did certainly. The strength of miners' protests owed much to the isolation of miners in their villages for there were few contacts with other groups. Miners believed that no one else cared about them unless they compelled their attention; they also realized that they were often scorned. In Britain miners were figures of fun on the popular stage and when miners reached London in the early days of the labor movement as politicians or union leaders they were often ridiculed for their strange clothes and speech. Unskilled workers also knew that they were regarded at best as inferiors. Dockers were widely believed to be the scum of the earth, depraved failures from all classes and all nations. Sailors had somewhat the same reputation, enhanced perhaps by the growing use of Asians and Africans by the maritime companies. Unskilled workers were frequently treated as potential beggars or criminals; many for example were arrested as vagrants when they were out of work. From workers of this sort labor protest could assume a peculiar intensity for workers sought not only material improvements but also a recognition of their human dignity.

Workers in general however were not so completely cut off from the rest of society. Many still retained attachments to the peasantry, often commuting to work from small villages. A large segment of the Belgian labor force lived in the country, traveling up to sixty miles a day on the cheap and ubiquitous electric railways. In bigger cities workers were more segregated into their own residential sections but they did have contacts with other elements of society; many were in fact moving into the suburbs by this time in cities like London. The participation of many elements of the middle classes in labor politics was another sign that the workers were not entirely cut off. Even aside from this middle-class reformers tirelessly investigated the conditions of the poor in this period. Shopkeepers and other groups frequently sympathized with labor strikes and contributed funds and leadership. Only around 1910 in many countries did public opinion turn against labor agitation in general. Finally throughout the period many workers moved up into other classes of society. This was a period of substantial mobility in which unskilled workers could gain some skill and skilled workers or their sons could rise to be foremen, small proprietors, or small landowners. The working class as a whole was not entirely cut off from the rest of society or from the values and expectations that other groups held dear.

Here then was the ambiguous background from which working-class protest emerged. There was potential for a truly revolutionary upheaval. The factory-labor force lacked a direct revolutionary tradition in any country for it was too new. But it had been drawn from both peasant and artisan elements which had revolted in many countries during the previous century, attacking the spread of commercialized agriculture and manufacturing. Now, with mature industrialization, commercialization—that is, the maximization of production for profit—had reached a new stage. It brought to the workers a new pace of work, new human relationships on the job, and a loss of some freedoms. Would they rebel against it—against the principles as well as the leaders of their society?

There were other possibilities. New hardships such as declining real wages might induce a vigorous protest which did not however call the bases of the industrial order into question. A new sense of progress might bring insistence that the control of the industrial order change hands or at least that this order grant workers far more than they were then receiving. Or workers could seek more minor gains limited by a recognition that conditions had improved in many respects and were still improving in some. Economic and political conditions combined with the prior creation of labor doctrines and organizations created a new stage of labor protest. It is time to turn to this directly, to see what it portended.

STRIKES AND VIOLENCE

The best starting point in determining what workers wanted is a summary of the goals and methods of strikes. There are three reasons for this. First, in many cases strikes were chronologically the earliest significant expression of labor grievance, with Socialist voting and even unions coming afterwards. Second, many strikes were uncontrolled or incompletely controlled by unions and parties; strikes allow the closest possible look at what workers themselves desired. Finally, strikes involved the greatest commitment to protest albeit episodically. There were far more risks involved in striking than in joining a union of voting Socialists; so strikes should tell us for what gains workers were prepared to make sacrifices. Reaching unprecedented intensity in this period, strikes were a major feature of the labor movement in any event although they have seldom been studied. (12)

In France and Britain a significant tradition of strikes antedated both durable unions and labor politics. French miners for example conducted important strikes in the 1830s and 1840s; they had some organization and leadership to guide these movements but no enduring union was formed until some decades later. The point was that strikes burst forth when workers reached the breaking point; they did not require elaborate advance planning or any clear ideology. They stemmed from the immediate material problems and aspirations of workers themselves. Even at the end of the nineteenth century many workers engaged in strikes before they entered any labor organization. They formed unions or turned to unions to aid in their strikes, and workers long regarded unions above all as combat units; one of the reasons workers quit and rejoined unions so often was their belief that membership was important only when a fight was in prospect. In Britain the basic pattern is clear—a new level of strikes beginning in 1889 led to the formation of new types of unions and the extension of old. From this movement, in turn within a decade, came the Labour Representation Committee; admittedly the Social Democratic Federation, not without fleeting importance, had more independent origins. In France the formation of major Socialist groups often preceded strike and union movements from the late 1870s onward but the development of a real worker constituency did not. Northern textile workers turned to the Guesdist party in the early 1890s after a vigorous strike movement that left them dissatisfied. Coal miners in many areas of France began to vote for reformist Socialists after considerable experience with strikes and union organizations.

In sum, workers first expressed their grievances through strikes because this allowed the most immediate and spontaneous protest. As they gained experience and realized how much organization was needed to maintain a successful strike they formed unions or joined existing unions to protect their ability to strike. As their unions proved inadequate to obtain all that workers wanted or, as in Britain with the Taff Vale decision when the unions were brought under political attack, the workers turned to politics. Strike movements that failed, or even successful ones that revealed the limitations on the gains that workers could expect, opened workers to Socialist voting and the more sweeping doctrines of labor protest.

This is not to say that all strikers turned to unions or socialism or that all working-class Socialists or even union members had a background of direct action. The pattern was clearest in the 1890s in both France and Britain during the first wave of new labor protest. Thereafter the attractions of union-benefit programs could draw workers not particularly interested in striking especially in Britain (indeed this had happened before among skilled workers, in the moderate New Model Union movement of 1850–90); while in France workers could turn directly to the growing attractions of the Socialist appeal. Even after 1900 however strike activity continued to pull new workers into the labor movement for the first time. In France even by 1913 over 20 percent of all strikes involved no union members at all though many still led quickly to the formation of new groups. Though not uniformly accurate this pattern seems useful: workers first awakened to new personal grievances or expectations, expressed them best in strikes, and then perhaps participated in more organized forms of protest.

But what of countries like Germany and Belgium where socialism developed before significant union organization or persistent strike activity? Workers in both countries had struck occasionally in the first two-thirds of the century, prior to the introduction of socialism, but the efforts had been sporadic. A wave of strikes comparable to that of Britain and France in the 1890s developed only at the end of the decade long after socialism was well established and even then it did not reach the same levels (and never did, before World War I). Many groups of workers did turn to socialism after experience in more direct agitation. In Belgium for example, mineworkers with a long tradition of strikes and unions were the bulwark of the Socialist party. But clearly many workers awakened to socialism before they developed new personal expectations; indeed for some socialism may have delayed the formation of such expectations. We will have to deal with this difference in patterns. Even in Belgium and Germany, however, strike activity does allow an insight into workers' most immediate reactions; and unions though they developed after socialism and under the party's control quickly developed many of the characteristics of unions elsewhere.

In all countries strikes were only incompletely under the direction of parties and unions throughout this period. Even the great strikes often had a spontaneous element. The 1905 miners' strike in the Ruhr was called by unions—but only after workers in several companies had walked out on their own to protest changes in the hours of work. The 1906 miners' strike in northern France spread like wildfire after a disastrous accident; unions could only follow their members' lead. The 1910 French railroad strike, though long discussed in the unions, burst out in fact without warning when maintenance workers in a Paris yard protested the reduction of overtime. The great British transportation strike of the next year had similar origins in Liverpool. (13) And this is not to mention the vast numbers of smaller strikes that had no union preparation. The spontaneous element was vital. Unions and parties influenced but could not completely determine the goals and the tactics of strikes. Gradually the two aspects of the labor movement—the spontaneous protest and the doctrinal organizational element—did draw together as workers gained experience and as union and party membership spread. This was one of the key developments in the emerging labor movement, but it had not been completed even by 1914. Hence strikes must be viewed somewhat separately, not as outgrowths of union resolutions or party dogma. They truly came from the grassroots, from the needs and desires of workers themselves. Relatedly they differed less from country to country than the more formal aspects of the labor movement did.

The strikes of this period were an unprecedented expression of lower-class grievance. Undoubtedly a higher percentage of the manufacturing labor force was involved in strikes than had ever before engaged in direct action. Certainly this was true for any period since the industrial revolution began; and these years would bear comparison with lower-class protest in all but the peak revolutionary periods before industrialization. Millions of workers were involved in all the leading industrial countries. These numbers were all the more impressive in that direct action, though easier than before, still entailed huge risks. Workers who stayed away from their jobs for more than a few days—and over a tenth of all strikes lasted for at least a month—suffered economic hardship for neither their own savings nor their aid from outside sources were sufficient to support them at their usual levels. They suffered possible loss of jobs; in many small strikes the entire body of protesters was dismissed while in large strikes dismissals of hundreds of workers were not uncommon. Some of these workers were blacklisted in a whole region or industry for years. Finally, as we have seen, strikers risked confrontations with police and often arrest. The strikes of this period were not simply ingredients of calm industrial bargaining; neither governments nor employers nor workers themselves fully recognized them as such. The sense of industrial warfare was widespread. Finally strikes not only multiplied in number and in participation beyond all past experience but also developed an incredible diversity of form. All the major types of strikes were attempted in this period, often for the first time. There were tiny strikes of workers in a single company, sometimes in a single category of skill. There were local general strikes, particularly in port cities. There were national industrial strikes, particularly in coal mines. And more tentatively there were nationwide general strikes, notably in Belgium, (14) Holland, and Sweden, but to an extent in France in 1906 and less formally in Britain in 1910–12. Workers might walk off the job calmly or they might be violent. They might sit down on the job instead of leaving or slow up their work rather than risk an outright strike. In these respects too the strike movement constituted a decisive new stage in the history of protest, a clear beginning of the modern period of industrial relations in which high rates of strikes serve as a basic element.

Despite all these undeniable and important signs of vigor however the strike movement was in many ways surprisingly moderate. The strike itself in a broad history of lower-class protest must be recognized as a more restrained form of complaint than the previous mainstay, the riot. It was better organized, probably more effective, and certainly capable of drawing in larger numbers of protesters, but by stressing a withdrawal of work rather than a direct, physical attack on an enemy it involved some control over the most immediate emotions. Furthermore strikes in the leading industrial countries did not compare with those in emerging nations like Italy or Russia. Despite the fact that these two countries along with Catalonia in Spain had far smaller manufacturing labor forces, strikes there increased far more rapidly than in western Europe; Italy for example had twice the strike rate of Germany. And this was in spite of a much higher level of police repression. Workers in the new industrial countries were protesting the bitter hardships of early industry and a hostile political structure as well. Their strikes commonly included demands for political reform; they were often informed by an ideological purpose; they were often violent, indeed revolutionary. The general strike of Russian workers was fundamental to the revolution of 1905; the five-day strike and riot in Milan in 1898 and the five days of mob rule in Barcelona in 1909, in which many churches and public buildings were burned, showed a similar revulsion against the existing order. Nothing like this happened in industrial Europe for workers there had come to terms with industrial society and to a considerable extent with the industrial state. Strikes in industrial Europe reveal workers in a mood of vigorous moderation; if the energy was new the restraint was equally important.

Direct political strikes were rare in this period in contrast to patterns later in the twentieth century and even in the years immediately after World War I. Workers in the industrial countries did not feel that strikes were a realistic political weapon and possibly did not believe that political goals were important enough to risk a strike. There were a few exceptions. The two general strikes in Belgium directly pressed for universal suffrage; and demonstrations and rioting in Germany over suffrage questions indicate that political strikes might have taken hold had they been called. We shall return to these points. In countries where reasonably universal and effective suffrage existed, however, political strikes simply did not develop. In 1911 for example the revolutionary-syndicalist Confédération générale du travail in France called a one-day strike against the army and militarism. Naturally they claimed great success but it seems that only a few thousand workers actually participated. Even May Day strikes, which were urged everywhere on the continent by revolutionary-syndicalists and Socialists as a demonstration of worker solidarity, were joined by relatively small numbers of workers though they had some significance on occasion. None of this proves that workers had little political interest; it does show that they took the risk of striking only for more immediate goals.

Some workers did strike to press their governments to take specific reform measures. Coal miners in France, for example, struck in 1912–13 for a better pension law. Other workers agitated for legislation on the hours of work. Even these strikes were rare until late in the period and they were clearly not political in the sense of calling a whole government into question. They were important in showing a pragmatic political awareness, an extension of the specific reform interests of workers into the legislative sphere. This aside, however, political strikes though widely discussed on the theoretical level were not an important phenomenon in industrial Europe.

The majority of strikes concerned wage questions, primarily wage increases. This is the most important single goal to assess. Labor leaders and many other contemporary observers often claimed that the vigorous pressure for wage increases stemmed from a deep-seated desire for a better material life and for a greater share of industrial revenue. Though the term was not used at the time something like a revolution of expectations seemed to be taking place. Governmental strike statistics listed the vast majority of wage strikes as *offensive*—that is, as seeking higher wages than before. It was noted that most wage strikes took place in prosperous years when workers were actuated by a positive desire to improve their lot and share in the general well-being. We can emerge then with a picture of a strike movement perhaps not revolutionary at least insofar as it largely ignored political goals but impelled by a sweeping desire for change.

There are problems with this view however. We have seen that many workers had reasons to strike simply to keep wages at their previous levels. Wages invariably fell during the slumps of this period. Workers might not protest the cut immediately for they realized that strikes in a recession are difficult to win because employers face little economic pressure to make concessions. But when the slump was over they would strike, apparently for a raise but actually for a restoration of a standard already known. The post-1900 inflation caused even more general demands for raises to maintain existing conditions. Everywhere after about 1905 there were claims that prices had outstripped wages. Strikers, in fact generally argued in defensive terms. That is, they justified their demands for a raise by past standards, pointing to a previous pay cut, or a reduction in hours that reduced pay, or to the inflation, or at most to higher wages that similar workers received in another company or another town. Only rarely did they argue that they deserved a greater share of industrial income or a raise beyond all precedent. Partly of course their arguments were intended to win maximum public support, for they knew that justifications in terms of existing or past standards were most popular. But there was more than debating technique involved. Workers were readier than ever before to defend what they had, and they were admittedly defending not just traditional conditions but the improvements of the past decades. In general they had not developed an explicit desire for much more than they already had.

This generalization demands some qualification of course. Many workers as individuals sought better pay, and they often could find it by taking a different job or moving to a different company. We are talking about a willingness to use collective action to win major improvements. Even here there was great variety. We can go back for a moment to a three-fold division of the sorts of workers most involved in the labor movement. Unskilled workers, particularly when they first burst forth in strikes and unions did seek a better life. They talked specifically of their misery, their hard work that was not sufficiently rewarded, their desire to share the standards of other types of workers. Workers in light industries, particularly textiles which so dominated strike activity in the period, were more strictly defensive. Wages often fluctuated in their industries and they sought above all to keep what they had. More sophisticated workers like printers, construction workers, and miners sometimes talked in terms of absolute gains and a share in rising prosperity. And this approach gained ground in the period. Groups of workers might conduct a first strike or two against a previous pay cut and then, realizing their power, move toward more postive demands. Glove workers in one French city struck often after 1900 against pay cuts or rising food prices, but in 1913 they had learned to insist on their "normal and constant raise." The growing ability to claim that other, similar workers were earning more and to ask for unprecedented money wages to meet the inflation encouraged this evolution. Demands were still moderate however by 1914. The most sophisticated workers and even many of the unskilled once their first demands were met asked for only small increases and were almost always ready to compromise. Very few strikes held out for a bigger raise than employers were willing to give. Hence in this first great period of the labor movement workers were unable to maintain their share of national income as profits outstripped wages and even suffered at best a substantial diminution in the rate of real-wage gains. My contention is that these developments resulted not simply from the weakness of organized labor but also from the persistently limited character of worker demands.

The instances in which real wages advanced in the prewar years tend to bear out this point. Germany and Belgium offered poorer living conditions to the workers than Britain or France; worker expectations were less developed; but the most important fact was that real wages did not decline, save in specific recessions, and so workers had less basis in terms of their overwhelming desire to maintain what they had, to press for money-wage raises. So the strike rate was considerably lower in these countries than in Britain or France. There was a notable decline in strike activity in Britain from 1899 to 1901, though these were prosperous years, and in France from 1911 to 1913. In both cases many workers had made good previous losses in recessions and were not at that point afflicted by overrapid inflation; again their motivation to strike was reduced. Conversely the greatest worker outburst in any industrial country, that of Great Britain after 1910, was directly caused by a rapid deterioration of conditions due to inflation.

The strike rate increased after 1890 and even more after 1895 because some workers acquired new expectations but even more because though free enough from prolonged recessions to be able to risk a protest, they still faced periodic deterioration in their living standards. They were not as far removed as has often been thought from the traditions of lower-class protest, which depended on an economic decline because the lower classes could not formulate positive material goals very easily. At the same time for most workers the level of deterioration was not great enough to induce revolutionary bitterness. For some, strikes themselves were sufficiently successful (and wage strikes had the highest success rate of any type) to eliminate the deterioration altogether. Wage strikes before World War I add up to a distinctive but transitional phase in the history of labor protest in which workers were realizing their strength as never before but still held back from demanding huge gains.

All this may seem surprising. It is easy to feel that everyone is an acquisitive economic man and wants more at all times; and of course we have not proved that workers did not want more, only that they were restrained in collective action to get it. There is no need to be patronizing in an approach that stresses the continued limitations on workers' desires. Most groups historically have been unable to risk novel expectations. Many have found other satisfactions and workers often still had some of these. We must stress again that workers were not far from peasant or artisanal origins in which material acquisitiveness beyond a certain range was frowned upon. They had not formed as distinctive or demanding a social class as is usually contended. Moreover some of them through socialism and other movements may have been looking for progress in less materialistic terms; their expectations may have distracted them from material demands and also may have comforted them in some continued hardship.

Most contemporary inquiries do not reveal that large numbers of workers had very specific notions of how they would spend more money if they had it except when their spending had fallen below a previous level. (15) It is possible for example to point out that German workers suffered terribly constricted housing conditions and had little money for recreation. But how much did most of them care? How conscious were they of deprivation? German rural-housing conditions which many workers had experienced in childhood were miserable as well. Many German workers continued to be satisfied with inexpensive recreation, notably strolls in the countryside. When they struck over wages they almost never mentioned housing or inadequate recreation, though the labor leaders often did. This does not mean that they were benighted and not even that they were satisfied but that they were still too traditionalist to phrase very clear positive demands.

Much of the character of the strike movement then was determined by the nature of wage demands and expectations. The same character pervaded strikes over working conditions. There are two points here. First, it was frequently difficult to persuade workers to strike for improved conditions. Most labor leaders believed correctly that such strikes were more important than wage strikes because their results were more lasting. A wage increase might be swept away by recession but a reduction of work hours usually remained. By the same token strikes for such goals involved a more active sense of progress than many workers had.

Time and time again campaigns to improve working conditions fell flat. Two such campaigns in France serve as illustrations though it must be noted that French workers have always been somewhat less ready to act on working conditions (as opposed to wages) than workers elsewhere. In 1906 the C.G.T. conducted a nationwide strike for an eight-hour day after three years of extensive propaganda. The strike was successful in many ways; we are by no means saying that workers ignored such issues. But it drew only 250,000 workers at most and mainly in Paris; less than a quarter of the C.G.T.'s membership participated. Equally important many of the workers who did strike turned out to be asking for higher wages rather than shorter hours. (16) A few years later an effort to induce workers to strike for an English week—with Saturday afternoons off—met with very little response. Relatedly in France and elsewhere, many workers who struck for and won hours reductions kept on working as long as before, merely taking the last hour or two as overtime for extra pay.

Many workers did strike directly over hours and other conditions. Again however they did so largely to protest change, not for positive gain. Metalworkers sought nine-hour days because the intensity of their work was increasing. Printers sought fewer hours to counter both the growing rapidity of work and rising unemployment. All this was important and in no sense denotes lack of vigor. Few workers however talked about hours reductions in the same terms as their leaders. They rarely spoke positively about the desirability of greater leisure for its own sake to benefit family life and cultural opportunities. At most they stressed that reduced hours for women were essential to permit shopping and housekeeping.

In this area too worker demands must be seen as pragmatic, not sweeping or fundamental. Workers were undoubtedly bothered by the new pace of work and new machines; German workers often mentioned their nervous tension as a result of work. They undoubtedly feared unemployment; the tenacious efforts of British workers to defend skilled workers' rights to certain jobs reflect this fear. But most workers were able to accept the broad lines of industrial change and only a handful fought it directly.

A few workers, as we have seen, damned machines altogether but they were isolated voices. Most workers sought reforms, such as a gradual reduction in hours, to palliate the change or simply demanded more money as a compensation of a different sort.

The final major category of strike demands is more difficult to assess for it sometimes conveyed an anger that precise requests for more pay or lower hours could not. A large number of strikes were conducted over personal issues, for the rehiring of a worker who had been dismissed or the firing of objectionable foremen or workers. Here workers could express their solidarity with a colleague who in their eyes had been unfairly treated whether for leadership in agitation or for poor-quality work. They could attack a harsh foreman or even a company director who seemed too money-mad. Leatherworkers in one French city blasted a new manager "who is only a financier anxious to get rich as fast as possible." Here was a major outlet in strikes for anxieties about the growing size and impersonality of industrial units and about the increasing pace of work. Here was an expression also of a desire to have greater liberty and humanity in industry. Workers could rebel against an employer who insulted them or treated them brutally. They could demonstrate class consciousness both in attacking employers as enemies and in uniting to defend their colleagues.

This personal element in strikes was exceedingly important. It showed that workers did not seek material goals alone; it showed that sometimes they felt an anger which was difficult to express in specific demands. Yet the fact that this anger had usually to be turned for or against a person was a severe limitation. Most personal strikes were small. Workers who had direct experience of a harsh foreman or close contacts with an abused worker were typically the only ones drawn into the agitation. Also, it proved difficult to generalize the motives of a personal strike into anger against employers as a whole or solidarity with workers in general. The potential for class-conscious action in strikes was rarely fulfilled in this period. There were large strikes of course but mainly over issues that affected all the strikers. The actual solidarity strike, in which workers supported other workers on grounds of class brotherhood, was rare. The C.G.T. in France tried many times to develop agitation in support of beleaguered postal or railroad strikers, but their success was very limited. Only in Britain after 1910 did workers show extensive willingness to strike in defense of general worker dignity; here national movements developed in support of workers fired for labor agitation or for drinking off the job, backed by workers who had no personal link with the people in question. More commonly however the personal link was essential, for what was involved was more clearly small-group loyalty than class loyalty. Finally workers proved willing to be somewhat pragmatic even in pressing personal demands. In most industrial countries as we shall see they accepted quite limited systems of collective bargaining that provided a mechanism for settling personal grievances. They did not insist on a more elaborate voice in the governance of industry.

Strike tactics generally displayed the same moderation as strike demands. Workers' frequent lack of experience in strikes raised many tactical problems, even in the years immediately before the war, that could make tactics more radical than expressed demands. Workers frequently walked off their jobs in anger, particularly when there was a personal issue involved, without much thought to preparing bargaining demands, selecting leaders, or raising funds. Even when this anger was due more to transitory than permanent factors it could bring violence and even an initial unwillingness to bargain. Furthermore lack of preparation often heightened violence during a strike. Poor funding meant that workers suffered as a strike wore on and their tempers were easily frayed. Many workers were unwilling to join a hasty effort and this was a sore point to those on strike. Strikers saw that they could not win without extensive participation and they resented lack of loyalty to their cause; so attacks on nonstriking workers were particularly common and they could lead to attacks on intervening police as well. As workers gained experience and prepared their effort better and as labor organizations became increasingly involved in strikes these symptoms often declined. There were fewer fights with workers when strikes were preceded by careful consultation with all potential participants and then enforced by union organizers and ample strike funds. Spontaneous anger waned in France and Belgium after 1906 or so; the pattern was admittedly less clear in Germany in part because police brutality was greater but only in Britain was it decisively reversed.

Despite anger and lack of experience most workers showed relative moderation throughout the period. They were rarely violent except against nonstrikers. They rarely attacked the persons or property of their employers. There are important exceptions to this but the general picture is more important still. Workers seldom hungered for a fight. Even in many agitated strikes violence was undertaken not by strikers themselves but by young urban toughs, primarily unskilled laborers—the same group whose strikes were most likely to be violent anyway. Workers were eager to bargain. They saw the strike as a tool for negotiation, not as a declaration of war. Often too they appealed to outside mediation, particularly by government figures—a sign not just that workers were willing to take whatever help they could get but that they recognized the state as a fair and relevant force. Almost never, despite many theoretical arguments against accepting contact with a bourgeois state, did workers reject mediation or decline a mediated settlement. Rarely did they refuse to compromise with employers directly.

Above all, as a result of workers tactics an impressive amount of collective bargaining developed after 1900. England led the way with major agreements in mining, textiles, and the crafts well before 1900. Bargaining spread to almost all French miners and many dockers, textile workers, construction workers, and others. German heavy industry largely resisted bargaining but agreements were widespread in the crafts and also in dock work. (17) This was an important development in industrial relations. Bargaining set general wage rates in a company or locality and often determined other conditions as well. It frequently gave workers a chance to argue for further gains without a strike at all, and increasing numbers of workers accepted compromise in advance. Where strikes did occur they were seen as part of the bargaining process not as expressions of anger. Finally many bargaining agreements set up committees of worker and management representatives to handle all sorts of grievances about the execution of the contract; this was a key factor in reducing the ubiquitous personal disputes in industry. All of this was a great gain for the millions of workers covered by collective agreements. But the system, inevitably both a product and a promoter of compromise, had many limitations. Worker voice in industry remained slight. Many grievances went uncorrected. Profits continued to mount more rapidly than wages, and the pace of work still increased. Yet most workers when they attained some agreement accepted the new framework of industrial relations. One of the key reasons for the decline or stabilization of the strike rate in Britain in 1899 or in France in 1911 despite prosperity was an acceptance of the collective-bargaining system. In terms of their expectations many workers no longer had to strike, for bargaining had given some stability to their conditions and some outlet for personal grievances. Here was another sign of the fundamental moderation of the active elements of the labor force.

Only in Britain was there a partial rebellion against the limitations of the system of bargains and compromises after 1910; only in Britain of the industrial countries did workers display a nearly revolutionary discontent in their strikes. (18) At the root was the massive deterioration of real wages after 1910. Much of the tone of this huge wave of strikes came from workers protesting for the first time, like the rural metalworkers in western England, or for the first time since the early 1890s, many dockers. Often on the edge of misery, these people had not been drawn into the bargaining system. But miners, textile workers, and machine builders protested forms of agreement that they had long welcomed now that agreements had proved incapable of assuring a maintenance of living standards. The rebellions were incomplete and new bargains were accepted but the discontent was clear. Miners for example signed a new agreement in 1912 but with the important innovation that under government legislation employers were to recognize a minimum wage for each area. And before this occurred miners in Wales had conducted a strike of unprecedented length and ferocity, attacking police and mining equipment on many occasions. Something new was in the air. Railroad workers attacked the bargaining system even more directly, claiming that grievance procedures established in 1907 were a sham and served only to dissipate complaints in a morass of red tape. Here again a new conciliation procedure was established but discontent still simmered. Some have claimed that England was on the verge of revolution when saved by the war in 1914, in large part due to the new fury of the workers. It is at the least clear that workers had been roused to a decisive new level of agitation, a level which brings the moderation of strike movements in other industrial countries and in Britain before 1910 into full relief.

Strike activities from about 1890 onward reveal then a pragmatic and rather moderate labor force. The high expectations that might motivate a radical protest were not widely spread. The demands that were most open-ended concerning worker dignity and freedom were limited by their common dependence on a personal spark. At the same time except for Britain after 1910 deterioration of economic conditions was not great enough to impel a massive outburst. To be sure, in years when many workers, particularly the unskilled, were striking for the first time moderation hardly seemed dominant. Demands were far-reaching and tactics violent. These periods were short-lived however and resulted more from inexperience and temporary excitement than from the sort of sweeping discontent that could sustain a violent mood. Hence after 1892 on the British docks, after 1896 in Hamburg, after 1904 in Marseilles—in other words after no more than three years of intense agitation—the most excited workers were either successfully put down by new repressive measures on the part of employers or calmed by benefits that the first strikes had won and by their own growing experience in protest. Spontaneous excitement, most visible in tactics rather than demands was an important element of many strikes but workers did not usually allow it to overcome a fundamental restraint.

If strikes accurately convey the mood of the labor force, they thus show an essential absence of radical or revolutionary discontent. The fact that more revolutionary strike movements were possible in this very period against far more repressive governments and employers in the newly industrializing countries heightens this impression. But there are several questions. We must ask why workers with this mood joined labor organizations that professed to be revolutionary (even if, admittedly, their action became more and more pragmatic in fact). Before this however we must qualify the judgment of the strike movement itself.

In the first place strikes may not have expressed the workers' most important desires. It was difficult to use strikes to resolve some purely material problems. It was hard to strike against unemployment for example since the victims had no work to abandon; yet this does not mean that workers did not fear unemployment greatly. There are many cases in which workers were aroused by recent unemployment but because of the difficulty of phrasing an appropriate demand managed only a mild wage strike. The riskiness of strikes moderated both demands and tactics. Workers had to couch demands carefully so that a strike would not be futilely prolonged and public opinion—vital to strikers' morale and financial support—would not be alienated. Many workers then may have had more extensive expectations or a broader range of grievances than strikes could convey. Socialism or another ideology could express such sentiments more adequately. Finally some workers could not strike at all because their employers were too well organized and repressive. This does not mean that they were satisfied with their lot, but only voting could serve as an outlet. In many cases workers turned to socialism precisely at the point that strikes became impossible. (19) For these workers too one must ask what socialism meant, how far if at all it went beyond the sorts of demands that dominated strike activity.

Furthermore the workers that took part in socialism or even unions were not necessarily the same as those who predominated in strikes. In countries like France and Britain an important minority of strikers even by 1914 participated in no other aspect of the labor movement. In other words they may have been too moderate to go beyond a pragmatic strike and their moderation affected even organized workers who had to avoid offending them in the interests of a large, successful strike. Here too the judgment of the nature of strike activity cannot be easily carried over into other aspects of the labor movement. In Belgium and Germany the same qualifications apply with the addition that far more workers were involved in labor voting and unions than took part in strikes; this may have been so precisely because strikes did not convey the essential worker demands. It was true however that the overlap between strikers and labor voters was considerable and increasing; industries that produced the most strikes also led in the other aspects of the labor movement. And many strikers who did not formally belong to a labor organization, often because they did not care to pay dues, sympathized with its aims and were loyal to it. So the questions of why workers essentially moderate in strikes participated in radical organizations and what radicalism meant to them still have general validity.

Finally we must stress again the diversity of interests involved in the strike movement. Demands and tactics varied greatly depending on the area and the industry. Most important many strikes revealed a profound difference between a minority of radicals and a majority of active moderates. In every country there were repeated instances in which a minority held out against concessions and even bargaining itself, who wanted to raise extreme demands, and who advocated violence. They could not dominate the strike movement, for strikes depended on extensive participation. But they might have far better luck in influencing labor organizations where only a minority was usually active anyway.

For various reasons then we must approach unions and labor politics separately, not as mere extensions of the strike movement or its overall character. With all the qualifications, however, it remains true that the strike movements springing directly from the working classes best conveyed workers' general goals. There is no point pretending that we will not conclude that these goals dominated the other aspects of the labor movement or at least came to do so as workers gained greater influence in them. Organizations that failed to bow to the fundamental moderation, and there were some, proved really irrelevant.

TRADE UNIONS

Unions, which so often developed from a strike situation, were the organizations closest to a broad segment of the working class. Their membership, far larger than the membership of Socialist parties though usually smaller than the Socialist electorate, showed a commitment to the labor movement probably greater than periodic voting did, in that union members usually paid dues and sometimes attended meetings. It is true that the commitment was often tenuous, not only for the many workers who dropped out of unions; there were many complaints about poor participation in meetings and union elections. Still it seems clear that unions were the groups that dealt most directly with the problems workers faced. Relatedly union leadership usually came from the ranks of workers themselves. A few local unions were spurred by outsiders with radical inclinations. Tavern owners, themselves often former workers, played a role particularly among miners and the unskilled. But generally local leadership was firmly in the workers' hands. At the national level ideological influence sometimes came from the outside—notably in aspects of French revolutionary syndicalism—but even in these cases men of working-class origin soon took over actual administration; Georges Sorel for example had only indirect links with revolutionary-syndicalist unions. In almost all respects unions were a creation of the working classes.

At the same time the specific origins of the major union movements and the types of unions were extraordinarily varied. In all the industrial countries, but particularly in France and Britain, a number of artisanal unions, purely local or at best loosely linked in a national group, antedated the rise of a broadly based labor movement. They were generally moderate to conservative, stressing bargaining rather than strikes and maintaining large benefit programs of their own. In France where the main union movement was radical they stayed out of national federations altogether; only half the unions in France were in the C.G.T. Nowhere did the small craft unions match the industrial unions or the vigorous artisanal national federations in influence and importance but the type served the interests of some workers still and should not be completely forgotten. In Germany one of the three national federations, the Hirsch-Duncker movement, represented this type of union and contributed clearly to inter-union rivalry. Catholic unions representing industrial as well as artisanal workers (most importantly many textile workers in Bel-

gium and Germany and many coal miners in the Ruhr) constituted another important type of union specifically hostile to
politically radical movements. This diversity of unions within a
single country reflected some of the diversity of interests within
the working classes and often promoted distracting conflicts.

The most significant diversity however separated the major
national union movements. Here we must return to the question
of national characteristics and the relevance of ideologies to the
working classes. Differences in origins and form were extremely
important and they often correspond neatly with the character
we tend to ascribe to the different peoples. British unions flowed
from the traditionally pragmatic artisanal organizations. The
flowering of industrial unionism after the strikes by unskilled
workers in the early 1890s modified rather than overturned the
traditions. The new union leaders had ideological interests but
they were usually vague and did not clearly influence their organizational activities. The new unionism meant simply that artisanal as well as industrial federations became larger, more
centralized, and more willing to strike. They still stressed bargaining and benefit programs. In France the major union movement had in revolutionary syndicalism a radical doctrine of its
own, antagonistic to the state and to capitalism and dedicated
to an ultimate general strike to bring down the whole existing
order. Hostile to organization of any sort, revolutionary-syndicalist unions hoped to be streamlined combat units with few
funds and benefit programs and without a big, entrenched bureaucracy. Revolutionary syndicalism in theory and practice corresponded to the individualism of French workers as well as to
their radicalism and fit well a nation in which small industrial
and artisanal units still predominated. In Belgium and Germany
the main union movements were set up rather belatedly by the
Socialist parties; they did not have independent origins. They
remained committed to Socialist theory and devoted a great deal
of attention to mobilizing their members politically; hence they
often had less time than British or French unions for purely
trade-union programs and strikes. They stressed big federations
tightly controlled from the center by a large bureaucracy. This
followed from the Marxist stress on hierarchical control and

from the fact that the main federations were organized at the center by the party rather than flowing from a large number of more spontaneous local groups. The same characteristics were obviously appropriate for countries in which relatively big industrial units seemed to predominate and where workers perhaps were accustomed to discipline from above.

Here then are three distinct orientations which have persisted in many ways well beyond the early twentieth century. German unions have remained centralized and often relatively reluctant to strike. French unions have remained poorer and less heavily bureaucratized though revolutionary syndicalism itself has vanished. There is no denying the reality or importance of the tone initially established in the union movements. And yet generalizations can be made about the union movement in industrial countries before World War I and for this period they may be more significant than analysis of national types. The generalizations are possible because all the unions faced comparable problems and because they all ultimately flowed from working classes that, though diverse, were far more alike than any national typology can imply.

On the most basic level union movements whatever their origins tended to grow more similar in the early twentieth century. Socialist and revolutionary-syndicalist unions had to play down their doctrines in order to attract workers who could not accept a radical ideology and to attend to the practical demands of even the radical members. French and German unions had to devote increasing effort to collective bargaining, benefit programs, and the like. German unions as a result became the most conservative element in the Socialist movement. French unions drew increasingly away from revolutionary syndicalism as they built up their funds and improved their organization. British unions on the other hand grew more radical. They found they needed a political arm though they still avoided a distinct ideology, and after 1910 they had to develop a more vigorous approach to industrial conflict. Something of a common dynamic was clearly at work in all the industrial countries.

Even before this the major union movements in fact were dealing with similar problems in similar ways regardless of their origins and ideologies. British unions, primarily because of their longer history and the friendlier attitude of employers, had worked out some of the problems already but even they fit the general pattern. All unions had to debate the question of collective bargaining. For Socialists and revolutionary syndicalists collective bargaining long was anathema: how could one negotiate with the capitalist devil and what good would negotiation do in a system where workers were doomed to increasing misery? Socialists and revolutionary syndicalists also feared that contracts would tie workers to the existing order by granting satisfying but limited gains. Similar debates occurred in Britain, for regardless of ideology many workers long hesitated to deal with employers, fearing that employers would win in any bargain and cheat on any agreement they disliked. On this issue radical doctrine could express the views of a minority of workers but the views could also develop independently. And in all instances the unions had to decide against doctrine and against the minority, for if they did not bargain they would alienate the majority of workers and waste themselves in endless industrial conflict.

Unions with industrial and construction workers faced related questions about the level of dues and the establishment of benefit programs. (20) Socialist and especially revolutionary-syndicalist theorists looked askance at elaborate benefits such as sickness and unemployment insurance; this sort of aid might tie workers to the existing order and would certainly bog union administrators in a mass of bureaucratic detail, distracting them from a greater struggle. Many ordinary union members even in Britain distrusted benefit programs because they viewed the union as a fighting organization above all; and they had the added fear of high dues to feed their concern. Again however reality forced all union movements to raise their dues and establish benefits. More money was necessary even to conduct strikes, for regular strike payments became essential. Workers had to be attached to unions—remember the general problem of fluctuating memberships—and benefit programs were a good way to do this even aside from their utility in assisting workers in times of misery. English unions could develop benefit programs with no qualms of conscience though a minority of workers resented the trend and some refused to pay high dues. Debate was more bitter on the continent where doctrinal questions were involved but doctrine at most slowed up the general trend; it could not stop it. Even revolutionary-syndicalist unions in France tripled their dues after 1900.

Related to dues and benefits were vital questions about the nature and power of union bureaucracy. Every union movement developed a tension between demands by workers for local autonomy and pressures for centralized control. As unions developed more elaborate funds more bureaucrats could be hired; and more bureaucrats had to be hired not only to administer the funds but to guard against foolish behavior—such as unauthorized, expensive strikes—by local units. Union officials proliferated to recruit new members, deal with collective bargaining and the administration of agreements, and so on. All this improved union services in many ways. Most basically a worker in Lancashire cotton or Leipzig machine building could count on having an official present to deal with any grievance on the job, any affront, within a matter of days. But growing bureaucratization increased the conservatism of unions for bureaucrats had their own interests to serve and were concerned with protecting the organization above all. Hence radical workers including convinced Socialists were often angered. Even more moderate workers could resent the loss of local control and of a voice in union affairs as general secretaries and paid officials took over more and more of the vital decisions.

The pace of bureaucratizaiton varied, of course, from one country to the next. The national types do have some relevance in this process although individual unions often departed from the national patterns. German unions developed the largest officialdom after 1900, tripling or quadrupling their bureaucracies within a decade. (21) British unions followed the same evolution but a bit more slowly. In both cases after 1900 the larger unions were controlled by a general secretary responsible directly only to a small council of regional representatives. In both countries crucial decisions such as calling a strike or even initiating negotiation for a raise had to be referred to the central administration for approval in advance—otherwise no union support was forthcoming. In France revolutionary-syndicalist doctrine posed a formidable barrier to this sort of centralization. French unions, poorer than their counterparts elsewhere, could not afford many officials anyway. And revolutionary-syndicalist practice placed great stress on the power of local assemblies to determine local action and on frequent reshufflings of elected officials. And yet inexorably officialdom crept forward. Workers constantly called for leaders to guide strikes and negotiations and this meant hiring more leaders. Parisian construction unions, the most fervently syndicalist of any important group, found they had to hire lawyers to defend their interests in court. Plagued by incessant local strikes French federations also began to introduce rules requiring authorization in advance for any agitation. Tensions between worker excitement and bureaucratic calm developed in France as in other countries though always to a lesser degree. The Metalworkers' Federation noted, in insisting that its members obtain permission from the union before striking: "The strike is perhaps a necessary revolutionary exercise, but it should not exclude some notion of reflecting about its consequences."

The development of trade unions in this period must be seen then as the result of several partially conflicting factors in which ideology or the lack of it played an increasingly minor role. The first fact was that many workers entered unions because they needed organizational backing, not because of the ideological coloration of the union involved. To be sure, some workers were so hostile to radical ideology that they consciously avoided calling for outside help or expelled any leader who spoke too radically or formed their own, conservative union. Far more workers went through a process something like the following. They had grievances either because of some deterioration in conditions or perhaps because they had been roused by the recent passage of a union or Socialist propagandist. They decided they wanted to strike then went ahead and did so. Then they discovered that they needed help to conduct their effort. They needed money—so many strikers made it their first duty to wire a union: "Strike called, send funds." They needed help in bargaining for without experience they feared that employers would easily intimidate them. So they called in union leadership and formed or expanded a union of their own. It did not matter necessarily what the leaders' ideol-

ogy was; as far as many workers were concerned this was almost
an accident. Once in the union and exposed to regular propaganda
workers might of course develop ideological commitments. This
was particularly likely during the excitement of a strike itself
when workers were pulled out of their routine. Hence strikers in
France, many of whom were not permanently converted to anarchism or revolutionary syndicalism, paraded with the black flag
during strikes; in one case about 200 babies were named after the
most popular of the anarchist leaders who had come in.

But there was irony here. The majority of strikers could not
maintain excitement for long periods of time. And unions were
forced by the realities of organizational existence increasingly to
play down the more persistent fervor of the minority. In other
words the factors that encouraged union radicalism and ideological commitment declined rather quickly. Most potential union
members were moderate. Whatever their excitement on occasion
they fundamentally sought solid, piecemeal gains. Unions in the
long run appealed to them most by offering calm guidance in
strikes and greater security through benefit programs. Union
leaders whatever their ideology realized this quickly, though revolutionary syndicalists were slower than Socialists. They saw that
they would have to play down ideology in their recruitment campaigns. German unions faced with Catholic opposition made frequent efforts to claim religious neutrality though they were never
fully convincing. French revolutionary-syndicalist leaders were
capable of leading a strike by conservative Catholic workers with
never a mention of their real program. More specifically union
leaders found that regardless of their ideology they had to be willing to bargain with employers. Otherwise the union would have
no gains to show and the majority of workers would turn from it.
They had to advise against violence for again the majority of
workers could not stand for it. In sum they had to become moderate and pragmatic in practice—increasingly like the nonideological British leaders.

The need for solid but moderate organization came not only
from the mood of workers themselves. Everywhere after 1900
trade unions encountered increasing opposition from employers,
government, and public opinion. Employers formed new associa-

tions with big strike insurance funds and the power to lock out recalcitrant workers. Governments at least discussed new laws against strikes and for the limitation of union power. The Taff Vale decision in Britain was an obvious step in this direction until it was rescinded by law for it made unions liable for damages in cases of picketing. The German government around 1900 discussed a ban on picketing while the French government without any new law stepped up police surveillance of union activities particularly in Paris after 1906. (22) Public opinion more generally turned against undue agitation. It became harder to obtain outside financial aid in strikes and in some cases notably in Britain after 1910 members of the middle classes served as strike breakers.

These various pressures bore hardest on the German and Belgian unions. Lockouts were most frequent in these countries, employer associations most powerful; and here governments grew particularly free, even brutal, in the use of police. Hence German unions became most cautious of all and most heavily bureaucratized. In contrast French unions could afford a continued dose of disorganized, revolutionary syndicalism because the employers were relatively weak and the government despite its action in a few key strikes was still partially friendly. But the pressure was general however much it differed in degree.

In theory unions might have responded to these new pressures with increasing radicalism as worker organizations in the newly industrializing countries were doing at this time. More police brutality could easily have been opposed by greater violence and so on. In fact the new pressures forced greater moderation for three reasons. First, the pressures were not complete; they were complemented by conciliation. Employer associations could be tough but they also frequently proved willing to bargain collectively. Outright resistance to repression was not necessary. Second, the majority of workers remained moderate and would not tolerate increasing radicalism. Third, union leaders now had a comfortable stake in the existing system. They could not contemplate turning their powerful organizations into subversive bodies. They knew that they were winning some solid gains for their members as it was and for their members as well as themselves they feared any outright, probably futile, resistance to authority. Even in French revolutionary syndicalism after 1910, Jouhaux, the leader of the C.G.T., thought increasingly in bureaucratic terms; he had none of the fire of the earlier leaders.

These various and increasing pressures for cautious action forced trade unions to try to discipline the zeal of a minority of members and the occasional excitement of a larger number. They warned against spontaneous unplanned strikes that might damage the organization. They were particularly hostile to strikes of personal anger where the issues were narrow and the unfairness sometimes imaginary. They cautioned against violence and against fruitless prolongations of strikes, here resisting the common impulse of a minority of workers to turn the strike into an all-out conflict. A C.G.T. representative devoted to revolutionary syndicalism in theory summed up the usual message in advising some striking leatherworkers: "You can cut wires, unload wagons, but this won't end the strike. An agreement will result only from discussion." In many cases and in many ways then trade unions had to discipline the most ideologically committed of their members though their principal effort was against workers whose momentary excitement had little to do with ideology.

The main function of trade unions after 1900 was to control industrial conflict rather than exacerbate it. Employers who grew increasingly willing to deal with unions implicitly realized this. The union effort had considerable though incomplete success. It was greatest in matters of tactics. With the power of the purse unions could induce many workers to obey rules on methods. They could require advance votes on strikes to limit spontaneous outbursts; they could require bargaining. Hence strikes in France and Belgium became shorter, less violent, increasingly a part of a bargaining process rather than a burst of anger. On the issues of strikes, however, unions had less success. All unions tried to encourage workers to press for better conditions in addition to or instead of better pay. They had notable success with the more sophisticated workers like printers and miners but not with workers in general, many of whom of course were not unionized at all. Hence strikes over pay and personal questions continued to be as common as before in countries like France and Germany. This persistent gap between worker demands and union programs was the result of the continuing traditionalism and inexperience of many workers, not of ideological differences.

Still, with all the correspondence between worker moderation and union restraint, important divergences were still possible. Unions did not represent the radical minority. They could let them sound off in meetings and on the continent appeal to them by ringing reassertions of socialism or revolutionary syndicalism but they could not let them determine practical action. Radicals would have to seek other outlets, usually in politics. Unions were also unprepared to handle an upsurge of economic grievance due to deteriorating conditions as occurred in Britain after 1910. Hence in all countries but particularly in Britain and Germany where the leadership was most cautious and central control so great there were periodic signs of frustration with union conservatism. Large numbers of German workers clearly were eager to strike for political gains though their leaders held them back. After 1910 there were a number of strikes over economic issues in defiance of union command, particularly among shipbuilding and metalworkers. (23) Symptoms of *malaise* were even more general in Britain with the unauthorized strikes of Welsh miners, railroad workers, and shipbuilders. These strikes were as much against the moderate, conciliatory policies of the unions as against employers or government. Unions then had grown to represent the desires of most active workers in times of relative stability at least in the area of bread-and-butter, economic interests. They were incapable of representing massive grievance or any mood of frustration that went beyond specific economic issues. So they could not constitute the whole of the labor movement nor did they pretend to.

Because of their pragmatism and preoccupation with day-to-day problems however trade unions were almost always fearful of radical political action and were feared by its advocates. (24) Here again the labor movement was not a coherent whole. French revolutionary syndicalists were a major exception of course. They rejected politics because they distrusted its compromises. But in Germany and among Socialist-led unions in France like the textile federation the unions were quickly to be found in the cautious wing of the Socialist party, distrusted by the ideologues, who were however incapable of defeating union moderation in most party councils. Trade unions played an obvious role in reducing the revolutionary fervor of the German Socialist party. They resisted programs for effective political strikes and so on. They sought a party much like the party that the English unions succeeded in creating that would defend the legal rights of unions in parliament and work for reform legislation that would generalize and extend the sorts of gains unions were making by economic action. Despite their great power however trade unions nowhere captured Socialist parties completely. There were always ideological impulses beyond their grasp borne in some cases by people who were not part of the working-class union movement at all. It is time to turn to the most clearly ideological components of the labor movement, particularly in politics, to see what role they played.

THE PROBLEM OF REVOLUTIONARY SYNDICALISM

Revolutionary syndicalism, apart from anarchism which had only slight importance among workers in the industrial countries was the most revolutionary labor doctrine and movement in the period and in many ways the most revolutionary ever developed in an industrial society. (25) This was only partially apparent in the syndicalist methodology which stressed the general strike as the means of overturning society, in part because direct revolution was judged impossible given the arms at the disposal of the modern state. Vague as they were in many ways revolutionary-syndicalist goals carried the crucial message. Workers were to rebel not just against capitalism but against the existence of any state; this was a radical plea for human freedom. More profoundly they were really to rebel against industrial society itself. Although revolutionary-syndicalist theorists did not talk about abolishing machines they were firmly resolved to do away with large organizations in any sphere of activity; and large organizations were the inevitable companion of industrialization. In contrast socialism accepted industrial society; as a result it was far more effective and important than revolutionary syndicalism but also far less radical.

Where revolutionary syndicalism existed in any sort of purity it was a sign of far-reaching discontent, like that of the Parisian shoemaker cited earlier who felt that machines were ruining everything. The problem is to determine where revolutionary-syndicalist theory had any significant hold. Too often content with discovering that a doctrine exists instead of assessing its audience, historians have pointed to the importance of revolutionary syndicalism in many places. It was born in France and its leaders controlled the *Bourses du travail* movement and then the C.G.T. But it won some converts everywhere in Europe. It spread most obviously to Italy where it was a serious rival to socialism in the union movement and to Catalonia. But revolutionary-syndicalist ideas, imported chiefly by Tom Mann and spreading to young, discontented trade unionists, have been seen in Britain after 1910 playing a significant role in the rising tension of those years and particularly in the attacks on older union leaders and methods.

Of course we cannot question the existence of revolutionary-syndicalist ideas. Nor can we question their importance in newly industrializing areas, notably Catalonia, where large numbers of workers and peasants rejected the very essence of industrialization and commercialization in favor of an idealization of older ways. These people could find real meaning in syndicalist urgings to return to local, cooperatively controlled units of production. In industrial countries however—and France must be included among these—there were few workers of this sort. Because of the recency and rapidity of her industrialization Germany probably had more workers, particularly among the artisanally trained, who really hated industrial forms rather than their misuse. But ironically revolutionary syndicalism took no significant root among available labor leaders in Germany and so these workers had no direct outlet for their feelings; socialism had to suffice. Elsewhere, and generally even in Germany, most workers accepted industrial society and the existence of government. Revolutionary syndicalism could gain no real hold over them.

Why then did revolutionary syndicalism exist at all? Partly of course it existed because workers could see many things in syndicalism besides the ultimate goals. Those workers in Britain who were attracted by the movement before World War I clearly valued syndicalist tactics, notably the general strike, and the local, democratic control of unions that revolutionary syndicalism encouraged; they did not preach a syndicalist society. (26) Socialists could be drawn to the general strike as well as syndicalists. It was widely discussed among radical German Socialists and twice put into effect by Belgian Socialists for political rather than syndicalist goals. More broadly many workers who were not necessarily radical could be attracted to the loose organization of revolutionary-syndicalist unions which gave them greater voice and more power to strike when the spirit moved them and to some revolutionary-syndicalist slogans and tactics that fit the excited mood of a strike.

Aside from these partial and usually transitory correspondences between revolutionary syndicalism and worker interests, the existence of revolutionary syndicalism must be explained largely by the different lines of causation that operated on labor leaders and actual workers whether from the working class or not. Revolutionary syndicalism had an important intellectual and political background in France. It drew from the native Socialist tradition of Proudhon whose followers had dominated the small, largely artisanal labor movement of the Second Empire, and from the revolutionary advocacy of Adolphe Blanqui. It appealed also to the traditional glorification of revolution that went back to some aspects of Jacobinism and certainly to the Commune of 1871. It expressed resentment against the Third Republic which had turned out to be so conservative and against socialism which seemed vowed to perpetual compromise. The entrance of a reformist Socialist, Millerand, into the bourgeois cabinet of 1899 shocked revolutionaries in France and elsewhere, and Millerand's failure to gain any distinctive benefits for the workers confirmed the condemnation of politics and socialism. Finally economic crises and the increasing industrialization of the French economy after 1895 provided obvious encouragement to the revolutionary-syndicalist attack.

In short there was a variety of good reasons for the existence of revolutionary syndicalism. Revolutionary syndicalism obviously motivated many leaders to set up unions and work tirelessly to advance their cause. But the main point is that the causes of revolutionary syndicalism did not in fact affect many workers, though they certainly might have done so in theory. Workers had some friendly relations with the government. True, the French government lagged in social insurance programs but it was relatively advanced in factory inspection laws and workers had many fruitful contacts with official inspectors. True, the French government sent police into strikes but it also aided negotiation and conciliation in many ways. Workers did not see it as a consistently hostile force. All but a small minority welcomed the entry of Millerand into the government although undoubtedly many must have been disappointed with the results. In general French workers viewed the government in terms of their present contacts with it rather than in terms of France's revolutionary traditions.

Similarly French workers accepted the growth of the industrial economy. French strike patterns revealed a relatively moderate labor force concerned with wage questions above all. (27) Time and time again French workers proved willing to accept new machines and even a rising pace of work in return for higher earnings. The economic motives that roused them were far narrower than a concern about industrial society as a whole. They wanted to maintain and possibly improve their standard of living and reacted particularly vigorously against price increases. This was the only industrial country in which market riots took place in this period and this reflected in its own way a French tradition of lower class protest that was perhaps more relevant to more workers than the traditions behind the revolutionary-syndicalist movement.

Stated simply all this means that many French workers joined revolutionary-syndicalist organizations primarily because they were there when an organization was needed, not because of any enduring attachment to revolutionary syndicalism. Because of this, revolutionary-syndicalist organizations seldom behaved in practice any differently from nonsyndicalist organizations in France. Miners around Saint-Étienne in the center of France, though syndicalist led were actually more moderate in strike tactics and less prone to strike at all than miners in the north who were led by reformist Socialists. We have already noted that French workers were not unusually violent in this period, despite revolutionary-syndicalist promptings of sabotage. Revolutionary-syndicalist leaders could not hold out against collective bargaining and even dealings with the government. Time and time again, a syndicalist-led strike meeting would blast the cops and perhaps the perversity of the whole government and then break up so that strike leaders could see the prefect or a minister to urge their aid in negotiations and perhaps the fulfillment of a new labor law. As the pressures against labor agitation increased revolutionary-syndicalist leaders had to make still greater concessions to the demands of practical organization such as higher dues and greater restraints against violence. Their unions did remain weaker than most and indeed revolutionary syndicalism's chief effect in this period was to delay the restraints that unions everywhere had to place on small, spontaneous strikes. Nevertheless the tendency was comparable to that in other countries. Revolutionary-syndicalist leaders had to bow to the moderation of most of their constituents and to the necessities imposed by their desire to maintain their organizations. Typically the only unions that even approached distinctive tactics in labor agitation were those of bakers and barbers whose membership was so tiny that little organization existed at all.

Syndicalist success in reorienting the goals of workers was slighter still. The revolutionary-syndicalists could not even attempt political, or more properly antipolitical, strikes. Their one effort, the strike against militarism in 1911, largely failed. Protests against police brutality, particularly in Paris between 1908 and 1910, had greater success but few workers could be induced to strike in sympathy with postmen or railroad workers in the same period despite syndicalist hopes that these movements could discredit the whole government. The one great revolutionary-syndicalist success was the strike for eight hours in 1906 which came after several years of intensive propaganda and drew many workers particularly in the Parisian building and metal trades. If this was far from the hoped-for general strike, it was an impressive movement. But the issue—an eight-hour workday—was essentially a reformist goal and many strikers saw that even it was too radical and scaled down their demands. Furthermore syndicalists failed to induce French workers to continue the campaign for hours reduction with any consistency thereafter. And insofar as they tried, as in the later effort to win a five and one-half day week, they were simply doing what labor leaders everywhere did —attempting to persuade workers to strike for gains that were more solid than wage increases.

Revolutionary syndicalism, then, did not touch the majority of organized French workers in a significant way. Many of the big federations inside and outside the C.G.T. such as the textile and railroad workers were largely immune to the revolutionary-syndicalist influence. Ironically the revolutionary-syndicalists had little contact with dockers and maritime workers though these were among the workers most prone to violence. Furthermore only the essential moderation of most French workers explains the impact of revoluntionary syndicalism on the rest of French society. Syndicalist slogans undoubtedly played a role in disturbing public opinion, the government, and employers, and this was an important development. But neither the government nor employers took revolutionary syndicalism too seriously. Revolutionary syndicalism created none of the sense of political crisis that developed in Britain after 1910 where syndicalist doctrine played only a minor role. The Third Republic could function with the outlook that French workers actually adopted; huge new repression aside from a few show cases was not necessary. Similarly employers could handle worker demands with some conciliation. Revolutionary syndicalism failed then even thoroughly to *épater les bourgeois.*

But was revolutionary syndicalism an important minority movement, even if it failed to capture most active French workers? We have suggested that a radical minority existed in most industrial countries. Was revolutionary syndicalism in France, and ultimately perhaps in Britain, an important outlet for this group? Syndicalism can be viewed, for example, as primarily a Parisian movement drawing on the special Parisian revolutionary tradition and the diverse discontent in the capital city. Parisian printers, railroad workers, and construction workers, for example, were more influenced by revolutionary syndicalism in periods of great excitement than were their counterparts in the provinces. If in Britain revolutionary syndicalism played little role in the better established unions did it help motivate the special discontent of groups like the Welsh miners? After all revolutionary syndicalism always professed to be a minority movement though its leaders clearly felt some need for a broader appeal.

Undoubtedly, some workers were fervently syndicalist in France; that revolutionary-syndicalist notions spread significantly in Britain is very doubtful. Even in Paris it is hard to see that more than a handful of ordinary workers were led by revolutionary syndicalism to behave in distinctive ways aside from attending periodic propaganda meetings; revolutionary syndicalism had its greatest influence on first- and second-level leaders. There was an important burst of agitation among Parisian construction workers under syndicalist leadership between 1906 and 1909. But Berlin workers mounted almost exactly the same sort of agitation in the same years. Again economic rather than ideological causes seem to have been most decisive. Admitting then that a minority believed in revolutionary syndicalism, we can go further and say that revolutionary syndicalism made little difference in terms of their actual behavior.

But what of syndicalism as a myth? Many French workers were exposed to revolutionary-syndicalist ideas through union newspapers, pamphlets, and speeches. Surely there were many workers who though they realized that radical action was not possible at present, in part because their leaders told them so, still had the syndicalist vision of the future. And of course revolutionary-syndicalist theorists, notably Georges Sorel, began to talk of syndicalism as a myth perhaps never to be a reality but educating workers and separating them from the rest of society all the same. No one can prove that many workers did not harbor radical-syndicalist hopes; we cannot penetrate so deeply into the minds of workers or any other social group. It does seem that the behavior of French workers and their expressed goals are hard to equate with any extensive devotion to revolutionary-syndicalist principles.

In France and elsewhere this does not mean that many workers who struck and joined unions and some who could not risk even this did not want something more. Their frustrations however were best expressed in politics, in socialist voting. Many revolutionary-syndicalist unions helped teach workers to press for favorable legislation. Many cooperated actively with Socialists regardless of their professed principles. Politics offered some hopes for sweeping change whereas syndicalism seemed more and more an empty dream. Furthermore socialism offered greater emotional or intellectual satisfaction than revolutionary syndicalism. Syndicalism could rival socialism in its passionate denunciations of the existing order and its preoccupation with tactics but it did not have a clear enough vision of the future or of the historical past to constitute a complete theology. The minority of workers that wanted a total approach, a new religion, usually demanded more. Revolutionary syndicalism also failed to provide the elaborate ritual and institutions to maintain the faithful in good cheer. There were meetings of course and some songs and flags but little that was syndicalism's own. The convinced revolutionary syndicalist was more alone, more alienated, than the convinced Socialist. Above all few dedicated workers were ready to take on industrial society instead of capitalism alone. Revolutionary syndicalism was doomed to failure.

After about 1910 revolutionary syndicalists in France began talking of a crisis of syndicalism. (28) French workers seemed to be turning to greater conservatism. There was some truth to the arguments, at least insofar as trade-union membership stopped expanding. But the levels of strikes held up fairly well, though there was no agitation to compare with 1906, and Socialist votes continued to mount. The syndicalist crisis occurred less because of a change among French workers than because of the syndicalists' realization of how moderate most workers had been all along. Changes in leadership and the increasing preoccupation with organizational problems to meet the growing hostility to the labor movement also heightened the irrelevance of revolutionary syndicalism at this point. On balance revolutionary syndicalism is a clear case of a movement that existed parallel to the aspirations of most workers without really touching them. There was little interaction until the revolutionary syndicalists gradually abandoned their hopes. We must now ask whether socialism, a vastly more important movement which was also brought to the working class to an extent from outside, had much greater success.

SOCIALISM

Workers were heavily dependent on formal leadership for their initial political orientation—a leadership frequently drawn from other social classes. The paths this leadership chose were largely determined by the intellectual traditions and political structure of each country—hence the great diversity in the early forms of Socialist or labor politics. After the skilled among them gained the vote in 1867, British workers were led by moderates like George Howell to seek pragmatic reforms through support of the Liberal party. This first political exposure proved quite durable and even when a Labour party finally developed it retained a pragmatic reformist approach. Largely Marxist socialism in Germany was created by the interweaving of a convoluted Hegelian philosophy, the power of the German state, and the twelve-year period of repression against nascent socialism from 1878 to 1890. The result was a centralized party devoted to Socialist theory, respectful of the strength of the state and the importance of politics while resentful of the present forms of each.

Again however the motivations of the early leaders of socialism were not necessarily the same as those of working-class followers. In the 1890s the political interests of British and German workers did not necessarily differ as much as would be implied by the fact that the former voted Liberal while the latter voted revolutionary Socialist. The excellent historical explanations for the evolution of British labor politics or of German socialism should not conceal the element of accident as far as many ordinary workers were concerned. German workers did not turn to socialism because they were steeped in German philosophical traditions of which few were aware; they may not have been heavily influenced even by the authoritarian form of the German state, for few of them had a developed political consciousness before they turned to socialism. In short many workers found they needed a political outlet but they did not initially determine the form of that outlet.

This was a period in which socialism, for the first time a real political movement, educated its followers and was educated by them in turn; the correspondence of interests was not complete. Socialism played a vital role in teaching many workers what political action was and what in Socialist terms could be expected from it. In their turn workers, who were in no sense ciphers to be dominated by even sympathetic leaders, taught their parties what they expected and what action they would countenance. A third element in the evolution of labor politics was increasingly the changing situation of the leaders themselves as they gained political power and a sense of the demands of the parties as institutions.

These factors were present in every industrial country. National differences cannot be ignored. British workers for example had the opportunity of accepting Marxist leadership. The fact that outside of London they largely ignored it is not simply due to accident or to inadequate efforts of the Marxist leaders though both played some role. It is clear that skilled workers who set the tone of British labor politics to an unusual degree because they received the vote first were schooled in a pragmatic approach by their union movement. They did not need socialism as an expression of class hostilities because their relations with their employers were relatively cordial. British labor politics then reflected the characteristics of British workers as well as the special causes bearing on potential leaders; the same pattern prevailed in every country. Still it is useful to discuss the reasons for working-class political behavior across national lines noting diversities within each nation and points at which formal party programs differed from worker interests.

Among the reasons for this approach is the rather obvious fact that labor-political movements in the industrial countries despite highly diverse origins and early histories grew more similar with time just as union movements were doing. Marxist parties like the German became more pragmatic. Many reformists like the Jaurès group in France or the British Labour party gave increasing attention to revolutionary rhetoric if not action. By 1914 the overriding fact was that all the Socialist parties in industrial countries had become fundamentally pragmatic and reformist, seeking gains here and now through the existing political system; and that everywhere this development left some radicals discontent either within the main party as in Germany or outside it as in Britain and to an extent in France. In broad outline this situation came about because most workers, even those who were willing to be politically active, did not really expect a revolution. Unlike many workers in countries like Russia or Italy they were fundamentally satisfied with many of the elements of the existing political and economic order. Ironically, for some, participation in a Socialist movement actually increased their satisfaction. At the same time their leaders unlike those in Russia or Spain had substantial political freedom and could develop positions of power which helped their conversion to pragmatism. But the revolutionary element of socialism was not dead. It meant something quite real to many workers throughout the period and often became more explicit shortly before World War I as the radicals realized the moderate character of both the existing parties and their own worker comrades.

Most workers who turned to labor politics hoped for some immediate results. Few could turn their attention solely to the society of the future and parties from the German Social Democrats to the British ILO expanded largely as they filled their platforms with reform proposals. As we have seen conversion to Socialist voting often resulted from frustration in a strike movement as workers sought legislated gains that would establish and generalize direct economic improvements. Belgian journalists, with admittedly a conservative bias, who interviewed workers in the two great general strikes of 1902 and 1912, which were called to demand universal suffrage, found that the goals workers could express were seldom really political at all. The workers said they wanted the vote but almost uniformly went on to say that they wanted it because it would bring higher pay, better hours, and so on. And these were workers who went to the risk and nuisance of striking for a Socialist political goal; surely many who merely voted Socialist were even more pragmatic in their expectations. For many workers socialism was simply an extension of material demands—and not necessarily very sophisticated demands at that. Gradually socialism and the spread of welfare legislation taught workers to phrase such demands not just in terms of higher pay, for which Socialist politics were not very relevant, but in terms of factory legislation and insurance schemes. (29) More and more workers saw socialism as a means by which pensions could be increased or the work of children better regulated. This was an important change but it constituted less a heightening of the pragmatic interest in socialism than a growing sophistication in its direction.

The pragmatic interest in socialism was not simply national in scope. Historians tend to exaggerate the attention which ordinary voters, particularly when newly politicized, give to the national arena. (30) Local political interest was often quite strong and workers could gain many benefits from Socialist influence in local government. Better housing inspection, new sewage or park facilities in working-class districts, more public works and welfare payments in times of crisis—these were only a few of the benefits that workers could derive from representation in city governments. This could be fully as important a reason to vote Socialist as expectations of national legislation. From this time onward influence in or control of key local governments played a big part in the power of Socialist and labor parties even when they fell far short of national dominance, because of the range of material improvements that local government could undertake.

Finally at both national and local levels socialism could serve workers pragmatically by protecting the trade-union movement. The growth of the British Labour party followed obviously from the unions' realization after the Taff Vale case that they needed political representation to defend their right to strike. German unions, initially a weak offshoot of the Socialist party, virtually wagged the dog during the decade before the war and used the party vigorously to guard against hostile legislation. Many continental Socialists were hostile to trade unionism and the short-run gains it sought but they could not refuse to defend it against government attack. In so doing they provided another practical reason for even moderate workers to vote Socialist particularly as much public opinion hardened against unions and strikes.

The pragmatic bread-and-butter interest of workers in labor politics explains much of the evolution of socialism. As Socialist parties grew they won more and more workers who sought immediate gains above all. Given the moderate mood of the class as a whole the expansion of Socialist voting guaranteed increasing reformism. This same expansion, propelling Socialist parties into important positions in parliaments, allowed new reforms to be won. The Taff Vale decision was rescinded by law, new welfare legislation was passed; here was another reason for persisting in the reformist effort. To win reforms at all, Socialists had to cooperate with middle-class parties on the national level and in many localities. This was possible even in conservative Germany and promoted further moderation. It was difficult in Germany for any but the most fervent ideologues to rail quite so bitterly against bourgeois liberalism after bourgeois liberals had helped defeat a government effort to ban picketing. It was even more difficult for a Socialist municipal councilman to maintain his theoretical hostility to middle-class politicians when he worked with them daily to improve the sewers or build a new primary school. The pragmatic gains that the working class expected from its politics led socialism into increasing involvement with the existing order. There was no betrayal here but it is true that the result was a major change in the activities and outlook of Socialist leaders.

Certainly after 1900 Socialist leadership on the continent tended more and more to become a settled bureaucracy. The interests of the parties were far-flung now and demanded many men to serve as deputies, councilmen, and the like. There was need also for newspaper editors, theater directors, and administrators of worker cooperatives. Inevitably many idealists drawn into these activities became increasingly impressed by the necessity of pragmatic realism; inevitably many administrators were now recruited who were not idealistic at all. Some Marxists have claimed that the new central and local leaders were drawn increasingly from white-collar ranks instead of worker ranks as before and that this was the reason for growing opportunism. (31) On the contrary worker representation in Socialist leadership particularly on the local level was rising as socialism changed from a movement of middle-class theorists to a largely working-class effort. Some of these workers did see socialism as a means for their own advancement into white-collar or professional work. But they also accurately represented the desire of most workers to see Socialist politics bring rapid, tangible gains.

Socialism and even labor politics in Britain never meant pragmatism alone however. Of course we cannot know what motives were most important in attracting workers to socialism. Some types of workers seem to have been drawn fairly consistently to a particular Socialist tone. Miners almost everywhere served as a mainstay of reformist socialism. In Britain they switched from the Liberal to the Labour party after 1900 but continued to see politics as a means of gaining beneficial legislation such as limitations on the hours of work in the mines. In France miners in all the main basins—even miners who belonged to revolutionary-syndicalist unions—supported reformist groups. The character of the vigorous but moderate Belgian party was set by the miners above all. On the other hand textile workers outside of Britain seemed more attracted to the larger Socialist vision as in France where they backed the most orthodox Marxist movement. Even here however generalization is difficult. Some individual self-educated miners were among the most knowledgeable exponents of Marxist theory. (32) The type of commitment to socialism depended greatly on the individual personality. The main point is that socialism offered far more to many workers than material benefits alone.

Workers wanted political rights. During most of the period there were obvious gradations among national Socialist movements that corresponded to workers' political power. France had universal male suffrage and a predominantly moderate Socialist movement. Britain's suffrage was not complete but did give effective rights to the majority of workers including the most articulate and again the result was a moderate movement. In Germany workers were able to vote but because of the three-class voting system in Prussia and other states had not attained equal voice; the situation was somewhat similar in Belgium. Here the revolutionary rhetoric of socialism had wider appeal and greater durability; and with or without the full support of the party, workers were willing to agitate directly for full political rights. Still the political gains that had been made were sufficient to hold most Socialists back from persistent extraparliamentary agitation. Socialist parties constituted a potentially revolutionary force only in countries like Italy, where most workers had no vote at all until 1912. Socialism then expressed a real demand for political rights; in the industrial countries this demand had been satisfied enough for socialism to work largely within the system.

Was socialism an expression also of the workers' sense of alienation from his whole society whether he had formal political rights or not? German socialism for example can easily be seen as the product of a political and economic system that excluded workers from any political voice. (33) Big companies with heavy-handed paternalism controlled the material lot of many workers while an authoritarian government stood behind the employers' authority. The workers' answer, socialism, was a rebellion against the impotence in which they were held. The workers really wanted a revolution or at least wanted a revolutionary rhetoric that would terrify the good bourgeois society that had rejected them.

This approach should not be carried too far. Popular and appealing as words like *alienation* are in describing the industrial proletariat they imply a sense of isolation that many workers did not have. We have seen that many workers were able to advance, that many developed positive contacts with employers and government even in Germany through collective bargaining and the like. We must also stress once again that many of the most fervent Socialists were not employed in big firms at all but were textile workers or even artisans who were not faced with impersonal, paternalistic employers. It was not true in this period that the larger the firm the more radical the workers; (34) relatedly German workers were not really as radical as many British or French workers. Still some workers in a variety of industries did feel cut off from their society. Socialism helped explain their isolation and promised to remedy it.

Particularly in Belgium and Germany but to an extent everywhere socialism in fact helped remedy the workers' isolation by its very existence regardless of whether workers believed in an ultimate revolution or not. Socialist victories in local and national elections undoubtedly gave workers a new sense of power and dignity. Even more important were the institutions Socialist parties established. We cannot know precisely how alienated workers felt before the advent of socialism. We can assert however that socialism significantly reduced such feelings by setting up an elaborate environment of its own in which many off-the-job interests could be pursued.

Socialist groups provided extensive facilities for recreation and culture. Local centers had libraries and dance halls; they sponsored music groups, picnics, and sporting events. The party in Germany sponsored a peoples' theater of high quality. All the parties of course produced a volume of reading matter from newspapers through scholarly treatises to some fiction. Legal services and even personal advice were offered, particularly in Belgium. In Belgium also the Socialist Peoples' Houses often had cooperative market facilities; one could sustain body as well as soul directly through the party.

In sum the Socialist parties as they developed their institutions from the 1890s onward could absorb much of the energy and much of the leisure time of workers who, for whatever reason, felt alone in a hostile world. This was undoubtedly one of their chief attractions but it may also have curtailed the revolutionary fervor of potentially radical workers. Busy in his separate Socialist society the worker could to an extent ignore the larger environment. In fact the separate Socialist society helped integrate many workers into the industrial world in a variety of ways. It discouraged and provided alternatives to heavy drinking. It encouraged literacy and acquaintance not just with Socialist work but with traditional culture as well. For many it provided organizational experience and even upward mobility in the Socialist administration itself. Socialism drew many of the lonely. It gave them an ideology which they could sincerely maintain but it also made it difficult for them to preserve their sense of isolation. Along with workers who looked to socialism for pragmatic gains almost exclusively were workers who turned to the movement out of a greater hunger but actually received from it pragmatic benefits of a somewhat different type. These were workers—and we cannot pretend to know their number—who believed much of Socialist theory but with decreasing fervor

and with almost no relationship to their actual political behavior.

Finally there were workers who believed thoroughly in Socialist ideology and who actively hoped to put it into effect,
possibly by revolution. These were the true faithful who saw in
socialism an explanation for existing evil and a truly sweeping
remedy. Enthusiasts of this sort could be found in many areas
among many types of workers. Even in Britain, despite the
relative unimportance of dogmatic Socialist theory in the formal
labor movement, individual workers demonstrated an enthusiasm
for doctrines of class war and a new society that was quite comparable to continental patterns. A rebellion against the liberal
economics and general stodginess of the worker-education program at Ruskin College was led by young self-taught workers
who had read widely in Marx and other theorists and had a
deep commitment to socialism as a philosophy. (35) To be sure,
a higher percentage of workers in countries like Belgium or
Germany may have had a commitment to socialism as a theory.
The greater doctrinal interests of the leaders led to more thorough
propaganda and more widespread discussions of Socialist philosophy while political disabilities and greater economic hardship aided the reception as well. It may even be that British
and some French workers, having developed an awareness of industrial problems prior to any elaborate Socialist movement and
being actively interested in personal gain, were more immune to
elaborate doctrinal interests. Belgians and Germans on the other
hand were converted to socialism often before new personal expectations had developed; their more widespread enthusiasm for
the ultimate aims of socialism continued to distract them from
more limited agitation—hence the lower strike rates in countries
with extensive Socialist parties. Still some workers everywhere
developed a thorough emotional and intellectual commitment to
Socialist doctrine. Their importance to the Socialist movement
exceeded their numbers. These were the faithful who regularly
attended meetings, signed manifestos, and served as local leaders.

Interest in Socialist doctrine could take many forms of course.
Many workers doubtless were drawn to a few slogans and nothing
more; many found Socialist doctrine appealing in times of excite-

ment but were never durably converted. Of the workers who were in any sense converts some were preoccupied with the tactical issues raised by socialist doctrine rather than with stated goals or historical concepts. Socialism was vitally important to them but their principal concern was in planning what to do next. It is no accident therefore that many of the most vigorous debates in the Socialist movement concerned somewhat abstract questions of tactics—whether to countenance the general strike, whether to co-operate with a bourgeois ministry, and so on. Still others fed upon the class hatred element in socialism, the better condemnation of what existed. A smaller number probably were genuinely concerned with the whole range of Socialist theory including the nature of society to come.

Socialism has often been seen as a new religion for the workers. Marxism like Christianity provided everything from an explanation of history to a prediction of heaven to come; it had its sacred books, its martyrs, its ritual. Workers having lost their traditional Christian beliefs in the transition from peasantry to proletariat needed this new, sweeping movement not simply as a defense of their material interests but for their emotional and intellectual integrity.

The analogy had meaning for many workers. Several German metalworkers told a middle-class visitor to their factory: "What Jesus Christ was until now someday Bebel and Liebknecht will be." (36) Without question the ideologically committed workers could regard socialism as a theology and the party as church. There may even have been some real transference between Christian belief and socialism in the period. Many French and British workers had lost their religion before the advent of socialism. They had replaced it not so much with another doctrine as with a devotion to individual well-being. German, Belgian, and many Italian workers, on the other hand, had preserved a more traditional faith, and certainly workers' children in the late nineteenth century still received religious training. Some of them of course remained religious. Others under the impact of industrialization and Socialist propaganda transferred their religious sentiments to socialism. They were accustomed through their religious training to accepting directions from above, they thought in terms of theological unity, they wanted a cosmic hope for the future, and they found in Socialist activities an opportunity even for a sort of daily devotion. Hence again Belgian and German workers were more receptive to the religious aspect of socialism than the French or British were; but there were many French and British workers in the same situation. Within France it may be more than accidental that the industrial base for Marxist socialism was in the north where industrial concentration was greatest but where religious sentiment had persisted to an unusual degree as well. This notion of religious transference rather than simple de-Christianization followed by conversion to socialism may help explain some of the differences in the type of Socialist fervor from one region to the next and from one person to the next.

But to see socialism's impact on workers generally as religious we must take a broader view of religion. (37) Long before the advent of industrialization the commitment of most ordinary people to religion had been episodic. We tend erroneously to see a deep general piety in too many centuries of the past. Among the common people religion long has had the occasional churchgoer (for baptisms, Easter and the like), the regular communicant, and the truly fervent soul. Socialism insofar as it became a new religion reproduced these gradations. It had its voters whose commitment was episodic indeed. These voters may have known a bit about Socialist doctrines but they cared little. Many of them continued to be occasional Christians just as they now were occasional Socialists. Their main interests were elsewhere. Along with this group were the members of the party—people who paid dues and occasionally bought Socialist literature but whose doctrinal interests were slight. Many of these people actively used the institutions of the party as well, deriving from them a sense of comradeship as well as material benefits. Finally as we have seen there were the true believers. These workers avidly followed doctrinal debates and kept up with the party's literature. On the continent they were just as fervently anti-Christian as their Christian counterparts were fervently anti-Socialist, for they shared a similar type of uncompromising zeal.

Hear the true believer, a Ruhr miner who hated his work and found his wages no solace:

What am I? What is my meaning in this great world plan where brutal physical and psychological forces feast themselves in orgies? Nothing! Nothing at all! Zero! But why should I be a zero if I do not wish to be one? And I absolutely do not want to be one . . . I therefore adhere to socialism with every fiber of courage and idealism.

Hear also the more common type of Socialist, who saw in the movement material support and an appeal for justice but who took neither doctrine nor ritual too literally:

You know, I never read a social democratic book and rarely a newspaper. I used not to occupy myself with politics at all. But since I got married and have five eaters at home I have to do it. But I think my own thoughts. I do not go in for red ties, big round hats and other similar things. All that does not amount to much. We really do not want to become like the rich and refined people. There will always have to be rich and poor. We would not think of altering that. But we want a better and more just organization at the factory and in the state. I openly express what I think about that, even though it might not be pleasant. But I do nothing illegal. (38)

Socialism then meant many things to many people. This is hardly surprising, for any successful political movement it is true. Equally obviously socialism had a difficult time pleasing its varied constituents. Too much attention to purity by avoiding parliamentary bargains for example would antagonize those who looked to socialism for reforms; too many reforms would antagonize the ideological purists. The debate that raged among the leaders of socialism mirrored the diversity within the working classes.

In every industrial country however the debate had finally to be resolved in favor of a pragmatic approach. The pressures on Socialist leaders as administrators of an increasingly complex institution played a role in this resolution but more vital still was the fact that the majority of Socialist supporters were only vaguely committed to the doctrine of the movement. Practical interests predominated although admittedly some workers like many leaders doubtless continued to delight in Socialist revolutionary slogans while ignoring them in day-to-day tactics.

The evidence of majority reformism is overwhelming, admitting still that we cannot fathom the exact sentiments of such a vast array of people. Party membership was small—much smaller than union membership and far below Socialist voting figures. Socialist libraries in Germany reported that 80 or 90 percent of the books withdrawn were light fiction rather than works with any relationship to socialism. Socialist leaders complained in many ways of the apathy of their charges though there were a few factories in which large numbers of workers eagerly debated social questions. As with the unions there was much absenteeism at meetings and many local groups had to be dissolved each year. In sum, the evolution of socialism toward a reformist position corresponded to the interests of most party constituents and occurred in large measure because of these interests. Was there a lost opportunity here? Many Socialist theories including Marxism spoke of the vital role to be assumed by a working-class minority, the proletarian vanguard. There was in many countries a revolutionary minority available, devoted to Socialist doctrine. Many leaders urged that the movement remain true to this group; and in Russia Lenin planned tactics based on a zealous minority that proved ultimately viable. Socialist leaders in industrial countries did not do this; they yielded increasingly to majority sentiment. The minorities were put down, thrown at most a few doctrinal bones through affirmations of revolutionary purpose at the party congresses. By 1914 it was obvious that there were not only leaders but also many ordinary workers to the left of the major parties in countries like Germany or Britain, willing for example to challenge their governments by essentially political strikes. Socialist leaders were often complacent about their own power and prestige. They were preoccupied in aiding to their electoral following which had long meant stressing practical reforms above all. They were conscious of the difficulties of planning revolution in an industrial state. Perhaps in terms of the interests of ultimate Socialist goals they had made a wrong turning.

Aside from the fact that historians are usually more comfortable describing what has happened than what ought to have happened, it seems difficult to imagine a different evolution. The majority of workers in the industrial countries were not simply tradition-bound or confused, compared to the vanguard. Though heavily dependent on formal leadership for the initial impetus in political activity they had increasingly well-defined political and economic interests of their own. Socialism was their vehicle for important reform efforts and a more vague yearning for something more; something like it would have arisen even if Socialist leaders had devoted themselves to real revolutionary efforts. Parliamentary democracy even if incomplete in many cases offered opportunities for action that were attractive, if not completely adequate, in terms of working-class aspirations. Workers might have wanted more but in large part due to their adjustment to the industrial economy most of them did not revolt. Collectively they were not in a revolutionary mood and revolutionary theory had to bow before this fact.

CONCLUSION

There are two obvious and important objections to the approach this essay has taken. We have consistently stressed the vigor but essential moderation of this phase of the labor movement; and we have played down national peculiarities in the interests of generalizations about the nature and structure of the movement. Both of these premises can be questioned and both deserve a brief final statement.

The focus on general rather than national features, which is not a denial of some significant national peculiarities, is based on fundamental similarities in the working classes of industrial countries and the idea that these classes had largely determined the tone of the labor movement by 1914. There were some distinctive characteristics in each national labor force. German workers rather, recently exposed to industrialization, remained unusually attached to nature and the countryside and in this sense remained unusually conservative. This may be related to the ultimate conservatism of the German labor movement just as the docility and lack of imagination of German workers, noted by contemporary foreign observers, could be related. But such distinctive features must not obscure two points. First, no national labor force had uniform characteristics; each was divided into various industrial types and these types almost always bore striking resemblances to their counterparts elsewhere. Second and more important, the protest orientation of any large group of workers was largely determined by economic factors and relationships on the job and these factors were fundamentally comparable in all the mature industrial countries. France's industrial economy was a bit backward and this encouraged revolutionary syndicalism to an extent; but France's economy was not sufficiently out of line to allow revolutionary syndicalism to be a real or enduring force among large numbers of workers. No argument that insists on national economic peculiarities can explain the increasing similarities in the national labor movements by 1914, which contrast so vividly with labor movements in the newly industrial areas of Europe.

National differences in the ideology of the labor movements cannot be denied of course. Our thesis rests heavily on the notion of largely separate lines of causation for initial leaders on the one hand, most constituents on the other. For those in real contact with the ideologies whether they were workers or not distinct national political and cultural traditions had real force; however the ideologies did not determine most workers' goals. Yet leaders did shape the broader labor movements to some degree. They could not shake the fundamental moderation of the workers but they could teach them different ways to express their goals. German workers were taught to work through politics rather than strike and this remained an enduring characteristic of German labor later in the twentieth century. This was a conversion more to method than goal but it was important. Workers were heavily dependent on leaders for tactical guidance and this could shape national characteristics, some of which were more evident after 1914 than before. The organizational forms determined by ideologies could have a further impact. Certain features of the French labor movement were not set directly by revolutionary-syndicalist ideology but by the fact that syndicalist leaders due to their theories failed to discipline the spontaneous impulses of French workers as early or as firmly as occurred elsewhere, despite the fact that the impulses were not particularly unusual initially.

So the merging of the leaders' efforts with worker interests could create important national differences. Also the impact of the labor movement differed from country to country. Obviously we have been discussing the nature more than the results of the labor movement. Where the movement professed a radical ideology even when its behavior was moderate it could frighten outsiders. Differences in national political structures and upper classes created different receptions as well. The labor movement was far more disturbing in Germany than in Britain and not simply because German workers professed Marxist socialism; this was evident despite the fact that British workers had expectations in many ways more advanced than the Germans. The reactions of employers and governments to the labor movement could in turn affect the nature of the movement itself. Again some of the results in distinctive national characteristics might be more visible after 1914 than before.

On the whole, however, discussion of the impact of the labor movements brings us back to the similarities that overrode national differences. Everywhere the fundamental moderation of the movement allowed governments and most employers to come to terms with it regardless of the fears they professed. No government in the industrial countries was really behaving as though it anticipated revolutionary attack after 1890, though the Germans were more nervous than the British. Hence repression did not notably increase. Most employers could bargain with their workers; those whose firms were large enough to resist any compromise—and they existed in all countries—were able to win out. It was true that everywhere regardless of the professed ideology of the labor movement a general reaction against labor's excesses set in after about 1906. This reflected the growing power of the labor movement despite the fact that most leaders were becoming more conservative. It led to few important measures before 1914 but set the stage for more bitter class conflict after the war. Again however we are talking about a roughly common pattern.

Most historians would agree that the labor movements were becoming more similar by 1914 on the basis of a growing pragmatism combined with minority dissent. But have we exaggerated the pragmatic character of the organized labor movement for the period as a whole? We have stressed the relationship between labor organizations and large groups of workers, including those on the fringes of the movement, rather than the proclamations of the organizations and their committed minorities. The tone of the proclamations did evolve toward greater moderation. Within the quarter-century after 1890 the mood of the participants and potential participants in labor agitation did not change so decisively. Some unskilled workers calmed down after a first enthusiasm. Some angry workers were increasingly preoccupied and even satisfied by the extensive activities of their labor groups. But most participants in the labor movement were essentially reformist even in the 1890s. This is particularly evident when one views the labor movement as a whole—as strikes and unions as well as politics— and when one recognizes that for many workers politics was the last element in the order of precedence. The very real evolution of the labor movement was inevitable because workers had reached a stage of protest that was vigorous but directed to specific and rather limited goals and would not quickly change. Leaders, subjected to growing organizational pressures anyway, increasingly realized this and behaved accordingly; ideological causation diminished in importance for most of them. This was what changed.

Labor leaders had a difficult task in this period. They needed the support of an energetic ideology and the backing of some like-minded followers to persist; they worked extraordinarily hard —they had to. Aside from some of the older British trade-union chiefs they faced deep-seated hostility from the so-called right-thinking elements of society. Moreover they had to try to educate their followers in many ways. Obviously they tried to teach their ideology. They preached class consciousness to workers who felt mainly personal loyalties though they might welcome class slogans. They had to persuade skilled workers that class interest included the unskilled both now and in the future society. They had to show the evils of the present state. They had a long list of lessons. As we have seen they had mixed success, convincing

some workers but drawing many others for nonideological reasons; and all the while they had to handle the daily details of administration—fund raising, editing, scheduling, and the like—
with small staffs or no staff at all.

Their task was complicated by the need to educate most workers not just in ideology but in more elementary matters as well.
The labor movement in this period must be seen not simply as a
major innovation in politics and industrial relations but as a stage
in the adaptation of workers to industrial life. Workers with at
most only a few generations of experience in industry had not fully
adjusted to the key innovations of the new economy—steady technical change, disciplined subjection to large organizations, and
rising material standards and expectations. They had not yet fully
accepted the notion of change and progress itself. Our approach
to the labor movement from the bottom up has revealed that most
workers were not angry at the whole industrial system; their adaptation had already begun. But most workers still lacked habits
of discipline and expectations necessary to increasingly complex
industry and to the labor movement alike. This is where labor
organizations played a great role. To maintain themselves they
had to have greater discipline; and in socialism most leaders had
an ideology that accepted industrialization. Hence gradually
workers were taught to curb spontaneous anger and to play down
personal disputes. As their representatives gained some voice in
industry some workers gradually abandoned old habits of frequent job changing. As fairer conditions of work were set labor
leaders encouraged workers to avoid absenteeism and bad quality
work. Through the labor movement many workers gained active
expectations of rising wages for the first time. This created new
frictions but it also helped industry establish new machines and
methods of work in return for better pay. In sum, labor leaders
encouraged a variety of industrial virtures in their efforts to increase the sophistication of working-class protest. Here again the
principal factors were the nature of the working classes and the
organizational necessities of any labor movement that went beyond small subversive units.

The labor movement did not end in 1914 of course. Having
learned some of the requirements of a disciplined labor movement

by 1914 workers were in a sense ready for greater efforts. They had learned more realistic tactics and were able to restrain immediate and personal reactions to problems; and they were increasingly aware of the relevance of politics. Except in Britain their mood was still calm; but new hardships or new expectations could change this. New ideologies might win a greater devotion than the older ones had; the later twentieth century would reveal that no fixed relationship between workers and ideologies had been established. The war and the Russian Revolution were soon to create a new set of radical leaders and a new radical ideology. These and the experience of the war itself at least temporarily shattered the workers' calm while also creating new differences in the national forms of the labor movement. The period 1890–1914 was only a first step in the modern labor movement, a primary education. It did reveal however that workers had their own dynamic, their own limitations and goals, that might merge with a formal ideology to some degree but could seldom be swallowed by it. This ambiguity in the labor movement has never disappeared.

NOTES

1. For what I would regard as highly competent surveys of the labor movement which err in relying too heavily on formal ideas and pronouncements, see W. A. McConagha, *Development of the Labor Movement in Great Britain, France, and Germany* (Chapel Hill, N.C., 1942); Paul Louis, *Histoire du mouvement syndical en France* (2 vols., Paris, 1947); and most recently, Hedwig Wachenheim, *Die deutsche Arbeiterbewegung 1844 bis 1914* (Cologne, 1967).
2. The most elaborate treatments of material conditions are by Jürgen Kuczynski: *Darstellung der Lage der Arbeiter in Deutschland von 1871 bis 1917–18* (2 vols., Berlin, 1962–67); *Die Geschichte der Lage der Arbeiter in Frankreich von 1600 bis in die Gegenwart* (Ber-

lin, 1949); *Die Geschichte der Lage der Arbeiter in England von 1640 bis in die Gegenwart* (Berlin, 1955). Examples of contemporary surveys of workers' habits as well as conditions include B. Seebohm Rowntree, *Land and Labour: Lessons from Belgium* (London, 1911); and Fritz Schumann, *Auslese und Anpassung der Arbeiterschaft in der Automobilindustrie* (Leipzig, 1911).

3. Examples of recent approaches are: Gerhard A. Ritter, *Die Arbeiterbewegung im Wilhelminischen Reich* (Berlin, 1959); Guenther Roth, *The Social Democrats in Imperial Germany* (Totowa, N.J., 1963); Claude Willard, *Les Guesdistes; Le Mouvement socialiste en France* (Paris, 1965); H. A. Clegg, Alan Fox, A. F. Thompson, *A History of British Trade Unions since 1889* (Oxford, 1964), I.

4. Two contemporary studies that deal with the question of worker contentment: Richard Ehrenberg and Hugo Racine, *Krupp'sche Arbeiter-Familien* (Jena, 1912); Clément-Eugène Louis, *Cantonnierposeur de voie du chemin de fer du Nord* (Paris, 1904).

5. Robert Tressell, *The Ragged Trousered Philanthropists* (London, 1955).

6. See Clark Kerr and Abraham Siegel, "The Interindustry Propensity to Strike—an International Comparison," in *Patterns of Industrial Conflict*, eds. A. Kornhaus, R. Dubin, and A. M. Ross (New York, 1954).

7. Good accounts of each of these strikes exist: Llewellyn Smith and Vaughn Nash, *The Story of the Dockers' Strike* (London, 1899); Léon de Seilhac, *Les Grèves de Marseilles* (Paris, 1901); Ferdinand Tönnies, "Der Hamburger Strike von 1896–97," *Archiv für Gesetzgebung und Politik* (1897), 673–720.

8. See Schumann, *Auslese . . .* ; Max Morgenstern, *Auslese und Anpassung der industrieller Arbeiterschaft betrachtet bei den Offenbacher Lederarbeitern* (Freiburg i.Br., 1911).

9. See the various works by Jürgen Kuczynski cited in note 2. Also: Ashok V. Desai, *Real Wages in Germany, 1871–1913* (Oxford, 1968); Robert Kuczynski, *Arbeitslohn und Arbeitszeit in Europa und Amerika* (Berlin, 1913); E. H. Phelps-Brown and S. Hopkins, "The Course of Wage Rates in Five Countries 1860–1939," *Oxford Economic Papers* (1950), 226–96; Arthur L. Bowley and Josiah Strong, *Three Studies on the National Income* (London, 1938); Marcel Peeters, "L'Evolution des salaires en Belgique de 1831 à 1913," *Bulletin de l'Institut des sciences économiques* (1939), 389–420; Jean Lhomme, "Le Pouvoir d'achat de l'ouvrier français au cours d'un siècle; 1840–1940," *Le Mouvement social* (1968), 41–69.

10. Note that workers did not see the state very directly as a tax collector, a role that in earlier times (and in places like Spain and Italy in these same years) provoked popular attacks on the state or its agents. Most taxes and tariffs were indirect for people who owned

little property; labor movements might rail against them as they did in Germany for they did discriminate against workers, but there is no sign of great popular anger. In contrast some workers did complain about deductions for the social-insurance programs which they could see easily. Here as in other connections if we place workers in the history of popular protest as well as view them through Socialist pronouncements, we can see that hostility to the state might in many ways have lessened.

11. See the penetrating autobiography of a man who began in the Welsh mines: Wil Jon Edwards, *From the Valley I Came* (London, 1958).

12. The most important studies of strikes only touch on this period, but they provide a useful framework: Robert Goetz-Girey, *Le Mouvement des grèves en France, 1919–1962* (Paris, 1965); E. T. Hiller, *The Strike* (Chicago, 1928); Arthur M. Ross and Paul Hartman, *Changing Patterns of Industrial Conflict* (New York, 1960); Robert Gubbels, *La Grève, phénomène de civilisation* (Brussels, 1962); and above all, K. G. J. C. Knowles, *Strikes—A Study in Industrial Conflict* (Oxford, 1952).

13. On several of these strikes, see Max Koch, *Die Bergarbeiterbewegung im Ruhrgebiet zur Zeit Wilhelm II* (Düsseldorf, 1954); Ben Tillett, *History of the London Transport Workers' Strike* (London, 1911); A. G. Rouchy, *Les Grèves dans les chemins de fer* (Paris, 1912).

14. See Cyr van Overbergh, *La Grève générale* (Brussels, 1913).

15. See Maurice Halbwachs, *La Classe ouvrière et le niveau de vie* (Paris, 1913); and *L'Evolution des besoins* (Paris, 1933).

16. A. and Z., "Pour la réduction des heures du travail," *La Revue socialiste* (1906), 129–44, 307–23, 433–51, 592–605, 718–33.

17. George Askwith, *Industrial Problems and Disputes* (London, 1920); Sidney and Beatrice Webb, *Industrial Democracy* (London, 1902); Hans J. Teuteberg, *Geschichte der industriellen Mitbestimmung in Deutschland* (Tübingen, 1961); Peter N. Stearns, "Against the Strike Threat: Policies of French Manufacturers," *Journal of Modern History* (1968).

18. See George Dangerfield, *The Strange Death of Liberal England* (paperback, New York, 1961), for a statement of how near revolution was; but for an important corrective, see E. H. Phelps-Brown, *The Growth of British Industrial Relations* (London, 1959).

19. For one such case, see Leo A. Loubère, "Coal Miners, Labor Relations, and Politics in the Lower Languedoc, 1880–1914," *Journal of Social History* (1968).

20. Fanny Imle, *Die Arbeitslosenunterstützung in den deutschen Gewerkschaften* (Berlin, 1903), gives a clear exposition of the tensions created in the development of benefit programs.

21. See Philipp A. Koller, *Das Massen-und Führer-Problem* in den *Freien Gewerkschaften* (Tübingen, 1920).

22. One indication of the general trend is sketched in Leo A. Loubère, "Left-Wing Radicals, Strikes, and the Military, 1880–1907," *French Historical Studies* (1963).

23. Koller, *Das Massen.* . . .

24. Heinz-Josef Varain, *Freie Gewerkschaften, Sozialdemokratie, und Staat* (Düsseldorf, 1956).

25. Two good surveys of syndicalism, though dated in some ways, exist in English: J. A. Estey, *Revolutionary Syndicalism* (London, 1913); and Louis Levine, *The Labor Movement in France* (New York, 1912). For syndicalist theory, see Robert Goetz-Girey, *La Pensée syndicale française* (Paris, 1948). See also Peter N. Stearns, *Revolutionary Syndicalism and French Labor: A Cause without Rebels* (New Brunswick, N.J., 1971). For general French labor history, see Val R. Lorwin, *The French Labor Movement* (Cambridge, Mass., 1954).

26. The most important document issued by the new radicals came from the Welsh mines: *The Miners' Next Step* (Tolypandy, 1911).

27. See Goetz-Girey, *Mouvement des grèves.*

28. Paul Louis, *Le Syndicalisme français d'Amiens à Saint-Etienne (1900–1922)* (Paris, 1924).

29. Maurice Bruce, *The Coming of the Welfare State* (London, 1961); Karl E. Born, *Staat und Sozialpolitik seit Bismarcks Sturz* (Wiesbaden, 1957).

30. Ritter, *Die Arbeiterbewegung* . . . , opens the investigation of the local impact on the character of socialism.

31. See the summary by Harry J. Marks, "The Sources of Reformism in the Social Democratic Party of Germany," *Journal of Modern History* (1939); the more elaborate statement is G. Sinowjew, *Der Krieg und die Krise des Sozialismus* (Vienna, 1924).

32. Adolf Levenstein, *Aus der Tiefe, Arbeiterbriefe* (Berlin, 1908), a fascinating collection of radical statements by workers who had no share in labor leadership.

33. See Roth, *The Social Democrats.* . . .

34. The general statement of the relationship between company size and political mentality can be found in Seymour M. Lipset, *Political Man, the Social Bases of Politics* (Garden City, N.Y., 1963). I am not sure that this pattern is accurate for Europe, at least until later in the twentieth century.

35. Edwards, *From the Valley.* . . .

36. Paul Göhre, *Drei Monate Fabrikarbeiter* (Leipzig, 1890), 111.

37. A very suggestive discussion of many of these points, for a later period, is Serge Bonnet, "Italian Workers in the Metallurgical District of Lorraine," *Journal of Social History* (1968).

38. Levenstein, *Tiefe*, 70; Göhre, *Monate* . . . , 115.

Comment on Stearns's Essay
by Harvey Mitchell

Two approaches, yet remarkably similar findings: this is certainly one of the conclusions which may be drawn from a comparison of the two essays in this small volume. While I reason that much can be still gained from pursuing what Mr. Stearns terms the traditional viewpoint, and argue that a comparative one runs the risk of excessive schematization, Mr. Stearns presents cogent reasons for preferring to shift attention from the national framework and from the emphasis on ideology and labor elites—which he claims have dominated the writing of labor historians—to those problems the labor movement shared irrespective of geographic boundaries; and he also believes that it is time to examine more closely than has hitherto been the case the nature of the movement from below—that is to say, from the perspective of the working-class constituency. Since the first of his aims demands comparative analysis, he could not but approach the second in the same way. Mr. Stearns is, of course, aligning himself with a number of historians of other social problems in previous periods of history by looking more closely at the grass roots of social movements, and although a few efforts to apply the comparative method have been made, the results, as matters now stand, are still in the experimental stage. Be that as it may, the reader will have discerned that neither Mr. Stearns nor I rigidly dismiss the other's position. Mr. Stearns, for example, does not ignore—indeed, he constantly takes into account —the distinctive aspects of the national movements, and he does not neglect the views and activities of the leadership. Although

I focus on both, I also pay attention to the enormous importance of the working classes in shaping the organized movement; nor do I fail to recognize how like one another many characteristics of the separate labor movements were. Furthermore, on many points of controversy and interpretation, both large and small, Mr. Stearns and I seem to be in agreement.

The purpose of this volume will not have been met, however, if we were to gloss over our differences. At the same time, space forbids an exhaustive airing of all the challenges that have emerged from our separate treatments of the subject. What I propose to do instead is to fasten on the question of reformism, because it is unquestionably the single most important development within the labor movement in the advanced industrial societies before 1914. Moreover, both Mr. Stearns and I make it the focal point of our essays. Mr. Stearns maintains that reformism was the inevitable outcome of both aspects of the movement —the spontaneous protest of the working classes and the doctrinal-organizational element. I suggest, on the contrary, that the labor elites who altered the doctrinal foundations of the organized movement—and I might say once more that there were important differences in the way this was accomplished in each of the labor movements—were chiefly responsible for the diversion of the working classes from the ideology and tactics of confrontation to the search for greater conformity to the ethics of industrial society, the demands of social harmony, and the rules of organized political life. Mr. Stearns, if I judge his position fairly, acknowledges as I do the increasing indifference shown by labor elites to doctrinal questions. He also stresses, far more than I am prepared to admit, that the policy of compliance they urged on their followers did no injury to their deepest yearnings, and in fact responded to them, because apart from a minority for whom socialism or revolutionary syndicalism meant a great deal, the vast majority of workers had neither the desire nor felt the necessity to challenge the nature of industrialism. In Mr. Stearns's eyes, the goals of those at the top and the aspirations of those from below converged when, as a result of mutual interaction or education, both realized that in reformism lay the best solution to the problems of the working classes in an industrial society. Among a number of reasons responsible for this identity of interests were the bureaucratization of the unions and the Socialist parties, the provision by both of some improvements in the quality of working-class life, the incipient welfare programs established by the state, the development of machinery for the settlement of industrial disputes, and the general appeal of Socialist parties to groups outside the industrial working classes, including groups which had only recently passed from the latter to assume a new status in society. These are developments within the labor movement which cannot be overlooked; indeed, we both take note of all of them. Nevertheless, the point that is worth making again is that each of them operated in different ways in each of the societies in question, and as I try to show, not all of them had the same impact everywhere, however similar the results appear when taken together.

It is also important to make another observation in this connection. Mr. Stearns—and I must confess I may have been equally remiss—tends to equate ideology with revolutionary action, and does not allow that reformism or moderatism was believed by its exponents and supporters to constitute a valid ideological position. This was certainly not as true of those who consciously and deliberately sought to accommodate themselves to the prevailing social norms—the bureaucrats and the pure trade unionists, for example. Revolutionary socialism in western Europe was seriously diluted by 1914, but those who still employed its rhetoric or tried to reassess their ideological commitments in the light of changing conditions believed in the appropriateness and wisdom of the fresh doctrines they were proposing as alternatives to the combative traditions of the immediate past. In another sense, they maintained that they were not in fact denying the essentials of those traditions and were necessarily adjusting them to the realities of the present. Jaurès and Bernstein, for example, always defended themselves against the charge of revisionism with the reply that their understanding of Marxism was superior to that of their opponents. It would be a serious distortion of the past to assume that the men and women in the parties, and even in some of the unions, who were providing greater amenities for the working classes through a number of their agencies, were motivated simply by the expectation that such action would help them achieve power, though the prospect of its conquest certainly was an important ingredient in their calculations. They sincerely believed that they were helping create the conditions of a better life, the antechamber, so to speak of a Socialist society. This was clearest in Germany where both the party and the unions offered their members the protection and security denied them in the larger society. Although such a development was less evident in France and Britain, the attempt to create alternatives to the existing order in this way was also being made. The contradiction lay in the fact that the enclaves thus created were not self-sufficient, but rather rested on the most fundamental of ties with their host societies—the economics of employment. While some of the reformists accepted this, others refused to acknowledge that sooner or later they would have to come to terms with the consequences of their theoretical gymnastics. This was the reason for the bitter attacks on the latter by the revolutionaries, especially in Germany; they knew what the moderates could not willingly or easily admit—that trade-unionism and reformism meant the end of authentic change as they conceived it.

But it is on the outlook of the majority of the workers that I find I am most in disagreement with Mr. Stearns. To be sure, long-range ideological goals were, for the most part, the concern of the labor elites, most of whom in the Socialist parties, if not in the unions, were of bourgeois origin. Doctrine meant something rather different to the rank and file. Mr. Stearns reminds us of this point again and again; and he is right to do so. However, he also insists that most workers were traditionalist, not radical, and draws on a rich variety of evidence in support of this view. To drive his point home, he compares the experiences of workers in the less industrialized societies of Russia and Italy with those of the advanced western societies of France, Britain, and Germany. I consequently have the impression that Mr. Stearns is positing a general proposition that ideology or doctrine is a necessary feature of the early stages of working-class protest, at least insofar as a body of distinctive beliefs and principles is required to educate, mold, and direct the working classes, but that it comes to lose its urgency, in fact, is increasingly seen as cumbersome and stifling, and can therefore no longer serve the goals of labor movements in maturing industrial societies. I might have been prepared to accept such an interpretation had Mr. Stearns taken care not to dismiss the importance of ideology in the later development of industrial labor movements.

In the long term, Mr. Stearns also tells us that workers in similar occupations, notwithstanding national origins, acquire rather uniform attitudes towards authority, make the same kinds of demands, express the same expectations—in short, develop a world view that distinguishes them from other workers. Mr. Stearns offers many striking illustrations of such tendencies. Yet, in the present state of research, the evidence is inconclusive, as Mr. Stearns implicitly recognizes, for example, in his contrast between British and German railway workers. Mr. Stearns was wise to do so. He might have made more of another example, this time afforded by miners. They were, on the whole, moderate, deeply tied to the mining regions in which they lived, but they were also not slow to strike, and, indeed, often demanded reforms and innovations not narrowly confined to their own specific needs. True. Yet in France their earlier demonstrations of violence gave way to caution after 1890, for a variety of reasons all peculiar to that country. In Britain, on the other hand, moderation was overtaken by a new militancy. British miners increasingly moved after 1893 to a new and unprecedented call for more radical action, so much so that whatever the exact nature of the permeation of revolutionary-syndicalist ideas in some mining districts, after 1912–13 there occurred a distinct break between the traditional leadership and the militants who believed they understood the mood of the workers.

Finally, the shift that did take place in doctrinal positions may have been more appropriate to the needs of the better organized, relatively better educated, and better paid sections of the working classes in western Europe. Did, however, the new outlook answer the needs of the unorganized workers, the growing numbers of unskilled who were seeking to improve their conditions, the younger generation of workers, or even all the expectations of the more advantaged workers in the last years before 1914? The question is worth asking even if, as it has been suggested, a more homogeneous working class was emerging which was tending to erase the differences between its upper and lower strata. Though such a trend was being established, important distinctions remained, most obviously between poorer and better off workers, and there is no overwhelming evidence as yet to support the contention that the latter were more attracted to militancy than the former. The massive strike action in Britain was, in a sense, quasi-revolutionary, even if finally tamed. Important groups within the German movement were prepared to strike for political objectives, and were also ready to challenge the bureaucracies of their unions. Although revolutionary syndicalism was beginning to lose its vigor and appeal after 1909 in France, I find it hard to believe that the *crise de conscience* of such figures as Monatte was not related to the ideological perceptions of many workers, however unstructured and contradictory they were. In brief, I am suggesting that the legacies of ideological disputes within the labor movement had hardly exhausted themselves before 1914 and that reformism, though it captured the general staffs, had not completely eliminated the opposition, either at the top or among certain elements at the bottom. Call it romantic, retrogressive, or unrealistic, the residues of belief in revolutionary action were still very visible. So much was it in evidence that the policymakers in the various movements took measures to combat it not only in their annual congresses, but in the less salubrious atmosphere of the factory and the local union halls. The persistence of revolutionary appeals in some of the most advanced industrial societies today may be ascribed to the force of retardative factors in the economy, to the weight or memory of revolutionary action hallowed by tradition, to a heightened consciousness of continuing injustice, and to a host of other causes. While in the long run they may pass into history, they continue to exert their attraction and force.

By looking closely at the working-class constituency, Mr. Stearns has helped clarify our perceptions of the labor movement and its political expressions. Both of us recognize the importance of the changing shape of ideology for the elites of the world of labor. My quarrel with Mr. Stearns can be reduced to his reluctance to attribute to the grass roots of the movement its own ideological commitments. To be sure, I offer no substantial body of empirical evidence to explain the development of such an ideology and the functions which it performed, but my reading of Mr. Stearns's essay convinces me more than ever that it ought to be explored.

Comment on Mitchell's Essay

by Peter N. Stearns

It would be idle to pretend that Mr. Mitchell's essay and my own clash directly either on fundamental principles or on specific facts. It would be equally silly to adopt a combative tone in this comment or even to hold forth at particular length. I can say in all candor that I find Mr. Mitchell's essay an elegant, useful, and accurate summary of the development of the labor movements in the three main industrial countries. We agree obviously in the final conclusion about the increasingly reformist character of the labor movement although Mr. Mitchell, with his chronological approach, stresses a more definite evolution than I do. We agree in a more basic conclusion, despite differences of phrasing, that the labor movement moved into increasing integration with the capitalist or at least the industrial order. Mr. Mitchell stresses the integration of the labor organizations in largely political terms, while I emphasize the broader integration of the working classes, but the approaches can be easily and usefully combined. Finally Mr. Mitchell and I even anticipate the most likely criticisms. He says that he does not believe a supranational approach is possible and indicates why the national peculiarities are so important; I say that generalizations are possible above the national level particularly when one examines the labor movement as a combination of working-class characteristics and formal leadership. We have then indicated already that we differ and that we have made a fairly explicit choice of the approach each of us has adopted.

For it is a difference of approach not a direct disagreement that we are dealing with. Mr. Mitchell and I talk about quite different things. Where I feel that strikes were a basic component of the labor movement for example Mr. Mitchell cites them only in brief outline as indications of growing unrest or individually only where they affected the formal labor movement directly. We approach causation differently in some instances. Mr. Mitchell stresses the ideology, or lack of ideology, and the organizational pressures on leadership—in essence the choices that leaders made whether knowingly or not—while I emphasize the imperatives created by the nature and position of working-class constituents. A specific illustration of our differences occurs in the explanation of the changes in the C.G.T. after 1910, where Mr. Mitchell, with a very brief note on changing economic conditions, focuses on new Socialist attitudes under Jaurès's aegis that I do not mention at all. There are many cases in which Mr. Mitchell and I are talking about different topics altogether. Nothing in my essay would indicate the reasons for some French workers choosing one revolutionary group and some another, for I do not feel that these divisions are of first importance. But they did exist and Mr. Mitchell describes them well and raises important questions about what elements in each group, personal or doctrinal, attracted any given set of constituents.

Obviously, examples of this sort could be multiplied but to little purpose since the essays are open to direct comparison in this volume. Mr. Mitchell's approach is, I think, more conventional than mine but this is in no sense a criticism; it may by the same token be far more important. Certainly Mr. Mitchell makes a real contribution by offering such a concise description of formal political and trade-union developments. My own essay is possible only because this sort of information has been established so thoroughly.

Still, having said that our essays complement each other far more than they conflict I cannot leave everything in sweetness and light. Mr. Mitchell and I disagree on a few facts of importance. We obviously clash on wage trends. Mr. Mitchell sees

French real wages rising until 1910 then declining due to inflation; I claim the reverse. Mr. Mitchell has the support of almost all the scholars (few enough, to be sure) who have worked on this question (largely because they all use the same government statistics without question), and so he may of course be right. But oddly, even Mr. Mitchell says that while prices rose faster than pay after 1910 living standards improved, which seems an unlikely combination. And he says that French workers became more moderate because of inflation, which is improbable. Here of course is the important point, for if Mr. Mitchell is right about French wage patterns, then workers, or at least French workers, grew cautious not just in recessions but also when conditions deteriorated more modestly, whereas they were ready to ask for much more in prosperity. As I try to show, this is incorrect. I must add that Mr. Mitchell goes against even the usual scholarly judgment in claiming that German real wages declined after 1910.

Another partly factual disagreement must be noted. Mr. Mitchell implies, particularly for the SFIO in France, that middle-class support not only grew but was a rather new element in the 1900s and that it helped lead the party to greater conservatism. (He does, admittedly, note middle-class support for Guesdism in southern France, but in an earlier section.) As I try to suggest, the question of middle-class participation needs a much more careful assessment. It seems to have been important for most Socialist parties all along, in France possibly preeminent until the 1890s. And it is not clear that it necessarily led to a more reformist party than purely working-class support would produce. This is a complex issue and a significant one, not to be disposed of by simple statements of class differences.

Mr. Mitchell does not, in my opinion, pay enough attention to the actual working classes. He does at one point suggest the different types of workers in the labor movement but thereafter ordinary workers appear only in statements about wage trends. There is little attention paid to workers' expectations, without which neither material conditions nor the activities of organized labor can be understood. Mr. Mitchell cites for example the huge inequalities of wealth in Britain in the 1890s. Fine. But these inequalities say little about the labor movement unless we know how and to what extent workers perceived and resented them. Too many labor historians believe that a brief summary of material conditions tells us all we need to know, for worker response is supposed to be easily induced from this. This approach begs a difficult but vital question: did workers react to their living standards as we think they should have, or as labor leaders said they should, or as workers later would? Did they react in any uniform way at all?

Mr. Mitchell obviously places far more weight on ideological factors than I do. This is partly a matter again of different interests rather than different interpretations. Mr. Mitchell pays attention to the procolonialism of German revisionists whereas I am more concerned with the degree to which workers in Germany and elsewhere were nationalistic and put at least implicit pressure on their leaders to modify an antinationalist approach. There are also several instances in which I believe Mr. Mitchell's stress on ideology is simply wrong. He easily assumes that the post-1910 strike wave in Britain was syndicalist inspired. He says at one point that the "rank and file" of British unions "were eager to accept" much of the new Socialist and revolutionary-syndicalist attack on society. I think this is highly doubtful, demanding clear proof at any rate. Many British workers were very angry but neither their strike goals nor the bargains they were still willing to accept indicate general penetration of a new ideology. Further, the most violent workers, largely unskilled, were also the least likely to have ideological interests at all.

Mr. Mitchell overstresses ideology in the French union movement too. Here again our differences of approach are clear. I do not see how French unionism can be summed up simply by looking at the C.G.T. or even by judging the C.G.T. by its formal pronouncements alone. Mr. Mitchell correctly notes that only a minority of unionized workers in France were in the C.G.T. To me this suggests immediately that the importance of the C.G.T. and its doctrines need careful assessment in judging the character and the probable evolution of French unionism. As a result of his preoccupation with revolutionary-syndicalist groups, Mr. Mitchell errs several times in implying that heavy industry was unimportant in the French labor movement. The miners were vital though admittedly most of them were not syndicalist; so were railroad workers. It is true that votes in the C.G.T. were substantially based on France's small shops; but this is the same as saying that the C.G.T. was not and could not be the whole union movement and that many unions even in the C.G.T. ignored its policies. The stress on ideology leads to mistakes about the syndicalist unions themselves. Mr. Mitchell says that the syndicalists sacrificed immediate for long-range goals and he makes this judgment on the basis of formal resolutions against collective bargaining and the like. In fact many syndicalist unions took the lead in collective bargaining and almost none resisted it; France did not lag much behind Germany in collective bargaining, though it was true that the loose structure of French unions and French employers encouraged local rather than national agreements. Ideology must be tested constantly against the professed desires of its constituents and against the behavior of its supporters.

Obviously Mr. Mitchell thinks that national differences were far more important than I do. Neither of us denies some common elements or some important peculiarities; but the stress placed on each is very different. In my opinion Mr. Mitchell misses a number of opportunities to talk about the general incidence of developments that he discusses in one country alone. Why not discuss the Socialists' increasing concessions to nationalism generally instead of merely in Germany? (I use this example because I think neither of us did justice to this important topic.) French Socialists after all faced quite similar problems and were very restrained in their comments on French imperialism. National differences might still emerge but they would be far more precisely stated and undoubtedly quite narrow in a real comparative study. Again examples of this sort could be multiplied but there is no need.

One of the bases of Mr. Mitchell's reliance on national units must be directly challenged however, particularly since if accurate it would force substantial modifications in my claim that ordinary workers were more similar than the ideologies of each national labor movement imply. Mr. Mitchell in my opinion greatly exaggerates the national peculiarities of each industrial economy, especially in the cases of France and Germany. I have already tried to suggest that Mr. Mitchell gives inadequate attention to French heavy industry and its importance in the labor movement. As a result he too easily concludes that French industry was backward, artisanal, and so on; there is a touch of the self-fulfilling statement in all this, when attention is paid only to the more backward and artisanal industries. Equally erroneous is the repeated effort to sum up German industry in terms of big industry alone. I think it is far more important to discern two industrial economies in Germany—a modernized sector, growing rapidly but still employing only a minority of manufacturing workers, and a traditional sector of small shops and domestic production. It was the latter that was most important in the labor movement. Mr. Mitchell is simply wrong when at one point he says that Germany had little room for small capitalists; small business still existed and in fact the number of units was increasing though less rapidly than the great firms. Mr. Mitchell also cites the importance of the state in German industry and here I cannot disagree; but I am not sure that this produced decisive peculiarities in the German working class. In all this I am not denying the possibility of important differences from one national economy to the next. I am urging a recognition that national economic characteristics are to an extent statistical abstractions, masking great differences within the nation; and that comparisons must be made with great precision. It would be simpler if we could accept the conventional view, which Mr. Mitchell largely repeats, that France is small shops and Germany is heavy industry but this just is not so. On this point at least Mr. Mitchell's insistence that each nation be considered individually rests on false bases.

Still, the most consistent differences between Mr. Mitchell's essay and my own do not emerge in direct disagreements but in a different judgment of what is most important. I find greater reality for the labor history of this period in the roughly common developments of industrial Europe than in national characteristics. Exclusive focus on the latter, it seems to me, involves the historian in needless detail, some repetition, and some real inaccuracy. I find a study of formal ideas and leadership inadequate without consideration of the condition and motives of ordinary constituents. Indeed I think the future in labor history lies in studies of the working classes, so long neglected; some of these studies should deal with working-class activities that have little or nothing to do with the labor movement, but others will certainly deal with the complex, often ambiguous relationship between workers and the labor movement. This obviously is the framework within which I approach labor history. But each historian must choose his own framework, his own means of determining what is most real. The reader will hopefully be able to decide for himself which of the approaches toward European labor presented in this book is most appropriate. He may take elements of each or, heaven forbid, reject them both; he cannot accept them both in their entirety, for Mr. Mitchell and I have a different sense of what labor history is.

Bibliography

WORKERS AND WORKING CONDITIONS

Little has been done on the conditions and quality of working-class life in this period, aside from studies of wage patterns. The best coverage by far is given by contemporary investigations such as those conducted by most governments into domestic manufacturing, or by private groups like the Verein für Sozialpolitik, or by individuals [e.g., Charles Booth, *Life and Labour of the People in London* (London, 1891), or R. Seebohm Rowntree, *Poverty, a Study of Town Life* (London, 1901)].

A few sociological studies are useful for general orientation, though they draw their materials mainly from later periods: T. B. Bottomore, *Classes in Modern Society* (New York, 1966); Ralf Dahrendorf, *Class and Class Conflict in Industrial Society* (Stanford, 1959); S. M. Lipset and R. Bendix, *Social Mobility in Industrial Society* (Berkeley, 1959); Heinrich Popitz *et al.*, *Das Gesellschaltsbild des Arbeiters* (Tübingen, 1957). A short general survey is Jürgen Kuczynski, *The Rise of the Working Class* (paperback, New York, 1967). A more general social history is Peter N. Stearns, *European Society in Upheaval* (New York, 1967).

GREAT BRITAIN:

Arthur L. Bowley, *Wages in the United Kingdom in the Nineteenth Century* (Cambridge, 1900) and, with Josiah Strong, *Three Studies on the National Income* (London, 1938); John Jewkes and E. M. Grey, *Wages and Labour in the Lancashire Cotton Industry* (Manchester, 1935). Two books discuss workers as a factor in production in the period: Charles P. Kindleberger, *Economic Growth in France and Britain 1851–1950* (Cambridge, Mass., 1964) and especially A. L. Levine, *Industrial Retardation in Britain* (London, 1967). Sidney

Pollard, *A History of Labour in Sheffield* (Liverpool, 1959) is a local study that goes well beyond the formal labor movement. Alfred Williams, *Life in a Railway Factory* (London, 1915) is a valuable discussion of conditions by a worker.

CONTINENT:

In English: R. Seebohm Rowntree, *Land and Labour: Lessons from Belgium* (London, 1911).

Ralf Dahrendorf, *Society and Democracy in Germany* (New York, 1967), for provocative suggestions about the nature of German workers. W. H. Dawson, *The Evolution of Modern Germany* (London, 1908) and *Industrial Germany* (London, 1912) provide excellent summaries of welfare systems and other matters. Another contemporary study of English and German workers is useful: Arthur Shadwell, *Industrial Efficiency* (2 vols., London, 1906). On wages: Ashok V. Desai, *Real Wages in Germany 1871–1913* (Oxford, 1968) and Jürgen Kuczynski, *A Short History of Labour Conditions under Industrial Capitalism* (3 vols., London, 1944–45).

Henry Steele, *The Working Classes in France, a Social Study* (London, 1904).

Foreign Language: Léon and Maurice Bonneff, *La Vie tragique des travailleurs* (Paris, 1904); Michel Collinet, *L'Ouvrier français; essai sur la condition ouvrière* (1900–1950) (Paris, 1951); Maurice Halbwachs, *L'Evolution des besoins* (Paris, 1933); Jürgen Kuczynski, *Die Geschichte der Lage der Arbeiter in Frankreich von 1600 bis in die Gegenwart* (Berlin, 1949); Jean Marczewski, *Introduction à l'histoire quantitative* (Geneva, 1965); Georges Mauco, *Les Étrangers en France* (Paris, 1932); François Simiand, *Le Salaire, l'évolution sociale, et la monnaie* (3 vols., Paris, 1932).

Wilhelm Brepohl, *Industrievolk im Wandel von der agraren zur industriellen Daseiform dargestellt am Ruhrgebiet* (Tübingen, 1957); Wolfgang Köllman, *Sozialgeschichte der Stadt Barmen* (Tübingen, 1961); Jürgen Kuczynski, *Darstellung der Lage der Arbeiter in Deutschland von 1871 bis 1900* (Berlin, 1962); . . . *von 1900 bis 1917–18* (Berlin, 1967); Robert Kuczynski, *Arbeitslohn und Arbeitszeit in Europa und Amerika* (Berlin, 1913).

STRIKES AND CONCILIATION

General: Eduard Bernstein, *Der Streik* (Frankfurt a.M., 1920); also in French, *La Grève* (Paris, 1906); Robert Goetz-Girey, *Le Mouvement des grèves en France 1919–1962* (Paris, 1965); Robert Gubbels, *La*

Grève, phénomène de civilisation (Brussels, 1962); E. T. Hiller, *The Strike* (Chicago, 1928); K. G. J. C. Knowles, *Strikes—A Study in Industrial Conflict* (Oxford, 1952); Arthur M. Ross and Paul Hartman, *Changing Patterns of Industrial Conflict* (New York, 1960).

GREAT BRITAIN:

George Askwith, *Industrial Problems and Disputes* (London, 1920), by Britain's chief mediator in the period; George Dangerfield, *The Strange Death of Liberal England* (paperback, New York, 1961); David Evans, *Labour Strife in the South Wales Coalfield 1910–1911* (Cardiff, 1911); Llewellyn Smith and Vaughn Nash, *The Story of the Dockers' Strike* (London, 1889); Ben Tillett, *History of the London Transport Workers' Strike* (London, 1911); Sidney and Beatrice Webb, *Industrial Democracy* (London, 1902).

CONTINENT:

Laurent Deschene, *L'Avènement du régime syndical à Verviers* (Paris, 1908); Léon Delsinne, *Les Grèves générales au XXe Siècle en Belgique* (Brussels, 1965); Cyr van Overbergh, *La Grève générale* (Brussels, 1913).

A. G. Rouchy, *Les Grèves dans les chemins de fer* (Paris, 1912); Antony Schoux, *Des Grèves maritimes* (Paris, 1910); Léon de Seilhac, *La Grève du tissage de Lille* (Paris, 1910); *Le Lockout de Fougères* (Paris, 1907); *Les Grèves du Chambon* (Paris, 1912); and *Les Grèves du Tarn* (Paris, 1910). On conciliation: Albert Aftalion, Arquembourg, and Fagnot, *Le Règlement aimable des conflits du travail* (Paris, 1911); on strike law, Jean-Pierre Bouère, *Le Droit de grève* (Paris, 1958).

Max Koch, *Die Bergarbieterbewegung im Ruhrgebiet zur Zeit Wilhelm II* (Düsseldorf, 1954); August Winnig, *Der Grosse Kampf im deutschen Baugewerbe 1910* (Hamburg, 1911). On conciliation: Hans J. Teuteberg, *Geschichte der industriellen Mitbestimmung in Deutschland* (Tübingen, 1961).

TRADE UNIONS

General: Selig Perlman, *A Theory of the Labor Movement* (New York, 1949).

GREAT BRITAIN:

Henry Pelling, *A History of British Trade Unionism* (London, 1963), provides a convenient summary. Far more detailed is H. A. Clegg,

Alan Fox, and A. F. Thompson, *A History of British Trade Unions since 1889* (Oxford, 1964), I; see also Eric Hobsbawm, *Labouring Men. Studies in the History of Labour* (London, 1964).

There is a vast array of studies of individual unions; what follows covers only the most important unions and most recent work. R. Page Arnot, *The Miners* (2 vols., London, 1949–53) and *South Wales Miners* (London, 1967); Alan Fox, *A History of the National Union of Boot and Shoe Operatives 1874–1957* (London, 1959); Ellic Howe, *The British Federation of Master Printers 1900–1950* (London, 1950); James B. Jefferys, *The Story of the Engineers* (London, 1946); Ben Turner, *History of the General Union of Textile Workers* (Herkmonwicke, 1926); H. A. Turner, *Trade Union Growth, Structure, and Policy: A Comparative Study of the Cotton Unions* (London, 1962). On a special topic, see Branko Pribićević, *The Shop Stewards' Movement and Workers' Control 1910–1922* (Oxford, 1959).

CONTINENT:

In English: See the works by W. H. Dawson, above. Val R. Lorwin, *The French Labor Movement* (Cambridge, Mass., 1954). W. H. McConagha, *Development of the Labor Movement in Great Britain, France, and Germany* (Chapel Hill, N.C., 1942) is a useful brief sketch but obviously this is not a field that English-speaking scholars have extensively surveyed.

Foreign Language: Laurent Dechesne, *Syndicats ouvriers belges* (Paris, 1906); Léon Delsinne, *Le Mouvement syndical en Belgique* (Brussels, 1936); S. H. School, *De Historiografie der Arbeitersbewegung in België* (Brussels, 1959).

Robert Brécy, *Le Mouvement syndical en France, 1871–1921: essai bibliographique* (Paris, 1963); Edouard Dolléans and Gérard Dehove, *Histoire du travail en France* (Paris, 1953), I; Georges Lefranc, *Histoire du mouvement syndical français* (Paris, 1937); Paul Louis, *Histoire du mouvement syndical en France* (2 vols., Paris, 1947); Jean Reynaud, *Les Syndicats en France* (Paris 1963). On individual unions, Guy Chaumeil, *Histoire des cheminots et de leurs syndicats* (Paris, 1948); Henri Facdouel, *La Fédération française des travailleurs du livre* (Lyons, 1904); Max Ferré, *Histoire du mouvement syndicaliste révolutionnaire chez les instituteurs* (Paris, 1955); Raymond Joran, *L'Organisation syndicale dans l'industrie des bâtiments* (Paris, 1914). A fine regional study is Jean Charles, *Les Débuts du mouvement syndical à Besançon: la féderation ouvrière, 1891–1914* (Paris, 1962). Hedwig Wachenheim, *Die deutsche Arbeiterbewegung 1844 bis 1914* (Cologne, 1967); this is the best survey and contains an extensive list of trade-union histories published before World War I;

unhappily, few studies have been written since that time. Dieter Fricke, *Zur Organisation und Tätigkeit der deutschen Arbeiterbewegung* (Leipzig, 1962) gives a Marxist view. On special themes, Philipp A. Koller, *Das Massen-und Führer-Problem in den Freien Gewerkschaften* (Tübingen, 1920) and Heinz-Josef Varain, *Freie Gewerkschaften, Sozialdemokratie, und Staat* (Düsseldorf, 1956). A very suggestive study of the development of group consciousness and early organizations is Leo Uhen, *Gruppenbewusstsein und informelle Gruppenbildungen bei deutschen Arbeitern im Jahrhundert der Industrialisierung* (Berlin, 1963).

SYNDICALISM AND ANARCHISM

In English: J. A. Estey, *Revolutionary Syndicalism* (London, 1913); James Joll, *The Anarchists* (paperback, New York, 1966); Louis Levine, *The Labor Movement in France* (New York, 1912); Peter N. Stearns, *Revolutionary Syndicalism and French Labor: A Cause without Rebels* (New Brunswick, N.J., 1971); George Woodcock, *Anarchism. A History of Libertarian Ideas and Movements* (Cleveland, 1962).

Foreign Language: Félicien Challaye, *Syndicalisme révolutionnaire et syndicalisme réformiste* (Paris, 1909). Elisabeth Georgi, *Theorie und Prexis des Generalstreiks* (Breslau, 1908); Robert Goetz-Girey, *La Pensée syndicale française* (Paris, 1948); Paul Louis, *Le Syndicalisme français d'Amiens à Saint-Etienne, 1900–1922* (Paris, 1924); Jean Maitron, *Histoire du mouvement anarchiste en France, 1800–1914* (Paris, 1951); André May, *Les Origines du syndicalisme révolutionnaire* (Paris, 1913). Also useful is a recent biography: Bernard Georges and Denise Tintant, *Léon Jouhaux: cinquante ans du syndicalisme* (Paris, 1962).

SOCIALISM

General: There are a few general works which aim at comprehensiveness and broad interpretation, but each of the studies listed in this section achieves neither aim with startling success, with the possible exception of George Lichtheim's all too brief but stimulating *A Short History of Socialism* (London, 1970). Unfortunately it appeared after the present study was completed. Since some of the studies devoted to the Second International necessarily deal with the Socialist parties of individual countries, the most noteworthy are included here also. Werner Sombart, *Socialism and the Social Movement* (New York, 1909), though old, is still useful, as is Robert Michels, *Political Parties* (paperback ed., New York, 1962), because he was the first to discern and to analyze the growth of a Socialist party bureaucracy.

Joseph A. Schumpeter, *Capitalism, Socialism, and Democracy* (2nd ed., New York and London, 1947) retains its originality, but Arthur Rosenberg, *Democracy and Socialism. A Contribution to the Political History of the Past 150 Years* (New York, 1939) is disappointing. Much more interesting are Elie Halévy, *Histoire du Socialisme Européen* (Paris, 1948) and Leo Valiani, *Histoire du socialisme au XXᵉ siècle* (Paris, 1948), the first compiled from the lectures of a scholar who despaired over the future of socialism in his declining years, and the second written by a veteran Italian Socialist. Jacques Droz, *Le Socialisme démocratique 1864–1960* (Paris, 1966) is a fine example of the French genius for subtle synthesis. The most ambitious works are the encyclopedic studies of G. D. H. Cole, *A History of Socialist Thought* (7 vols., London, 1953–60); and Carl Landauer, *European Socialism: A History of Ideas and Movements from the Industrial Revolution to Hitler's Seizure of Power* (2 vols., Berkeley and Los Angeles, 1959), although the latter omits a consideration of Great Britain. Written in a different spirit is George Lichtheim's *Marxism: A Historical and Critical Study* (New York, 1961), which must be singled out from a vast literature on the development of Marxism. For works dealing with the theoretical aspects of socialism, S. Ossowski, *Class Structure in the Social Consciousness* (London, 1963) and Schlomo Avineri, *The Social and Political Thought of Karl Marx* (Cambridge, 1968) cannot be neglected. It is tempting but obviously not possible to note more books of this nature. Of works on the Second International which add perspective to the histories of the individual Socialist movements, the most recent is Georges Haupt, *La Deuxième Internationale 1889–1914* (Paris and The Hague, 1964). It is also a splendid bibliographical guide. Others are: Julius Braunthal, *History of the International 1864–1914* (New York and Washington, D.C., 1967), which deals with both the First and Second Internationals; James Joll, *The Second International 1889–1914* (London, 1955); and Patricia Van Der Esch, *La Deuxième Internationale 1889–1923* (Paris, 1957).

GREAT BRITAIN:

Max Beer, *A History of British Socialism* (London, 1919) is a good place to begin and might be followed by A. B. Ulam, *Philosophical Foundations of English Socialism* (Cambridge, Mass., 1951). Essential is Royden J. Harrison, *Before the Socialists: Studies in Labour and Politics, 1861–1881* (London, 1965). For a reliable and stimulating overview, see Cole, *A History . . .* vol. III, pt. 1. His older *British Working Class Politics 1832–1914* (London, 1941) and the later *Studies in Class Structure* (London, 1955) cannot be ignored. Both E. J. Hobsbawm and Henry Pelling are major contributors to the study of British working-class politics. Though not specifically concerned with British socialism, Hobsbawm's *Industry and Empire: An Economic History of Britain since 1750* (London, 1968) is thus far the best statement of Britain's economic development written from the viewpoint of a Marxist. He has also edited a convenient collection of documents, *Labour's Turning Point* (London, 1948). His other works are cited in other sections of the bibliography. Pelling has also edited a useful book of documents, *The Challenge of Socialism* (London, 1954). On the background to the establishment of the Labour party, see his *The Origins of the Labour Party 1880–1900* (paperback ed., Oxford, 1966) and *Labour and Politics 1900–1906: A History of the Labour Representation Committee* (London, 1958), the latter coauthored with Frank Bealey. Pelling has also just published a collection of essays, *Popular Politics and Society in Late Victorian Britain* (London, 1968). Asa Briggs and John Saville (eds.), *Essays in Labour History* (rev. ed., London, 1967) brings together a group of studies on various aspects of British socialism and labor. Other studies on the Labour party include those by J. H. S. Reid, *The Origins of the British Labour Party* (Minneapolis, 1955); P. P. Poirier, *The Advent of the Labour Party* (London, 1958); and Carl F. Brand, *The British Labour Party* (Stanford, 1964).

The various strands of British socialism have attracted investigation. On the Social Democratic Federation, there is no full-scale study. The closest approach to one is C. Tsuzuki, *H. M. Hyndman and British Socialism* (Oxford, 1961). The same historian has recently devoted a study to Eleanor Marx, *The Life of Eleanor Marx 1855–1898. A Socialist Tragedy* (Oxford, 1967). There are no adequate studies of most of the other personalities in the movement, but both Quelch and Bax wrote memoirs: H. Quelch, *Literary Remains* (London, 1914) and E. B. Bax, *Reminiscences and Reflections* (London, 1912). The Fabians have naturally inspired a much fuller exploration, but only the most important can be mentioned here. One cannot omit Beatrice Webb's very subjective yet revealing series of self-exposures: *My Apprenticeship* (London, 1926); *Our Partnership* (London, 1948); and the *Diaries, 1912–1924* (London, 1952), edited by Margaret Cole. The new biography, *Beatrice Webb, A Life 1858–1943* (London, 1967) by Kitty Muggeridge and Ruth Adam is one of those rare books; it really throws new light on its subject. The oldest and still exceedingly valuable assessment of the Society is by E. R. Pease, *The History of the Fabian Society* (London, 1916). Margaret Cole has edited *The Webbs and Their Work* (London, 1949) and written a personal evaluation, *The Story of Fabian Socialism* (London, 1961). The best account, however, is A. M. McBriar, *Fabian Socialism and English Politics* (Cambridge, 1962). Bernard Semmel, *Imperialism and Social Reform* (London, 1960), reveals

the Fabians' connections with and sympathies for imperialist policies.
Shaw was his own highly efficient press agent. A good antidote is
provided by A. Henderson, *George Bernard Shaw, Man of the Century* (New York, 1956). On Annie Besant, see A. H. Nethercot, *The
First Four Lives of Annie Besant* (London, 1961). An appreciation
of the Socialist League's role can be obtained from E. P. Thompson's
voluminous biography, *William Morris. Romantic to Revolutionary*
(London, 1955). See also a newer study of Morris by Philip Henderson, *William Morris: His Life, Work, and Friends* (London, 1967).
The Independent Labour party was recently surveyed by Robert
E. Dowse, *Left in the Centre. The Independent Labour Party 1893–
1940* (London, 1966), but, though useful, it is not entirely satisfactory. One has perforce to turn to the biographies of the I.L.P.'s
chief figures, most of whom still await serious study. One of the most
impressive regional studies, of which hopefully there will be more,
is Paul Thompson, *Socialists, Liberals, and Labour. The Struggle for
London 1885–1914* (London and Toronto, 1967). It is a good example of a regional study having a wider value, as is S. Pollard,
A History of Labour in Sheffield (Liverpool, 1959). On the churches
and socialism, we have nothing of a specialized nature, but one can
refer to K. S. Inglis, *Churches and the Working Classes in Victorian
England* (London and Toronto, 1963), a book which, it is hoped,
will stimulate additional studies.

Foreign Language: Very little has been written on British socialism
outside the English-speaking world. Some exceptions are two works
by E. Guyot, *L'Idée socialiste chez Morris* (Paris, 1919), and *Le
Socialisme et l'évolution de l'Angleterre contemporaine 1880–1914*
(Paris, 1924). For those who read Italian, Edoardo Grendi, *L'avvento
del laburismo. Il movimento operaio inglese dal 1880 al 1920* (Milan,
1964), demonstrates a quite unique perceptiveness and is painstakingly thorough.

FRANCE:

In English: Although English-speaking scholars have increasingly
turned toward a study of the French working classes and socialism,
there are only a few full-length treatments of the pre-1914 period.
Of these the most noteworthy are Samuel Bernstein, *The Beginnings
of Marxian Socialism in France* (New York, 1933); Margaret Pease,
Jean Jaurès (London, 1917); Harold R. Weinstein, *Jean Jaurès. A
Study of Patriotism in the French Socialist Movement* (New York,
1936); J. Hampden Jackson, *Jean Jaurès* (London, 1943); and Aaron
Noland, *The Founding of the French Socialist Party, 1893–1905*
(Cambridge, Mass., 1956). The most impressive of the recent studies
in any language, however, is Harvey Goldberg, *The Life of Jean*

Jaurès (Madison, Wis., 1962); and the first chapter in George Lichtheim, *Marxism in Modern France* (New York, 1966) is excellent.

Foreign Language: There are several general studies of French socialism. One of the early attempts to encompass the major parties in a multivolumed but individually authored study was due to Alexander Zévaès, who edited *Histoire des partis socialistes en France* (12 vols., Paris, 1912–23), but their quality is uneven. The same reservations may be made of the *Encyclopédie socialiste, syndicale et coopérative de l'Internationale ouvrière, publiée sous la direction technique de Compère-Morel* (11 vols., Paris, various dates). Mainly the work of men involved in various facets of the French movement, some of the volumes embody material pertinent to other parts of Europe. A work that has gone through several editions is Paul Louis, *Histoire du Parti socialiste en France 1871–1914* (Paris, 1922). More recent are Daniel Ligou, *Histoire du socialisme en France 1871–1961* (Paris, 1962) and Georges Lefranc, *Le Mouvement socialiste sous la Troisième Republique 1875–1940* (Paris, 1963); the second of these is better, but both perpetuate errors of detail. J. J. Fiechter, *Le Socialisme français de l'Affaire Dreyfus à la Grande Guerre* (Geneva, 1965) is totally based on the debates at the party congresses and in the Chamber of Deputies. Much more interesting is the study by Milorad Drachkovitch, *Les Socialismes français et allemand et le problème de la guerre 1870–1914* (Geneva, 1953). Nor should one neglect François Gaucher, *Contribution à l'histoire du socialisme français 1905–1933* (Paris, 1934). Two brief but originally conceived studies are Michelle Perrot, *Les Socialistes français et les problèmes du pouvoir 1871–1914* in *Le Socialisme français et le pouvoir*, eds. Michelle Perrot and Annie Kriegel (Paris, 1966) and Claude Willard, *Socialisme et communisme français* (Paris, 1967).

Specialized studies on the different problems of French socialism have been dominated by the attention given to Jean Jaurès. Oddly enough nothing in French is better than Goldberg, *The Life . . .* , although there are treatments which challenge his interpretations. New perspectives are offered by a collection of essays, *Actes du colloque Jaurès et la nation* (Toulouse, 1965). For a very human study of the great tribune, see Marcelle Auclair, *La Vie de Jean Jaurès ou la France d'avant 1914* (Paris, 1954). Of the Socialist factions, only the Guesdists have been properly examined in Claude Willard's superb study, *Les Guesdistes. Le Mouvement socialiste en France 1893–1905* (Paris, 1965). For the Allemanists, Independents, and Broussists, see the volumes by Charnay (1912), Orry (1911), and Humbert (1911) in Zévaès, *Histoire. . . .* The Vaillantists are studied by Maurice Dommanget, *Edouard Vaillant, un grand socialiste 1840–1915* (Paris, 1956). Two earlier studies retain their interest: Léon

Blum, *Les Congrès ouvriers et socialistes français* (Paris, 1901) and Daniel Halévy, *Essai sur le mouvement ouvrier en France* (Paris, 1901).

We are only now beginning to get regional studies which are of great importance for understanding the social and economic background of the implantation of industry and socialism, though this is not the purpose of all of the following: Daniel Vasseur, *Les Débuts du mouvement ouvrier dans la région de Belfort-Montbéliard 1870–1914* (Paris, 1967); Georges Dupeux, *Aspects de l'histoire sociale et politique du Loir-et-Cher 1848–1914* (Paris, 1962); P. Barral, *Le Département de l'Isère sous la Troisième Republique 1870–1940* (Paris, 1962); Simone Derruau-Boniol, "Le Socialisme dans l'Allier de 1848 à 1914," *Cahiers d'Histoire*, published by the Universities of Clermont-Lyon-Grenoble, 1957.

GERMANY:

In English: The outstanding contribution remains Carl E. Schorske, *German Social Democracy, 1905–1917: The Development of the Great Schism* (Cambridge, Mass., 1955). Guenther Roth, *The Social Democrats in Imperial Germany* (Totowa, N.J., 1963) is an insightful study with a sociological bent. For the early years, see Roger Morgan, *The German Social Democrats and the First International 1864–1872* (Cambridge, 1965). On the period of the anti-Socialist laws, Vernon L. Lidtke, *The Outlawed Party. Social Democracy in Germany, 1878–1890* (Princeton, N.J., 1966) is of high quality. Peter Gay, *The Dilemma of Democratic Socialism: Eduard Bernstein's Challenge to Marx* (New York, 1952) is valuable. J. Peter Nettl, *Rosa Luxemburg* (2 vols., Oxford, 1966) is a masterpiece. Older works that can still be consulted with some profit are Bertrand Russell, *German Social Democracy* (London, 1896), reissued in 1965; William Dawson, *German Socialism and Ferdinand Lassalle: a Biographical History of German Socialistic Movements during This Century* (2nd ed., London, 1891); William S. Sanders, *The Socialist Movement in Germany* (London, 1913); and in translation, Paul Kampffmeyer, *Changes in the Theory and Tactics of Social Democracy* (Chicago, 1908).

Foreign Language: Franz Mehring, *Geshichte der deutschen Sozialdemokratie* (4 vols., Stuttgart, 1898) is thorough, but only reaches 1891. Erich Matthias and Ebehard Pikart, *Die Reichstagfraktion der deutschen Sozialdemokratie 1898 bis 1918* (2 vols., Düsseldorf, 1966) collects the minutes of the Reichstag S.P.D. delegation meetings. Wolfgang Abendroth, *Aufstieg und Krise der deutschen Sozialdemokratie* (Frankfurt am Main, 1964) is critical of the right-wing in the movement. Other general works that should be singled out are: Helga

Grebing, *Geschichte der deutschen Arbeiterbewegung. Ein Überblick* (Munich, 1966); W. Conze and D. Groh, *Die Arbeiterbewegung in der nationalen Bewegung* (Stuttgart, 1966); Paul Merker, *Sozialdemokratie und Gewerkschaften 1890–1920* (Berlin, 1949); Rudolf Lindau, *Probleme der Geschichte der deutschen Arbeiterbewegung* (Berlin, 1949); Hermann Heidegger, *Die deutsche Sozialdemokratie und der nationale Staat 1870–1900* (Göttingen, 1956). Older but valuable is Edgar Milhaud, *La Démocratie socialiste allemande* (Paris, 1903).

More specialized studies range from biography, to briefer periods of the S.P.D., and to factions within the party. Horst Bartel, *Marx und Engels im Kampf um ein revolutionäres deutsches Parteiorgan 1879–1890* (Berlin, 1961) reveals a good deal of the two exiles' concerns over the party's tactics and future. Gerhard A. Ritter, *Die Arbeiterbewegung im Wilhelminischen Reich* (Berlin, 1959) is solid and reliable. On Bernstein, see Pierre Angel, *Eduard Bernstein et l'évolution du socialisme allemand* (Paris, 1961); and on revisionism, see Erika Rikli, *Der Revisionismus der deutschen marxistischen Theorie, 1890–1914* (Zurich, 1935). Vollmar has been served in a biography by R. Jansen, *Georg von Vollmar. Eine politische Biographie* (Düsseldorf, 1958). Horst Bartel *et al.*, *August Bebel. Eine Biographie* (Berlin, 1963) have given us a study of one of the movement's veterans. There is the first volume of a study of Ebert, Georg Kotowski, *Friedrich Ebert. Eine politische Biographie* (Wiesbaden, 1963). Kautsky's role has been explored by Erich Matthias, *Kautsky und der Kautskyanismus. Die Funktion der Ideologie in der deutschen Sozialdemokratie vor dem ersten Weltkriege* (Tübingen, 1957).

JOURNALS

Several journals publish articles devoted to the working classes, the labor movement, and socialism. The following list is a selective one, and includes journals of a general nature as well as more specialized ones. Not included are the more traditional periodicals, such as the *American Historical Review*, which will from time to time accord space to labor history. Journals in languages other than English, French, and German are not listed.

In English:

> *Bulletin of the Society for the Study of Labour History*
> *Comparative Studies in Society and History*
> *Economic History Review*
> *International Labour Review*
> *International Review of Social History* (formerly *Bulletin of the*

International Institute for Social History). Articles published in French and German, as well as in English.
Journal of Economic History
Journal of Social History
Past and Present

Foreign Language:

Annales. Economies. Sociétés. Civilisations
Archiv für Sozialgeschichte
Beiträge zur Geschichte der deutschen Arbeiterbewegung
Bulletin de la Société d'études jaurésiennes
Jahrbuch für Sozialwissenschaft
Jahrbuch für Wirtschaftsgeschichte
La Pensée
La Revue socialiste
Le Mouvement social
Preuves
Revue d'histoire économique et sociale
Sociologie du travail
Vierteljahrschrift für Sozial-und Wirtschaftsgeschichte
Zeitschrift für Geschichtswissenschaft

Index

248

DATE DUE

JAN 3 0 '73			
FEB 1 3 '73			
MAY 2 '78			
APR 25			
FEB 1 1 '86			
FEB 1			
MAY 8